UNDERSTANDING COMMUNITY LIBRARIANSHIP

Understanding Community Librarianship

The Public Library in Post-Modern Britain

ALISTAIR BLACK AND DAVE MUDDIMAN

Avebury

Aldershot • Brookfield USA • Hong Kong • Singapore • Sydney

Published by
Avebury
Ashgate Publishing Limited
Gower House
Croft Road
Aldershot
Hants GU11 3HR
England

Ashgate Publishing Company
Old Post Road
Brookfield
Vermont 05036
USA

British Library Cataloguing in Publication Data
Understanding community librarianship. - (Studies in
    librarianship)
    1.Libraries and community
    I.Black, Alistair II.Muddiman, David
    021.2

Library of Congress Catalog Card Number: 97-70015

ISBN 1 85972 243 1

Typeset by Brian Livesey, 48 West Park Grove, Leeds LS8 2DY

Printed and bound by Athenaeum Press, Ltd.,
Gateshead, Tyne & Wear.

Contents

Tables

Preface and acknowledgements

'Community' is today a very fashionable commodity. In recent decades an increasing number of activities in the social field have adopted a community perspective. Some, such as community policing and community care, are well known to the extent of attracting interest from the national media and becoming a familiar part of our 'social issues' vocabulary. Others, such as community architecture and community arts, whilst not obscure, enjoy less publicity, their content and purpose less well understood by the general public. A third category of community 'this and that' commands little or no public comprehension or familiarity, and it is here that we might locate such approaches to social and cultural practice as community pharmacy, community computing, or the subject of this book, community librarianship.

Aside from its attachment as a prefix to a variety of social service, practice, planning or policy initiatives, the term community is also frequently deployed with abandon in debates about social issues. It proliferates in the media and the public sphere as a whole, and it is a favoured aphorism of politicians, community leaders, bureaucrats, professionals of all kinds, cultural commentators and interested members of the general public with something to say about the problems they confront in society. It is invariably employed - if not always interpreted - in a positive way. More contentious words describing the social whole, like 'state' or 'society', have none of its allure: the former resonant with notions of control, the latter the preserve of the professional social scientist or the well-meaning do-gooder. 'Community', in contrast, is invariably seen to be a good thing, its usage in relation to the solution of social problems and to the meeting of human needs taken to be unproblematic.

However, in this book we take issue with the validity of such an unwaveringly positive perspective. 'Community' is not benign but is laden with value; it is, or should be, a contested concept. It is possible to look behind the facade of 'community' and, through critical analysis, attach negative features to it, to counterpoint its safe, reassuring connotations. Hence, we are committed here not to the delivery of an endorsement or superficial justification of community librarianship, but rather to a detailed deconstruction of its supporting discourses - the 'discursive formation' in authentic social science terminology - which initially propelled it to importance in the world of the public library. We are also intent upon pointing to the scepticism in both the professional library world and politico-administrative (local and national) sphere which has in recent years undermined the foundations of community librarianship and which we judge, albeit with the benefit of hindsight, to have been present at its inception.

In tracing the experience of community librarianship it has been our aim to contextualize it within a model of late twentieth century fragmentation and social change, which we characterise as postmodernity. Hence the book's subtitle, which may seem adventurous or even outlandish to some, but will to others appear to be a quite natural, logical and inescapable lens through which to view our topic. This book is therefore intellectually rooted primarily in social science rather than library, or information, studies. Although bringing to the research and to this discussion hands-on experience of public library work in both community information and outreach, we are eager to position ourselves as 'outsiders' in relation to the library world, viewing community librarianship as much as possible from a detached social science anchorage and mounting our exploration of the subject with reference to the sociologies of information, community, the professions, the welfare state and poverty/disadvantage. This said, we have not sought to divorce our analysis from the public library domain in which community librarianship emerged. On the contrary, we have drawn heavily on the surprisingly extensive - in view of the institution's rather innocuous social standing - literature of public library policy and practice. Indeed, one of the major objectives of our investigation has been to analyse, reflect and comment upon the wider issue and perplexing problem of public library development. It is categorically not our aim to decouple the 'community' in community librarianship from the 'public' in public libraries. Our interest in community librarianship is not based - as our focus on postmodernity might at first glance suggest - on a desire to promulgate an anarcho-progressive alternative to traditional public library service, either of the libertarian or market kind. Indeed, we reiterate the need for state involvement and its promotion of social justice in satisfying, through the agency of the public library, the information, literary and cultural requirements of the array of social groupings that populate the postmodern terrain, and especially those at its margins. In short, we are not peddling a postmodern agenda for the public library. Far from it; what we attempt, in fact, is to utilise that agenda as an analytical tool in order to retrieve from authentic community librarianship its modernist credentials of social commitment and community development.

It is important to emphasize that this is not a handbook of community librarianship. It has never been our intention to produce a 'how to do it' manual or guide; not least because, as we hope to show, there have existed since the birth of community librarianship a variety of interpretations, or models, of it. Our aim is to provide an account, sometimes descriptive but mostly critical, of its origins, rise, flourishing (in places) and decline, or perhaps more accurately, its metamorphosis. In conclusion we offer no detailed recommendations, but do suggest a possible new trajectory of public library purpose. We advocate openly an ethical perspective, and the tradition of the moral seriousness and ideological thrust of past public library reform. By inference, we call on others to re-examine the direction in which they are travelling and the use or misuse they may be making of the community librarianship concept or label.

Before reaching that point we build, in Chapter 1, a theoretical foundation for analysis centring on the multiple meanings attached to the word community and a sociological assessment of the profession of public librarianship. We comment on these in the context of the postmodern condition, of which a brief but multi-faceted definition is offered, inclusive of the shift, as some see it, towards a post-Fordist welfare state. In Chapter 2 long term historical influences on community librarianship are mapped out in relation to the development of the public library, of modernity, of post-Fordist service delivery and of social attitudes to poverty. Ways in which community librarianship might be considered to be discontinuous with the public library's past are also suggested. This theme is taken up more specifically in Chapter 3, where the rise of community librarianship is argued to be, in part at least, a reaction to the 'modern', post-war model of uniform public service. The chapter details the rise of community librarianship in the 1970s, and looks at its ideological roots in both the radical welfarism and emerging market individualism of the time. Chapter 4 argues that community librarianship reached its zenith in the early 1980s, and explores public library initiatives in community information, multicultural librarianship and services to unemployed people. It examines the factors which set limits on a 'community' approach, and contends that, despite its importance as rhetoric and philosophy, community librarianship remained relatively marginal as service activity. However in the late eighties, we argue, marginality became retreat. In Chapter 5, we detail the impact of the Thatcher revolution in local government on community approaches to library provision. We report on our own documentary research and fieldwork and examine the impact not only of financial constraint, but of neo-liberal and conservative/postmodern ideologies of public service such as public choice, managerialism and consumerism. The retreat of community librarianship is further explained in Chapter 6 where focal reference is made to the recent emergence in British society of a backward-looking, 'heritage' perspective. This corresponds, we claim, with a strong desire among politicians, administrators, cultural commentators and a growing number of librarians to reinstate in public librarianship, to the possible detriment of progressive creeds like community librarianship, core roles and a traditional identity. But, as we argue in Chapter 7, which examines the future of community librarianship in an 'information' society, such a 'heritage' vision of the public library will surely lead to marginalisation, cultural irrelevance and decline. Instead, we explore a possible future for community librarianship in a post-Fordist local public sphere based on networks, partnerships and community involvement. In our conclusion, Chapter 8, this leads us to reconsider the radical tradition of community (and much of public) librarianship, and to suggest ways in which this tradition is of continuing relevance in a postmodern society and culture. We hope, at least, that some of these arguments fall on influential ears.

At the basic level of organisation, therefore, our arguments are furthered by an essentially chronological approach. The chronological staging is then threaded through with various recurring themes: of postmodernity, welfarism, disadvantage, community, professional concerns and other aspects of community librarianship and public library provision. We trust that this intersection of thematic and chronological approaches has delivered a coherent exposition of our subject. However, in any co-authored publication there is potential for fragmentation and inconsistency. Hopefully we have avoided such pitfalls, but in a joint project there is inevitably a division of labour to be implemented and negotiated, both at the research and report stages. While this Preface and Chapter 8 were penned jointly, chief responsibility for Chapters 1, 2 and 6 rests with Alistair Black, and for Chapters 3, 4, 5 and 7 with Dave Muddiman. The field research that underpins this study, though a shared effort in terms of strategy, planning and analysis, was also organised by a division of tasks in respect of subjects interviewed, case studies undertaken and documentary sources consulted. How the research was done is explained in an appendix. This is essentially a note on methods (as opposed to methodology) and does not provide a comprehensive list of names that co-operated in the project.

It falls to us here, therefore, to acknowledge the many individuals who assisted us in our research. Our gratitude is extended to Ray Astbury, John Vincent and Joe Hendry for a wealth of helpful insights drawn from their long and rich experience of community librarianship; to Andrew Green and Howard Matthew of the Library Association Community Services Group; to Andrew Glen and Hugh Butcher of Bradford and Ilkley Community College and Kevin Harris of the Community Development Foundation for their generously given community policy perspective; to Juan Manuel Ros for his views on postmodernity and other socio-cultural theory; to Ken Worpole, Liz Greenhalgh and Charles Landry who gave us an opportunity to develop some of our earlier ideas as part of the Comedia research; and to Brian Livesey, Karen Simpson, Sheila Murphy and Jacqui Akkouh at Avebury for their assistance with the production of copy. We also wish to register our appreciation of the role played by Leeds Metropolitan University, in terms of funding for the project furnished by the Faculty of Information and Engineering Systems, as well as the feedback we have received from our students. In particular our PhD students Pen Jenkinson and Paul Johnson and also those postgraduates who over the last six years have opted to study our Master's module on community librarianship have provided us with ideas, criticism and encouragement. Repositories and organisations that have helped us with documentary evidence are noted in the Appendix. Further, we very much appreciate the efforts of the 73 English and Welsh library authorities who supplied us with policy documents and statements in the early phase of the research. Finally, we express our sincere thanks to those library authorities and their librarians who kindly co-operated with us in our programme of selected case studies, as well as the many other individual community and public librarians who came forward to provide evidence. Their anonymity remains intact; they know who they are and we are grateful for the arrangements they made, the time they afforded us and the interest they showed in our research and in our subject.

Alistair Black and Dave Muddiman
Leeds, November 1996

1 Introduction: The creation of community and its librarianship

Community librarianship is not what it used to be. A bold mode of public library service developed in the late-1970s and early-1980s by socially radical and committed librarians, over the past decade its content has been slowly transformed and its contours blurred by factors operating both within and external to professional librarianship. Buffeted by technological change, market pressures, uncertainties over professional jurisdiction and by growing competition from other expert groups in the information field, public librarianship has in recent years been experiencing a crisis of confidence that contrasts markedly with earlier phases marked by high optimism and a sense of direction, such as in the Carnegie era of expansion before the First World War, in the 1960s, or indeed, in the era of classical community librarianship which we suggest drew to a close around 1985. However, in investigating the tranformation of community librarianship - and at times, indeed, we are tempted to speak about its decline - explanations exclusive to the internal workings and culture of professional librarianship must also be considered, not least the historic tendency to favour administrative-technical over social concerns, and to prioritize cultural conservatism and conformity over the information and reading requirements of marginal or alternative social groups. Community librarianship, as it was originally conceived, represented a challenge to traditional public librarianship. But the failure to fulfil its promise of delivering a rejuvenated, egalitarian and more relevant public library cannot be laid at the door of the library profession alone. Libraries do not exist in a vacuum, isolated from the flux of social change. Consequently, this study pays close attention to the wider social environment in which public libraries and community librarianship have recently operated, and in particular to directly impinging developments such as: the reawakening of market economics; the (re)emergence of an underclass in British society; the emergence of 'heritage Britain'; the shift from a modern, Fordist to a postmodern, post-Fordist orientation in social policy; and the place of community, to which our attention is first turned, in our social thinking and in the sociological tradition.

Community theorized and romanticized: community as state, service and mutuality

Exploring the meaning of 'community' has become almost an obligatory ingredient in discourses on any form of public service or social practice prefixed by the word. Discussions of community librarianship are no different in this respect [1]. In his analysis of community librarianship in the inner city Dolan (1989, pp. 10-13) defines six different, though by no means mutually exclusive, types of community [2]:

- Territorial communities - people sensing membership of a group defined by location or geographical and, perhaps even administrative, boundaries.

- Communities of attachment - groups nurtured by a sense of belonging in terms, for example, of religious or political beliefs.

- Communities of interest - people who share common social practices and concerns arising from ethnicity, class, age, gender, educational achievement or lifestyle.

- Communities of action - autonomous groups pursuing change on particular issues.

- Communities of need - people sharing common needs, which are often unexpressed and thus require professional investigation to reveal them.

- Objective communities - people who wish to be involved in shared action or debate, but who are not necessarily the subject of need.

These definitions closely resemble the interpretation of 'community' offered by the *Oxford English Dictionary* from which a variety of meanings can be extracted: joint or common ownership; common character or identity; people sharing common practices; a body with common or equal rights; a body organized into a political or municipal unity; people living in the same locality; social intercourse and fellowship; and life in association with others.

2

On a more analytical level Butcher et al. (1994) have isolated three main views of community from which meaningful explorations of community practice can flow:

- Descriptive community - encompassing the communities of attachment, interest, geography and objectivity noted above.

- Community as value - a perpective rooted in the communitarian tradition of people associating to bring about a qualitative change in their lives, and in doing so building a shared, cooperative value system in a way which transcends, in spiritual terms almost, mere physical membership of an institution or group.

- Active community - the process whereby groups develop, or are helped to develop, their potential through purposive action.

For the purpose of this study the threefold notion of community given by the social historians Stephen Yeo and Eileen Yeo (1988) is particularly appropriate to the theoretical framework we have constructed. Their view of community 'as mutuality', 'as service' and 'as state' correspond helpfully with the configuration of community librarianship as a mode of community practice which in its purest form has addressed the needs of identifiable mutual, client groups through the policy formulation and practices of (local) state professionals who are motivated by an ethic of dutiful service to the disadvantaged. However, of equal importance to our analysis is the possibility, in the community librarianship context, of friction between these views of community: specifically, that the interests of autonomous, mutual communities can conflict with those of the state and its professionals.

Community has a long heritage. Always used in connection with the ethos of Christian communion - community being derived from the Latin 'communitatem' meaning fellowship (Yeo and Yeo, 1988, p. 231) - by the late Middle Ages it had taken on an additional, secular meaning as a description for the entire realm and its inhabitants. To this day community can be, and is, used as a synonym for the nation state, and is not uncommonly employed by authority in attempting to discredit alternative, radical, separatist or sectional interest groups seeking to build what they might see as *genuine* community, from the bottom up. Arguably the most conspicuous manifestation of a leap towards community 'as state' in Britain was the bureaucratic structures erected to support the war effort between 1939-1940 and to advance the welfare state after 1945. Statists often evoke communitarian values in calling or accounting for national success. Thus the tardiness of Western economies over the past quarter-of-a-century compared to the rapid advance of Pacific-Rim countries such as Japan, Singapore, Taiwan, Hong Kong and Korea is often explained by juxtaposing an individualistic West with organic, community oriented Eastern cultures, the inherent characteristics of which fit well with the imperatives of national planning (Hampden-Turner and Trompenaars, 1995, pp. 165-6). Community 'as state' is very much about the implementation and realisation of national plans and projects organized and run in a top-down fashion. Here, community is more a question of motivating rhetoric than the search for a community approach, the latter being seen not as central but largely as an adjunct to the formulation of national social policy, often being merely 'wheeled-in to the policy arena to address particular problems at particular times' (Butcher, 1994, pp. 18-19). There have been exceptions, of course, to the authoritarian tendencies of the community 'as state' approach and these are mostly evident in the symbiotic relationships which are sometimes formed between a collectivist state and grass roots organizations: in other words, the state resourcing of autonomous voluntary bodies, often of the local kind in urban priority areas (*Communities in Crisis*, 1985, pp. 8). In the public libraries sphere such an approach would entail a radical reformulation of service delivery whereby the information needs of groups are satisfied by the groups themselves, assisted only by professional guidance and resourcing from library authorities. Clearly, this very radical community librarianship path has rarely been trod, public librarians wishing to retain control over the community practices in which they engage. It is an alternative which powerholders, used to formal and 'establishment' approaches, find difficult to comprehend: hence the Department of National Heritage's preoccupation in recent years with the idea of a *national* Library and Information Commission, welcomed in many sectors of the library world, as well as the library establishment's fascination with the national review of public libraries, sponsored by the Department and published in 1995 [3]. Librarians achieved geographical centralisation of services over a century ago in the form of the branch library, something which the very earliest public library promoters had not foreseen. As for managerial decentralization [4], however, there has been a reluctance in public librarianship, despite the example set by some radical community librarianship initiatives, to endorse the politics of decentralisation about which so much has been written over the past twenty years (Boaden et al, 1982; Burns, Hambleton and Hoggett, 1994; Cockburn, 1977, ch.4; Hoggett and Hambleton, 1987; Smith, 1985; Stoker and Young, 1993, ch.5).

Community 'as service' is an outgrowth of community 'as state'. Just as national projects and policies generally have at their base a desire on the part of authority to provide for its subjects - albeit at times for the exercise of control in varying degrees - so also do individuals and social groups seek to offer their service and services to others in the name of social betterment. Such service *can* be rendered through voluntary association, but in modern societies is mostly delivered via formal organisations, institutions and built-forms which symbolize community life. Thus, linked into the idea of community 'as state', community 'as service' is often constructed by the provision of *public* facilities, like libraries, which are notionally available to all in society. Community practice here is very much the receptacle, or preserve, of the expert-professional who, in the liberal tradition, often seeks to undercut the objectives of those who form spontaneous communities or 'agitation', 'interpretive' groups. Such groups are seen to disturb the social relations upon which modern, professional society is built. Moreover, they are portrayed as disharmonious and lacking in true community spirit, due to their supposedly irrational state. Their alienation and segregation are seen to work against community. Hence, what is required is professional supervision, 'good works' and institutions for social class mixing - these being the precondition of authentic community feeling (Dennis and Daniels, 1981). Historically, the public library and its professionals have largely endorsed this controlling aspect of community 'as service'. Certainly in the nineteenth century, as allies of middle class reformers and benefactors seeking a consolidation of the dominant political economy, librarians can be seen championing in the name of social de-segregation the middle class and civic takeovers of irrational, organic, threatening and, to some, anti-Christian working class community activity [5]. Public librarianship has traditionally, therefore, coincided with the elite view of community power which states that: 'Communities, like nations, are governed by tiny minorities. The community itself, and the lives of the people who live in it, are shaped by a small number of people' (Dye, 1986, p. 29). Librarians, despite their traditional rhetoric of democratic access, have been reluctant to endorse pluralistic and participatory models of community power. In the past they have, most surely, sought to reach into society. But that reach has rarely stretched beyond the formal organizational level. The preoccupation with 'formal community' - which we propose as a synonym for community 'as service' - has been enthusiastically endorsed by one American library commentator: 'What is needed is a new concept of the community as a community of organizations, a concept that is realistic, descriptive of communities everywhere, and useful to the public library administration ... the contemporary community is in reality a community of organizations' (Howard, 1978, p. 3).

Public librarians might generally be termed good bureaucrats. While the citizen servant of the classical welfare state era may be a dying breed in some areas of social practice and service (Inglis, 1993), in public librarianship the desire to cling on to bureaucratic structures and procedures appears as strong as ever. There is much to be gained - if not admired, indeed, in terms of selfless service to others - from the rational planning of operations. In addition to this traditional role, however, account needs to be taken, in a way that community

5

'as service' at times does not, of the fundamental changes occuring in society, especially in respect of any pluralistic fragmentation that might occur and the consequent need for a flexible response driven by the grass roots and drawing on the very strong tradition of community as a function of mutuality.

Whereas community 'as state' and community 'as service' stress the importance of social cohesion they do so on authority's terms, unlike community 'as mutuality' which emphasises a natural, or organic, sense of community which is not imposed from above. Community is fundamental to the study of modern sociology and has become so largely because of the 'rediscovery of community' in the wake of the Industrial Revolution, a resurfacing viewed by Nisbet (1970, p. 47) as: 'Unquestionably the most distinctive development in nineteenth century social thought'. The conceptualization of community operates at two levels: the popular and, to be discussed below, that of the expert social theorist. At the popular level the early nineteenth century witnessed an explosion in the desire for closer social relationships, or mutuality. Torn apart by industrialization and urbanization, the social fabric of old was to be remade in the spirit of co-operation and of 'a fully liberated humanity living in supportive social relations' (Yeo and Yeo, 1988, p. 223) in order to realise the vision of a new moral order superior to the degrading and dehumanising code of the 'cash nexus' and market society. One of the most strident theorists of nineteenth century community was the historian E.P. Thompson whose *The Making of the English Working Class* (1968) [6] described the early Industrial Revolution as a phase of transition between two ways of life: the passing of 'old England' and its replacement by new strategies and discourses of discipline, the most prominent being the factory and the arguments of the classical political economists. However, faced with the prospect of *losing* their culture, particularly the tight community ties of pre-industrial society, working people developed an embryonic but identifiable working class consciousness characterized by an insistence on mutual aid. Working class self-help and agitational groups, institutions and movements (like trade unions, friendly societies, the Political Unions, Chartist lodges, Owenite socialists and co-operators) crystallized in their operations and activities, according to Thompson, a strong ethos of mutuality and made wholesale use of the word 'community'. A new sense of social cohesion was thus engendered. It was less organic perhaps than that evident in pre-industrial society, born as it was of a 'solidarity of antagonism' towards a new environment and new masters.

Less organic also was the sense of community, or social bonding, created by individuals who found themselves thrown together in close proximity by the forces of urbanization and burgeoning trade. The invisible hand of the market was promoted in the language of political economy as a means of harmonizing social relations through the healthy collision of independent, self-activating

6

individuals; a process that would deliver an appropriate balance of social relations and distribution of society's resources. Community here is constructed less out of basic human values than out of social necessity. This distinction, although fine, between organic and imposed or environmental community was noted by the nineteenth century German social theorist and philosopher Ferdinand Tönnies. In 'Gemeinschaft und Gesellschaft' (1887) Tönnies drew a line between, on the one hand, natural communities defined by intimate and enduring bonds of kinship, place and shared identity ('gemeinschaft' relationships) and, on the other, community characterised by contract and by 'calculated', rational association ('gesellschaft' relationships). In the 'gemeinschaft', said Tönnies, 'individuals remain essentially united in spite of all separating factors whereas in the "gesellschaft" they are essentially separated in spite of all uniting factors ... everybody is by himself and isolated ... nobody wants to grant and produce anything for another individual ... if it not be in exchange for a gift or labour equivalent that he considers at least equal to what he has given' (Banks, 1973, p. 110).

In the early twentieth century Tönnies' view of community was taken up by a number of social theorists, but most enthusiastically by the Chicago School of sociologists and anthropologists, in an effort to explain the paradox of an escalation in social problems in communities which were clearly advancing, or 'civilizing', in other respects, most obviously materially. The lens through which social stress came to be viewed was that of the rural-urban continuum, where the city and the country were positioned at opposite polls in the world of social harmony (Wirth, 1938), and where the 'health' of a community could be assessed by its place on the continuum (Redfield, 1947). The crude picture drawn was one of organic social peace and fellowship in communities of the pre-industrial kind, and social disharmony, or merely 'artificial' harmony, in industrial, urban communities; the level of disharmony being proportionate to the intensity of urbanization experienced. Others came to challenge the legitimacy of the continuum theory. Building on the criticisms of Durkheim - who argued that cities were 'homes of progress' exhibiting intimacy and 'a high moral density' (Banks, 1973, p. 111) - critics like Oscar Lewis (1949) sought to point up the social tensions caused by the claustrophobic nature of rural and village life. In this country, offering a critique of the thesis from the opposite end, Young and Willmott's (1957) study of social life in post-war Bethnal Green showed how a homogenous communal solidarity, based to a large degree on close kinship bonds and friendship ties, could thrive in the city.

Despite the discrediting of the 'gemeinschaft' thesis, the proposition persists that true community is anathema to modern, urbanized societies. As societies advance and increase in complexity, the tendency to romanticize community intensifies. Community often takes on an anti-modern endorsement of pre-industrial, or sometimes classical industrial (for example coal or manufacturing

7

communities) patterns of social life where moral commitment to others is conspicuous. The continuation of social criticism (of urban and industrial culture) into the late twentieth century (Williams, 1973) has engendered the widely sensed but simplistic conviction that 'past' community is 'purer' community. Authentic community is popularly seen as elusive, and yet society remains obsessed with the need to *create* it. The result of this obsession is the fabrication, or symbolic construction, of community (Cohen, 1989) through social agencies and cultural production which boast a potential for generating communal spirit. The public library is one such socio-cultural entity. Historically, it has championed the cause of community by promoting social class mixing, a democratic ethos and a mild doctrine of outreach/extension into society. This interest in community can be traced back to the idealist vocabulary of social fellowship uttered by early supporters and promoters, but has resurfaced in the post-war, welfarist era in a more virile form, backed by both community 'as state' and 'as service'. In the second half of the twentieth century the public library is seen in many respects to be even more communal in that it presents itself as having broken with the inaccessibility and cultural elitism of the past by making itself more 'marketable' and, for some, if technological change is accepted, in closer step with the community that flows from electronic networking (see Chapter 7). Others doubt its community credentials, particularly in areas of urban deprivation where libraries continue to be seen as unattractive, irrelevant and apart from the community (Darcy and Ohri, 1978). It was in response to the rhetoric of community which the public library has traditionally spoken that community librarianship arose. Community librarians believed they could assist genuine community by supporting self-forming, pre-exisiting, mutual communities of resistance, action, agitation and self-help - communities which are said to be at the heart of the postmodern condition of social pluralism and difference.

Postmodernity, community and the discourse of librarianship

Public libraries are a product of *modern* society. As promoters of individual and universal betterment, as investors in the idea of progress, as purveyors of rational science, education and recreation and as agencies run by expert-professionals often in accordance with strict rules and bureaucratic structures, public libraries match with astonishing precision the criteria of a modern social agency operating within the overall project of modernity. What Habermas (1985) called the Enlightenment project (of modernity) both gave birth to the public library in the middle of the nineteenth century and was itself subsequently enriched by its development as a forum for debate and as an institution for improvement within the public sphere. When modernity in

8

The Public library is engaged in the shift from a modern to postmodern age.

Britain reached its zenith in the era of the classical welfare state era between 1945 and 1970 (as many would have it), the public library also attained what many librarians and others regard as *its* peak of development, driven by purposeful planning and fuelled by a powerful ethical social vision. In the last quarter of the twentieth century, however, the public library has existed and adapted in the context of a postmodern society. Community librarianship, although forged in the dwindling flames of modernity, has similarly been forced to transform itself with reference to its new postmodern environment.

While theorists of information, culture and infrastructures do not hesitate to make use of wider socio-cultural theory, such as the concept of postmodernity, in order to contextualize and explain their subject (Collins, 1995; Allen, 1992), commentators on library issues, mostly librarians and library educators, have generally speaking fought shy of formulating wider theoretical frameworks, including the shift from a modern to a postmodern age [7]. It is our firm belief, however, that analysis of the public library, including its promotion of community librarianship, cannot proceed without reference to both social and cultural theory, each of which has in recent decades been characterized by a conscious adoption of postmodernism as a template for interpreting virtually any social practice. It is not appropriate here to engage in an exhaustive discussion of postmodern forms. This is due to reasons of space, but also because a lengthy exploration would reveal, in a way which would not let us retain the focus of our discussion here, the very fine texture of the debate and, in particular, our recognition of the notion of radicalized, or high, modernity promulgated by Giddens (1990) and others. It is therefore sufficient here to offer only a brief but hopefully useful definition of postmodernism, and indeed modernism, as a springboard for our ensuing analysis of community librarianship.

Postmodern forms of human behaviour can be organized into four basic categories: cultural, social, epistemological and economic. In the world of *culture* (used here in the sense of artistic pursuits), the shift to postmodern production has proceeded, as with the rise of modern forms, at a different pace in different areas, although current reference to postmodern styles - usually involving a movement away from standardized, established approaches towards freedom of expression, inversion and eclecticism - is now commonplace in, for example, architecture, literature, theatre, cinema and music. The most conspicuous manifestation of *social* postmodernity is the emphasis on pluralism (described by Jenks (1992, p. 11) as the leading 'ism' of postmodernism) - involving the search for social segmentation, fluidity and difference and the corresponding negation of homogeneity, centralization, bureaucratization, planning and any mass social form whether recreational, political, spiritual or consumerist. Regarding *epistemology*, posmodernism challenges the validity of the formulation of knowledge from objective, rational science. It questions the legitimacy not only of the Enlightenment scientific method of desinterested, systematic observation, but also of the experts and professionals who have pedalled the inviolability of scientific 'truth'. In particular, the social (including political) sciences and their contribution to social thinking and policy-making are viewed dubiously, while 'world views' or 'meta-narratives' offered as panaceas or as explanations are roundly condemned. Finally, postmodernism's *economic* dimension is most commonly conceptualized in terms of post-Fordism (Amin, 1995). The last quarter of the twentieth century has seen a movement away from Fordist mass production and mass consumption towards flexible 'regimes of accumulation'. Faced by a squeeze on profits in the late-1960s and 1970s capitalists have begun to implement - with the help of developing information technologies and a deregulation of the labour market - new regimes of production characterized by just-in-time methods, short-runs, greater customization and a much increased mobility of capital through the sectors and around the globe. This new approach to production has been essential in order to provide a swift response to the rapidly changing tastes and to the lifestyle packaging of postmodern society.

Post-Fordism has attracted considerable interest as a theory explaining recent social change. It has not surprisingly been applied outside the world of production and work, which in any case touches most aspects of our lives. It is not just economic life that is said to have undergone a post-Fordist transformation; sevices too have been subject to a similar trend. The welfare state is now seen to be striking a post-Fordist pose (Burrows and Loader, 1994). Elements of post-Fordism, and postmodernism indeed, are also clearly visible in the late twentieth century public library. At an operational-materials level the changes are obvious: fragmentation and flexibility in respect of team management, compulsory competitive tendering, devolved cost centres and the gradual switch from impractical (as some see it) print to adaptable, just-in-time electronic sources. More importantly, the public library might be viewed as a social institution in danger of having its historic, modernist, ideological heart transplanted by a postmodern, post-Fordist pragmatism where managers seek merely to respond to demand rather than make value judgements and set agendas according to what they believe is socially good.

The post-Fordist flight from ideology has implications for community in the postmodern age. As we have seen, the quest for community is a core characteristic of modernity. The modern, Enlightenment project is a global phenomenon driven by totalizing meta-narratives. In recent decades, however, community formed through grand discourses has become less popular, as manifest in the rise of individualism and the distrust of political and economic centralization and of logocentric remedies. But this does not mean that in the postmodern age the desire for community has been reduced. On the contrary, community has quickly resurfaced in a form rooted, not in the global

10

emancipation urged by classical liberal or Marxist theory, but in social 'difference'. Postmodern community, though suspicious of the selfish individualism of social atomism, materialism and the free market - witness the Blairite 'community' reaction against 1980's hedonism (Gutman, 1992) - is equally hesitant about the collectivist tradition. Supporters of postmodern community such as Etzioni (1993) see little role for the state as a contributor to community, arguing in the communitarian tradition that social problems should be solved mainly at the local level, with an input from autonomous forums and new social and political movements (which together might be described as 'interpretive' communities) in areas such as feminism, ecology, peace, sexual freedom and Third World liberation; and assisted of course by the communal networking provided by information technology. Such a view of community thus marginalizes and shames those who wish to make a contribution in the collectivist tradition - something which, notwithstanding our recognition of postmodern 'difference', we in this book regard as regrettable. However, we are equally disturbed by the instant, non-judgemental post-Fordist reaction of those delivering public services such as public libraries to the pressures imposed by the new pluralism. Librarians who become infected by a post-Fordist relativism of purpose, where the touchstone of policy is that of the market, are not inclined to prioritize social groups in respect of their information needs. Instead, librarians seek to be all things to all people (Astbury, 1994, p. 135). Society is perceived by librarians as a postmodern - even if there is little conscious recognition of the term - array of communities, each to be served without favour. Clearly, the modernism of authentic community librarianship, based on a targeting of the disadvantaged, stands in stark contrast to the postmodern, post-Fordist turn in public library policy and practice (more about this in Chapters 2 and 5).

The return of librarians to their long standing bolt hole of neutrality is in some respects a fall back to the public library's historic, comfortable cohabitation with community 'as state' and 'as service' where, although the emphasis was on helping to construct *one* community (unlike postmodern plurality), the guiding ethic of that strategy, even if the reality did not match it, was one of 'catholicism', universal treatment and the development of truly 'town' libraries open to all social factions. Mutual communities on the other hand, which the postmodern age champions, by definition stand apart from the consensus whole and are less likely, because of the postmodern emphasis on identities of difference, to be either homogenized or hegemonized culturally. Thus, in the context of their ethical inheritance, librarians have little choice other than to service, or at least say they will service, all social groups equally - this being the nearest they can come to replicating their traditional 'social binding' function. What they cannot do if they are to maintain a link with their past ethos, is to prioritize, judge or discriminate, as community librarianship in its heyday attempted to do.

This continuity in the social purpose of public librarianship points to the existence of a tremendously powerful and resilient professional discourse. Of relevance here, to pursue our analysis of postmodernism a little further, is the thinking of the French social theorist Michel Foucault, and in particular his perception of the relationship between knowledge and power. Foucault provided an interpretation of expert knowledge based on the reversal of the cliché that 'knowledge is power'. Far more important to an understanding of the proliferation and dissemination of knowledge, said Foucault, is the proposition that power delivers knowledge, as well as being delivered by it. He rejected Enlightenment assumptions that knowledge is neutral, or value-free, and is accumulated for the purpose of humanity's progress rather than in the interest of specific groups. Foucault denied the modern ideal of the disinterested knower, or expert, suggesting that 'truth', especially in the realms of the human sciences, is validated, not objectively, but by interested scholarly and professional communities (Grentz, 1996, pp. 131-4). Experts make knowledge true, said Foucault, through the construction of *discourses* of knowledge. But when these discourses are analysed, or deconstructed, in relation to the social position of the groups that produce them, and when factors of professional status and of subjective social belief are clearly seen to be at play, it is possible to term them 'regimes of truth' - inferring an imposition of truth as opposed to the pre-existence of knowledge waiting to be discovered.

Public, and to a degree community, librarianship lend themselves to such theorising. It is clearly possible to argue that, historically, the discourse of public librarianship has been constructed top-down rather than bottom-up. As we have argued elsewhere (Black, 1996b), public librarianship has furthered itself using the language of democracy, opportunity and pluralism, yet it is prone to a preoccupation with 'excluding' functions to do with order, bureaucracy, surveillance, control, elite culture and, not least, the achievement and maintenance of an occupational monopoly. Regarding this last point, it is possible to view public librarianship as merely another interest group pursuing a 'professional project' (Macdonald, 1995) - witness the current anxiety over competition from other professional groups and the continuing desire to move centre stage and colonize other information professions in the process (Abell, 1996) - as opposed to being primarily a social occupation exhibiting a burning desire to deliver social justice. Such a view is of course harsh, if not crude, in terms of analysis. However, there *is* evidence to support the notion that librarians tend towards the administrative and the technical rather than the social: 'library cultures have not encouraged', as recent research suggests, 'risk or experimentation', and remain essentially conservative in form and outlook

(White, 1993, p. 50). This was reiterated in the recent review of public libraries for the Department of National Heritage (ASLIB, 1995) which showed how, although librarians saw their institution as having adapted to new social demands - and certainly librarians are reluctant to see themselves as officious and out-of-touch (Atton, 1993) - the public viewed public libraries as unchanging, as places which offered 'coherence and continuity in an age of discontinuity' (Myers, 1994, p. 426).

Our analysis of the decline of community librarianship is founded to a large degree on the premise that the discourse of public librarianship and the regimes of truth that it purveys are rooted in social conservatism. Consequently, public librarians were woefully unprepared for the shift towards the pluralistic, postmodern society of recent decades. But more than this, a case can also be made for the rise and operation of community librarianship itself as a discourse founded on the power-knowledge paradigm. Just as public library work has always to a degree been characterized by 'the tyranny of the expert', so also have community librarians been accused of *preaching* a philosophy which the public does not really want to hear. In other words, too many community librarianship initiatives have been generated from above, directed by policy-makers, rather than arising from the grass roots; a manifestation of this distancing from the grass roots being the lack of understanding of the distinction between 'deserving' and 'undeserving' poor (to be discussed in Chapter 2) and the rather loose and at times meaningless use made of the word 'disadvantaged'. Community librarianship might be viewed as a form of community practice seeking to 'engineer' community (Crow and Allan, 1994, pp. 157-61). Here community would function ideologically and would be as imposed as that fashioned in the moulds of community 'as state' and community 'as service'. In this respect community librarianship has always found it difficult to break free from the shackles of public librarianship's controlling dimension. Indeed, aside from the very obvious and crucial fact that community librarians have rarely received community work training, what marks them out from other community workers is their close attachment to a parent professional discourse that has not moved with the times or with society as quickly as others, and which in any case has never fully recognized the importance of interesting itself in policy areas which are not its own. It is perhaps for this reason that, as our research has revealed, many community librarians have never felt truly convinced by the discourse they were promoting, *creating* in a way their professional rationale just as community is itself *created* by social tensions and anxiety (although the confidence of community librarianship practitioners in the relevance of their philosophy has always been greater of course than that sensed in the communities they served). On the other hand, it would be wholly wrong to dismiss community librarianship as merely a 'regime of truth', socially and professionally constructed from a desire to enliven a languid expert occupation. Those librarians who from around the mid-1970s onwards sought to challenge the conservatism of public librarianship did so out of keen ethical, social reasoning. Many believed that, by redirecting public library services towards mutual communities and grass roots social practices, they could achieve a redistribution of wealth and opportunity in society. Moreover, although this exciting departure at first presented opportunities for a higher and more relevant professional status, the reality would no doubt soon have been comprehended that community work, of whatever kind, offers few medals or bouquets and certainly little financial reward. In its infancy, community librarianship looked to break with the welfare state's bureaucratic past. Just as town and housing estate planners were mistaken in the belief that 'all that was necessary for neighbourliness was a neighbourhood unit, for community spirit a community centre' (Young and Willmott, 1962, p. 198), community librarians believed that public librarians were equally misguided in the conviction that buildings-bound, top-down, traditional library services could help deliver 'true' community. Authentic community librarians of the past, as well as those who *survive* in the present, would have baulked at the way some public librarians are now tempted to use community as a *creative* marketing tool. The postmodern conceptualization of community as an aid to marketing policy (community as marketing) conflicts starkly with the perception of community held by early community librarians as a synonym for mutuality and redistribution (community as social policy). This latter ethical perspective has patently declined, but the story of that decline can only be told fully by initial reference to community librarianship's historic baggage of past public library development.

Notes

1 Clarke (1991). See also, from an Indian perspective, Sahai (1973).
2 Borrowed by Dolan from Willmott and Thomas (1984).
3 'Library world welcomes national commission initiative', *The Bookseller*, 16 July 1993, p. 8. See Shimmon (1995, p. 376) for a summary of the review's findings.
4 McKee (1989, p. 72) notes the distinction between geographical and managerial decentralization.
5 The classic example of such a takeover in the library sphere is the closure of the Owenite Hall of Science in Manchester, criticised by some as a den of orgies, and its re-opening as the public library in 1852. See Black (1996b, p. 39).

6   See ch. 12 on community in particular. First published 1963. An exception here is Greenhalgh, Worpole and Landry (1995), although the authors themselves, and the Comedia research group they represent, stand 'outside' the library community.

2   Roots and discontinuities

Whatever version of community librarianship one considers - and it is a prime purpose of this study to identify and analyse a range of interpretations - its roots are closely intertwined with the broad historical development of both the practice and ethos of public libraries over the past century and a half. While not intending to base our discussion on retrospective analysis, it is none the less important to seek out those continuities in the history of the public library and its profession that have most directly informed community librarianship in its various late-twentieth century forms. The reason for this is simple. Any professional discourse is reinforced by an awareness that its tenets and activities are founded on a process of positive evolution, whereby the good and the bad, the effective and the ineffective, are pitched against each other in the cause of constructing, as a result of this dialectical process, a trustworthy expertise. In short, professionals thrive on an awareness of the 'wrong turns' and, indeed, the triumphs of the past. True, this is a Whiggish way of viewing professional consciousness and one which, moreover, invests heavily in the modernist optimism which society has tended to bestow upon groups of experts. Nevertheless it is evident that, in order to legitimise their social positions, many professionals require and seek a degree of historical consciousness, however small, that serves to emphasise professional continuity. Generally speaking, public librarians - including many of the community librarians questioned in the course of our research - display a healthy curiosity (though rarely a burning interest, admittedly) in their profession's past, even if that curiosity is often pitched at the level of folklore and myth, coloured by an 'ever onwards and upwards' perception drawn largely from an historic preoccupation with collections, administration and techniques.

However, rigorous historical investigation also requires that attention be paid to the possibility of *discontinuities* in the historical record. Thus, although it is inevitably the case that any model of professional service is to a degree the product of evolutionary forces, it is helpful to be alert to the likelihood of the 'radical redefinition', the 'new departure' or 'fundamental repositioning' in practice and, more importantly, ethos. Professionals can only be confident in proclaiming revolutionary pathways if they are able to locate and position their innovative advocacy on the historical landscape.

In seeking to explain the inheritance and the culture of community librarianship, this chapter extracts from the history of the public library evidence supportive of the proposition of continuity and, alternatively, that which might be employed to substantiate the position of those claiming a new status. An analysis of the short-term historical causes of community librarianship is provided in the next chapter. Here, the focus will be on the long period of public library development to around 1975. Two distinct phases are identified: the era of the 'civic' public library, 1850-1940; and that of the 'welfare state' public library 1940-1975. In a final section, these two phases of public library development will be commented upon further in the context of the shift towards postmodern society and in particular the post-Fordist reorientation in social policy.

The 'civic' public library and the 'undeserving' poor

Since their statutory inception in 1850 public libraries in Britain have been essentially parochial in character. Although they command national respect and commentary, and are familiar sites on the cultural landscapes of towns, villages and cities throughout the country, public libraries are local institutions founded upon, and operated by, municipal principles (Black, 1996a). The most obvious of these principles is the right of local citizens to tax themselves in order to fund services made open and accessible to all members of the local community. As such, public libraries have in a sense always served as *community* libraries. This was certainly the preferred term used by Stanley Jast (1939, p. 51) in his book *The Library and the Community*. Jast appears to have used the term, however, more as an unambiguous linguistic device, rather than as an ideological concept, to distinguish municipal libraries open to the public from historic 'public' libraries, like the Chetham Library in Manchester, and to avoid the misleading (as he saw it) word 'free'; although he did add conceptually that the term was warranted because 'this is what they are - libraries owned by, supported by, managed by and used by the community at large'. Others have reserved the term 'community library' for 'outlying' library points. Thus, community libraries have been defined by one library authority as 'all libraries not having "District Library" status and which serve villages or supplement the central and district libraries' (Cambridgeshire Libraries, 1984). The community library, historically and now, is therefore widely viewed as being synonymous,

17

on one level, with public libraries generally, and on another, with small satellite libraries deemed to be in closer contact with citizens than their larger counterparts. Similarly, community *librarianship* is often equated, rather simplistically it has to be said, with public librarianship and, in particular, its public service ethos, which in very small communities is perceived to be strengthened by social cohesion and familiarity.

However, as indicated in Chapter 1, interpretations of community are multifarious. Certainly, when public libraries were in their infancy, the idea of community as a means of furthering social solidarity was encapsulated in the *civic* ideal. Until the late 1880s public libraries were largely a phenomenon of the manufacturing areas of the north and the Midlands. (In London it was not until the quarter-of-a-century before the First World War that public libraries began to proliferate, doing so less as town-civic than as borough-municipal institutions.) A public library was promoted as the cultural powerhouse of a town. In an era when culture was viewed as both a contributor to and an outgrowth of economic progress, a town's cultural infrastructure was considered crucial to civic pride and to the competitive struggle with other towns for supremacy in urban social progress. This civic sense of community was frequently visually enacted by the grandeur of the public library built-form, in keeping with Raymond Williams' assessment that: 'For many people the sense of a community, the meaning of what it is to be living together in a particular place, is organized around some prominent mark or place' (Williams, 1978, p. 72).

Yet the civicness of early public library provision should not be mistaken for the type of close relationship between library and public which modern community librarianship infers. To the extent that public libraries were symbolic representations of a town's desire for success and prestige, their functional role as servant to the local citizenry in the matter of cultural enrichment, as opposed to their role as vehicles of civic pride driven by local elites, was inevitably weakened. For the public library to be truly accessible, argues Totterdell (1981, p. 40), it is necessary to make it an *integral* [our emphasis] part of community life'. In its early history, however, the public library can hardly be said to have displayed robust integration, as evidenced, according to Hendry (1981, p. 28), by the frequent use of the prefix 'branch', which tied local libraries conceptually to the civic centre, as opposed to the local community.

While it is important not to overstate and oversimplify the idea that public libraries in their early phase operated as mechanisms of social control (more about this later), where middle class reformers and librarians imposed their culture on a 'distanced' working class clientele, it is none the less a matter of historical fact that, generally speaking, an appreciation of plebeian cultural networks and popular culture was overshadowed by the need to propagate establishment, 'acceptable' forms of cultural production and political belief. There was clearly little recognition that public libraries should tailor their services to a segmented social body, especially to voluntary autonomous groups of the 'alternative' or 'social reform' kind which eras of rapid social change inevitably deliver and which authentic community librarianship has endeavoured to support [1]. Only in a piecemeal fashion have discrete groups of users (children, though a broad social grouping, being an early example) emerged as 'targets for specifically oriented library services', with group requirements commanding particular 'parameters, resource allocations and methods of work' (Martin, 1975, p. 9).

This said, the 'civic' public library was not an institution that stood entirely aloof from the populace. Nor did its librarians, as the mythology would have us believe, disengage from society in the tradition of the medieval scholar-librarian monk, most famously depicted in Umberto Eco's *The Name of the Rose*. Early public librarians often became leading figures in the civic and cultural life of urban communities (Black, 1996b, pp. 213-19). Societies and associations of all types - art, temperance, literary and philosophical, scientific, musical - were natural domains for librarians seeking to civilize urban environments and to further humanistic and material progress. Outreach - a word taken wrongly by many to be synonymous with community librarianship - was a prominent feature of public library provision even before the First World War, with services being developed for hospitals, the blind and even seamen (Kelly, 1977), and travelling libraries/collections being used for small reading rooms (Orton, 1980, pp. 13-15). Even more attention was paid to extension activities (often confused with outreach) such as lectures, adult education classes, reading circles, musical recitals, liaison with the National Home Reading Union, co-operation with the University Extension Movement and art exhibitions. Historically, the term 'library extension work' has been loosely used. As Jast (1939, p. 145) wrote: 'As originally employed it was meant to cover any and all activities which lay outside the work connected intimately with books - the essential services'. Extension work did not necessarily entail librarians positioning themselves in the depths of local communities. None the less, alongside early outreach, it did announce the willingness of librarians to look beyond the four walls of their libraries and the books they contained. By the inter-war period the concepts of outreach and extension work, even though definitions might have varied, were firmly entrenched in public library practice as illustrated by the obligatory references to them in standard texts about the public library, its history and its operational environment (Baker, 1922; Minto, 1932).

Enlarging the boundaries of library work in the late-nineteenth century beyond a merely docile provision of books and periodicals *in* libraries fitted with the emergent social and educational philosophies of the time. The very earliest public library enthusiasts were driven by a utilitarian desire to manufacture 'good citizens' whose improved moral outlook, practical skills and general intelligence would be appropriate to the political economy of modern capitalist, industrial society. As strong believers in the power of environment to shape character, utilitarians were naturally attracted to the moulding effects of a communal, civilized, civic space like a public library. From the outset, therefore, public libraries evinced a powerfully 'environmental' social and reforming purpose. However, the utilitarian philosophy that imbued the earliest public libraries was essentially reactive not pro-active. The onus was very much on citizens to help themselves by making use of facilities provided on a 'take it or leave it' basis. This approach was based to a large degree on the behavioural philosophy that the poor could be divided into two broad categories, the *deserving* (those who possessed, or had the potential to possess, the good character to work hard, seize the opportunities of material progress and act in a respectable way) and the *undeserving* (those who were beyond reform and who chose to follow lifestyles that resulted in impoverishment); or as one social historian (Jones, 1994, p. 48) has starkly defined the divide: '"Deserving" people were clean, sober, polite and grateful. They had fallen on hard times but might be assisted back to independence. "Undeserving" people were dirty, drunken and frequently abusive, lacking a respect for their betters'.

Particularly important was the prevention of the 'deserving' being subsumed into the 'undeserving' element of the population. In the late nineteenth century, especially in London but evident in other urban centres also, a wave of social anxiety swept across respectable society 'due to the perceived threat of the residuum uniting with an impoverished but politically intelligent artisan elite to challenge extant authority relations' (Marriott, 1996, p. 80). Hence, interest quickened in educational institutions like public libraries as a means of averting social dislocation and persuading the respectable working class not to be influenced by irrational demagogy. Educating the 'deserving' poor in public libraries would safeguard them from being dragged down into the 'submerged tenth' of society. At the same time it might even serve to reform, in some small way, the 'undeserving' element of the population. Indeed, this was a theme which had run through the public library movement since its inception. In commenting on the Manchester Public Library in 1852, one local newspaper expressed the hope that the 'thoughtful and intelligent' among the workers:

> might leaven, with their tendencies and sympathies, a large proportion of the inferior natures who come in contact with no higher standard of mental or moral worth than they find in their own ranks ... It is impossible to estimate the silent and unconscious power which a few thousand intelligently and rightly dispositioned minds distribute throughout the

20

whole mass of a large community .... This is the class of man for whom the Free Library will furnish the means of self-instruction - it will multiply their numbers, bring them together, and interest them conjointly in the common cause of good order and general enlightenment. [2]

In the last quarter of the nineteenth century attitudes to poverty and the 'deserving'/'undeserving' dichotomy began to change; and so with it, to a degree, the purpose and practice of public librarianship. The 'rediscovery of poverty' in the 1880s, which shook the Victorian middle class out of the social complacency into which it had fallen during the prosperous decades of the mid-Victorian boom, appeared to show that despite marked economic advance the question of poverty remained stubbornly and irritatingly insoluble. As a result, social commentators began to look less to the thesis that material misfortune and disadvantage were mostly a question of free will and personal responsibility, and more to the influence of a flawed and unstable socio-economic system. In addition, in the wake of Darwinist evolutionary theory, the idea that mental, moral and physical deficiency was hereditary gained in currency. Thus, battle lines were drawn, both in medical discourse and in social thought, between those who, on the one hand, viewed the persistence of poverty - seen in the extreme as an immovable 'residuum' of the permanently 'unfit' and unemployable - as resulting from a vicious downward spiral of insanitary environment, malnutrition and trade fluctuation, and on the other, those who pointed to the effect of 'hereditary predisposition', where physical, mental and even moral failings were passed naturally from generation to generation. This represented, in short, the appearance of a 'hereditary gap' whereby, according to degeneration theory, the very lowest elements of the urban poor were seen by some to be dragging down the standard of the race. Either way, the utilitarian, Malthusian idea that people *chose* to be poor, by virtue of exercising their freewill in favour of an immoral and slothful existence, lost ground. Poverty and disadvantage, it seemed, were not necessarily self-inflicted, for instead of being wilfully unemployed or casually underemployed - these being the chief causes of poverty - the poor were seen to be victims of either the 'system' or of the social delinquency and endemic (to capitalism) casualism of earlier generations which they had unfortunately inherited and would themselves inevitably self-perpetuate and reproduce (Harris, 1995; Marriot, 1996, pp. 83-4).

This shift in perceptions of poverty and its causes coincided with the replacement of utilitarianism by idealism as the leading school of philosophical thought and the main intellectual informer of social policy, including the public library movement. Idealists, often from a metaphysical position, denied the dominance of environment as the shaper of character, stressing instead the existence of innate qualities and knowledge. Every human mind, idealists taught, possessed latent potential and 'good' which it was the duty of society to nurture and exploit - for self-realisation of the individual was beneficial to the entire social body. It was believed that even those at the very bottom of the social pile could make some kind of contribution to the social whole; there was, after all, some good in everyone. Hence it was incumbent upon those in positions of social and educational privilege, including librarians, to stimulate in an active way the inherent qualities of citizens. This meant that the non respectable disadvantaged, who might previously have run the risk of being excluded from programmes of social amelioration by do-gooders because their individual shortcomings, were deemed to be self-formed, could now be incorporated into reform strategies. Thus, whereas social policy had once been defined according to the mechanical, stony philosophy of a deterrent Poor Law, in the late nineteenth century, when public library activity intensified significantly it should be noted, it became infused with the mission of *going to* the disadvantaged in a way not dissimilar to late-twentieth century community librarianship.

Moreover, that mission was one which purveyed and praised not just material but also spiritual benefits and gifts. For idealists, the spirit was of supreme importance; supplying its needs took priority over supplying those of the body, especially since material 'doles' were fraught with the danger of dependency. Idealists, like the working class housing reformer Octavia Hill, urged that the rich should help the poor as much through fellowship and solidarity as through pure almsgiving: the better-off should 'promote the happy natural intercourse of neighbours, mutual knowledge and mutual help' (Bell, 1942, p. 108). Aside perhaps from the settlement house movement, nowhere was this project of human fellowship, spiritual enrichment and social engagement more vividly displayed than in the late-Victorian and Edwardian public library movement. It is true that librarians did not *immerse* themselves in society to the degree seen, for example, in domestic missionary work. Nor did they carry Christian charity to the level of Christ himself who - like some but ultimately few community librarians have attempted - took a message to those at the very margins of society, to the destitute, the unloved and the downtrodden. Neither did they lose sight of their main constituency and of the fact that the public library was to a large degree a form of social policy which offered a 'lifeline to the "respectable" poor to divorce them from the "residuum" and from the "dangerous classes" who seemed to threaten both property and order' (Evans, 1978, p. 149). Nevertheless, what public librarians did begin to do was to take a wider view of the role of the public library in society, something which entailed a more sympathetic stance on the issue of popular fiction in libraries, as well as the promotion of 'good service' (for example open access and improved classification) and outreach and extension activities.

Reaching out and extending itself into communities represents, therefore, a long tradition in public library work, pre-dating the inception of community librarianship by a century or more. From the outset the public library concerned itself, albeit in a limited way, with the disadvantaged - the poor, the under-educated, the semi-literate, even the blind. But two very important qualifications to this statement need to be applied: public libraries were not just for the working class; nor were they ever really intended for the 'undeserving' residuum. These are important points which require elaboration.

First it is a misconception that the motivation behind early public library provision was to serve and civilize merely a working class clientele. Yet this myth persists and has been reinforced in recent years by historians' interest in theories of social control. Whatever its advantages the Industrial Revolution engendered, in organizational terms, a less controlled society. As a result, according to some historians, middle class reformers embarked on a successful campaign against working class culture, most notably in the field of leisure, in an effort to render the lower orders more rational and respectable (Donajgrodski, 1977; Bailey, 1978). The public library is one social institution among many which has been readily labelled as an instrument of control. For example, in respect of the Select Committee on Public Libraries (1849) Murison (1988) has written, originally in 1955, that: 'Little positive evidence was brought before the committee to show that there was a demand for the provision of municipal library services ... Where witnesses approved the need for the public library they almost unanimously showed themselves to be concerned with its effects as a counter-agent to evils rather than as a positive force for educational and recreational benefit'. An early critic of this line of argument was the City Librarian of Westminster, K.C. Harrison, who in 1963, long before the reaction against the social control thesis (Crossick, 1978; Thompson, 1981), questioned Murison's contention that there was little working class interest in public libraries and that they were simply 'thrust upon an unwilling world by do-gooders, moral reformers and sly capitalists who saw public libraries as soporifics, able to divert those members of the working classes who were beginning to ask awkward questions about the existing social system' (Harrison, 1963b, p. 2). Either way, the focus of this debate was, and has been, on the working classes and the extent of their compliance with public library initiatives. The general belief has been that the public library in its formative period was essentially for the underprivileged, whether controlled or not. Evidence drawn from the very early history of the public library movement has been very persuasive in this regard. It was said in the 1850s that Manchester Public Library was established as 'an acknowledgement by the wealthier class of its duties towards a vast industrial population' [3], and 'with a view to provide increased facilities for intellectual cultivation among all

23

classes, and especially to promote the education and self-culture of the poorer classes generally' [4].

In reality, however, the early public library was not simply a university for *poor* Victorians. What must be emphasized is its use - though the pattern varies, of course, according to location - by a wide range of social groups. The public library, proclaimed one local newspaper in 1887, was 'one of those mutual kind of institutions in which all classes may join with advantage, not only to the individual, but to the community at large' [5]. Earlier Edward Edwards (1869, p. 91) had described how the Manchester Reference Library was 'used by persons of every grade of society ... Clergymen, Professional men, persons engaged in all departments of mercantile pursuits, Clerks, Mechanics, persons out of work, boys in all positions of life'. Public libraries, he urged, were for 'all classes of the community'. Moreover, although for some in the 'superior ranks of society' the atmosphere, as Altick (1957, p. 238) wrote, 'of many libraries was disagreeable to even the moderately fastidious', for other well-to-do citizens the public library served as an invaluable source of literature and information. Certainly in some larger provincial towns they acted as minor versions of the British Museum Reading Room in London to which members of the professional, semi-professional and respectable classes generally had historically flocked. As the Select Committee on Public Libraries (1849, p. xii) reported: 'A great Public Library ought, above all things, to teach the teachers; to supply with the best implements of education those who educate the people, whether in the pulpit, the school or the press'.

What needs emphasising, therefore, is the healthy demand for public library services coming from middle class groups (Sturges, 1996). In some areas, in fact, middle class use of public libraries was greater, in terms of representation in the population as a whole, than working class patronage (Luckham, 1978, p. 83). So that while the working class featured strongly in early public library use (Kelly, 1966), certainly by the twentieth century any focus that had once fallen on the underprivileged had diminished markedly and was being rapidly replaced by a more catholic perception of readership (Luckham, 1971, p. 5). Given the *relatively* heavy use by middle - especially lower middle - class groups, it is therefore difficult to view community librarianship as an outgrowth of the usership pattern in the early public libraries. On the contrary, community librarianship's emphasis on the disadvantaged sets it apart from the pre-modern, as well as the modern post-1945, public library movement.

The second qualification to the statement that the public library has historically catered for the disadvantaged - to the image, if you like, of the working class 'soup kitchen' - is that, although workers were heavy users of the institution, by no means all sections of the working class patronized it. Only a small proportion of the working class was attracted to early public libraries (Noyce, 1974, p. 6). The public library in its formative period, despite its strong idealistic sense of social mission and outreach, was never intended as a cultural institution which could, or would, appeal to the very poorest sections of society, to the extremes of wretchedness - variously described as the residuum, the submerged tenth, the primitive tribes or savages, the abyss, the quagmire, the hopeless classes, the unfit, the unneeded, the dangerous classes or the 'other world' [6]. What Karl Marx called the 'lumpenproletariat' - a combination of the stagnant surplus of labour or 'reserve population', and the pauper classes - he described as 'social scum': an apolitical recruiting ground for criminals and loafers (Morris, 1994, pp. 13-16). Although early public librarians and their supporters would arguably have been less inclined to employ such strong and emotive language, they would probably have shared Marx's sentiments in respect of the very poor, and would certainly not have seen them as a natural constituency for their institution. From the outset the public library movement recognised the multiple divisions in working class culture - as marked as those between middle and working class (Thompson, 1963, p. 463) - and perhaps shared with respectable opinion generally the perception that the residuum was to be located even beyond the working class itself and thus outside the domain of respectable culture and self-improvement which sections of the working class and the public library inhabited.

Today, as in the pre-First World War era, it is difficult to view the public library - despite the language and legacy of community librarianship - as anything more than a social agency for the 'deserving' and the respectable. Although the distinction between 'deserving' and 'undeserving' poor is nowadays more blurred, in the popular mind it is still very real. The blurring between the two is a consequence of large-scale unemployment, commencing with the mass unemployment of the 1930s which even the most ardent Malthusian could not deny to have been generated by forces beyond the control of the individual. It was in the 1930s that the public library emerged as a truly *social* institution [7], serving a much wider range of social classes (middle and working) than had previously been the case. An unemployed worker describing in 1933 one of Liverpool's public libraries proudly announced that: 'Here the city has a reading room for the masses, a home from home, which is visited by old age pensioners, unemployed by the hundreds, down-and-outs, and all classes ... It is a model building for organization, comfort and good order, and I, as an unemployed man, have appreciated its facilities more than I can express' [8]. At the same time, however, running alongside the experience of mass poverty and the broadening of use of the public library, views on the persistence of a degenerate, alienated 'bottom tenth' continued to be broadcast. Ideas regarding the hereditarian causation of extreme poverty - the 'biologisation of class' in effect - reached a peak in the 1930s with the rise of racist Fascism (Macnicol, 1987, p. 299). One commentator, a sanitary inspector, argued at the time in respect of the nation's housing conditions that the bulk of the working class was being pulled down by a 'vicious slum element', the only solution in his opinion being 'segregation in the form of sanitary imprisonment ... It may be a very gradual and informal affair at first but ultimately will develop into a definite legal process, with these people forming a scheduled class, subject to special bye-laws and concentrated in blocks or groups of houses reserved for the purpose, where drastic sanitary policing will be possible' [9].

Despite the return of large scale unemployment in the 1980s and the impoverishment of previously 'deserving' and respectable groups that it has inevitably entailed, the perception of an unreformable bottom segment of the population has continued into the present day. Popular opinion, while a section of it accepts that the growth of an underclass is often due to forces beyond its control, also clearly believes that misfortune is to an extent endemic *and* inherited - if not for the most part biologically, then certainly socially in terms of the 'cycle of deprivation' [10]. Community librarians, like public librarians historically, have rarely engaged in detail with the debate on the distinction between 'deserving' and 'undeserving' poor, between the working class and the underclass. Instead, the tendency has been to avoid the past inability of the public library to address the needs of the very poor by employing the blanket (and some might say vague) word, the 'disadvantaged': a sociological description that can incorporate not only the poor, but also the handicapped, the sick or even those who merely experience, through particular social circumstances such as mere location, sub-standard access to library facilities. The disadvantaged are seen, through the community librarianship optic, to be chiefly characterised by *lack of opportunity*, rather than by 'innate inability or laziness or disinterest' (Martin, 1975, p. 12); that is to say, by weaknesses usually attributed to the 'undeserving'. In the tradition of public librarianship, community librarians have not formulated specific policy objectives for the society's underclass. Yet they have, however, built upon the outreach tradition of the public library forged during the era of idealist triumph in the half century before the First World War, applying that tradition, in fact, to groups further down the social scale than had previously been attempted. In the final analysis, however, those who stand outside the underclass, even professionals who declare an expertise to deal with its problems, may never come to understand it or be accepted by it. In this context community librarians of the late-twentieth century may wish to look back on 150 years of public library development and accept, realistically, that their institution has rarely shown an interest in the very poor and is therefore less than likely to depart from that historic position in the future.

26

The 'welfare state' public library

Whereas before the First World War the public library helped to engender a sense of community largely through localism and civic pride, in the inter-war period, and most emphatically after 1945, its idealist message of social fellowship was expressed more in terms of a *national* communal solidarity (community 'as state') in keeping with the ideology of the welfare state. The transformation in the public library's community commitment from a local to a national orientation began of course before 1914. This was illustrated by common and shared developments of techniques and purpose dating from the late nineteenth century such as the widening use of the Dewey classification scheme and the much vaunted argument that public libraries were key agencies for assisting in the reversal of national economic decline highlighted by the rapid advance of competing economies like Germany, which appeared to be reaping the benefits of good educational and, indeed, library systems. But it was in the 1920s and 1930s that the idea of the public library infrastructure as a national network and project took firm root. Thus, although contributing in 1935 to a publication celebrating a century of *municipal* progress, Stanley Jast (1935, p. 246) was able to announce in his essay on public libraries that: 'The centenary of the municipal corporation sees the public library firmly established as a thoroughly democratic organ of the national life'. Elsewhere Jast (1939) expressed the need for a national 'library grid', a suggestion which reflected the contemporary preoccupation, from London to Leningrad, with national plans and schemes for economic modernization, not least electrification. Another librarian, Ernest Baker (1924, preface), hoped that libraries would soon be co-ordinated into 'a national system, or group of systems, worked on economic lines, and empowered to act the part they were surely destined for in a civilized world'.

Increasing interest in the public library as a truly national service ran parallel with the growth of collectivism in the early twentieth century. In trumpeting the welfare state as a 'great departure', it has been considered ideologically correct, as well as methodologically sound from the historian's viewpoint, to view the pre-1945 period as a social policy wasteland, where any welfare or cultural provision that did occur was minimal and should certainly not be located in a Whiggish line of ascent culminating in the social and legislative triumphs of the late 1940s (Fraser, 1984, pp. xxii-xxiii). Others testify to greater continuity, arguing that by the Second World War there was 'a substantial tranche of public social provision in place' (Midwinter, 1994, p. 65), and that the First World War, and the inter-war years in particular, saw significant advances in social policy and in government intervention generally (Digby, 1989, p. 48). This creeping collectivism was both local and national in character: from municipal trading to the inauguration by central government of

27

an embryonic regional policy in the 1930s. Naturally, most social and cultural provision was undertaken by means of an alliance between localism (in the form of day-to-day administration of services) and centralism (through the passing of facilitating legislation, financial assistance and the expression of a national political will). This was clearly the case in respect of the public library which drew its statutory legitimacy from the Public Library Acts yet was envisioned and operated, certainly in its formative period, as a parochial institution. But just as with other areas of social policy - mass council housing being a prime example - the inter-war years witnessed a growth in perception of the public library as a national concern, with national objectives and national problems.

Although there is evidence in the 1920s and 1930s of an advance towards the type of consensus welfare state that emerged after 1945, that advance was not purposeful (Digby, 1989, p. 50). Pre-war collectivism proceeded by 'stealth and haphazard degree' (Midwinter, 1994, p. 73) rather than by virtue of a grand design. The opportunity for the preparation of a social blueprint did not arise until 1940. It was in that year that the welfare state, including the modern 'welfare state' public library, was truly born. The defeat of the British forces in France, followed by what was portrayed as a national triumph at Dunkirk, shook the nation out of both its military and social complacency. The end of the 'phoney war' left Britain facing the stark choice between defeat and the prosecution of a war of attrition involving considerable sacrifices by the civilian population. Total war required the inception of a benevolent 'war socialism' incorporating social reform and the promise of social reform, for the purpose of improving the nation's morale and rendering the civilian and military populations healthier and more efficient. The country's military war aims were thus inseparable from the project of building a new Britain. Moreover, the new society envisaged was much more egalitarian. The more 'total' the war, the more shared were its dangers and the greater the involvement and contribution asked of everyone. The war demanded, in the public's perception and in reality, as no war had previously, a rigorous 'equality of sacrifice'. Even before the official inauguration of the welfare state after 1945, therefore, the nation was experiencing and expressing a new and powerful desire for social justice, a national mood which delivered a surprising Labour victory at the end of the war (Addison, 1975).

The welfare state emerged from a silent revolution in social policy occurring during the Second World War. The Beveridge Report (1942) and the Education Act (1944) are prime examples of the abrupt shift towards collectivism occasioned by the war. The McColvin Report (McColvin, 1942) on public libraries is another. While earlier seminal reports on public libraries had stressed the dangers of central government influence and the value of municipal autonomy - the Kenyon Report, for example, had urged that the library service should remain on a permissive footing, local in character and free from government grants (Board of Education, 1927, pp. 38 and 150) - McColvin emphasised the appropriateness of centralization, mainly in the form of an amalgamation of library authorities and the creation of a department within government with direct responsibility for libraries, including the awarding of financial assistance. McColvin saw libraries as a chief means of planning a better world: they would inevitably become, he explained, 'necessary elements in the reconstruction of most things' (McColvin, 1942, p. v). As such, he viewed his report not simply as a statement of principles, but as a detailed blueprint for future operation (McColvin, 1942, p. viii), a perspective reflecting the intense wartime desire for social and national renewal.

The grand and adventurous vision of the public library which McColvin provided, defined as it was by a perception of the public library as a fully-fledged national cultural and, indeed, economic agency to be organised along universal lines, resurfaced time and again in the post-war period. In 1955 the Library Association formally repeated the recommendations McColvin had made (Kelly, p. 345) and much the same advice flavoured later government reports on public library structures (Ministry of Education, 1959), and on standards of service (Department of Education and Science, 1962), the latter re-emphasising (p. 6) 'the importance of the public library service as a great and developing national asset'. The period from 1939 to the mid-1970s witnessed a remarkable nationwide boom in the popularity of the public library, despite the austerity of the immediate post-war years. In the Second World War, as in the First, the everyday social changes wrought by total war, such as the enforced confinement of the blackout or of mass military service, as well as increased interest in social affairs generally, had resulted in a marked increase in public library use. Thus, whereas in 1939 the number of registered borrowers stood at 8.9 million, this figure had increased by 1949 to 12 million (Library Association, 1950, p. 5). There was also a widening in the institution's social base (more about this later). The development of libraries in the counties, driven to a degree by a suburban drift of urban populations into semi-rural areas and into new towns, was especially notable.

The post-war advance of the public library was unprecedented, more impressive even than the achievements of the Carnegie era, if not in bricks and mortar (initially) then certainly in terms of ideological commitment. As befitted the times, librarians themselves expressed considerable optimism: 'The period ahead holds great promise for British librarianship in general ... The interest shown by Central Government is beginning to yield results', reported Ealing Public Libraries (1964). Government's most notable contribution was the passing of a new Public Libraries Act (1964), which for the first time made the provision of a public library by local authorities obligatory and referred to the supply of a *comprehensive* service to all sections of the community. It appeared that the truly *modern* public library had arrived, reflecting the rational planning and universalism of the welfare state itself. Since 1945 the state, ostensibly benevolent in its outlook, had become much more interested in the public library question; this echoing the theory that in modern societies the state's record-keeping infrastructure - the public library being a form of record-keeping institution - is consolidated and centralized, as opposed to pre-modern, segmented societies where its administrative reach is limited (Giddens, 1985). Public libraries became an integral part of the climate of planning. This was clearly the case in post-war new towns (Tonks, 1975). In Stevenage, for example, a new social environment appeared to offer the perfect backdrop against which the public library could prove its modernist credentials: the town's library, it was reported, 'destroyed the old [librarian] image of the dreamy-eyed philosopher lost amongst his books' [11].

For the first time, therefore, it was possible to refer with confidence, in a thoroughly modernist way, to the existence of a public library *system*, even if the reality of the network that existed was more a question of co-operation than of full integration directed from the centre. Systems, their construction and a reliance on them, are a key component of modernity. In a mechanical sense, systems are assemblages of interdependent things forming a complex unity. Thus, it is not surprising to see in the 1960s: a heavy investment in ideas about inter-library co-operation (Ministry of Education, 1962); or the development of poly-purpose cultural centres - such as the Abraham Moss Centre in Manchester (Kelly and Kelly, 1977, p. 266) - where the public library formed an indispensable and sometimes core component of an educational and recreational complex; or the amalgamation of library authorities in accordance with local government reform; or talk (made known to one of our respondents who headed a very small library authority in the 1960s) in higher political and library circles of the establishment of giant regional library authorities with overseeing supremos. But systems can also be conceptualized on a non-material level, as activities working towards a common end. Thus, the public library system of the post-war years, particularly from the 1960s onwards, should also be viewed as a child of the *ideological* commitment to social justice, public betterment and increased opportunity forged in the Second World War and its immediate aftermath. The optimistic post-war era witnessed a strident rejection of the past: the 'better Britain' was 'modern and ahistorical' (Meller, 1996, p. 20). It was a society where historic fears concerning government intervention and planning were swept aside by a strong sense of social purpose that was nowhere more real than in the efforts of librarians and their local authorities to rejuvenate and expand, as well as make more relevant, the nation's public library service; and to do this by constructing a strong public service ethos. In many respects, therefore, the 1960s witnessed the high water mark of public library development and confidence with periodic crises, certainly after the mid-1990s, setting in thereafter; although some continue to deny, of course, the decline of public libraries and the immense funding problems they have faced in recent years [12]. It is the notion of 'the system' as *purposeful* planning - in this case social, ethical and egalitarian in nature - rather than planning based on technical rationality, which community librarianship came to inherit as its chief characteristic from the objectives and operations of the 'welfare state' public library.

The social commitment that to a large degree defined post-war public library policy did not feature, however, a *specific* concern for the disadvantaged. The most vivid attempt to isolate, label and target the disadvantaged occurred, in fact, in the context of underdeveloped public library services abroad and the need to encourage, in the post-colonial world in particular, modern library systems along British lines in order to promote independence and national self-help. When Lionel McColvin (1950) and others spoke of public library extension, they did not always mean the type of traditional non-book work which public libraries had undertaken since the nineteenth century, but often the business of exporting British public library know-how and a liberal social purpose to the rest of the world, especially its underdeveloped and developing nations [13]. In the 1950s and 1960s public librarianship's missionary spirit manifested itself most clearly in advice given to the world's, not Britain's, disadvantaged. Regarding library provision at home, far from broadcasting a message emphasising the need to incorporate those working class sections of the community previously excluded, the welfare state public library, in keeping with the ideological consensus of the day, adopted the language of universalism. The needs of the poor - cultural, literary, informational and educational, as well as material - would be met by a blanket provision which avoided stigmatizing the disadvantaged citizen. Many public librarians enthusiastically adopted ideas concerning universal provision, hoping that their institution's mythical soup-kitchen image and its stigma as a public charity might be banished for good. This strategy, drawn very much from the fight for liberty and social solidarity during the war, was to mould the public library into the modern, democratic institution it had always claimed to be, offering its services across the social body, to be truly 'libraries in the service of the community' [14], without discrimination or favour. The widening perspective described here was explained to the nation in 1957 in a BBC television news broadcast by McColvin, then City Librarian of Westminster. Asked to describe what people were reading nowadays McColvin answered: 'They're reading about everything. We cover the widest possible range of material. We try to provide books in everything in which people are interested, and our readers cover every type and class of person, from the Members of the Houses of Parliament down the road, to the children from the nearby housing estates'

31

[15]. Later, McColvin's successor at Westminster, K.C. Harrison, confirmed the democratic strategy when he wrote: 'Nowadays, the libraries which are provided by all are indeed used by all .... This is a right and proper state of affairs for a public service, but it is one that would have been quite unthinkable a generation or two ago' (Harrison, 1963b, p. 6). Evidence of the non-discriminatory, universal approach can also be found in the efforts to bring library services to Britain's new towns of the late-1940s and early-1950s. One of the main objectives of new towns like Stevenage was to construct mixed communities, to contrast with the divided cities inherited from the Victorian age. Public libraries in new towns, invested with the ethos of universalism and drawing on the democratic traditions of the public library movement, appeared to be ideal agencies for serving the experimental, socially-mixed communities which planners attempted to establish.

But despite the rhetoric of modernity and universalism engaged in by representatives and supporters of the public library - not to mention a helpful social climate of massification as seen in education, for example - the reality of 'across the board' patronage proved to be an elusive dream. Far from appealing to a potentially huge working class readership, public libraries succumbed to even greater middle class influence. The middle class grip on public libraries became a stranglehold. Thus, by 1962 David Gerard could justifiably describe the public library's 'public' as 'a narrow band taken from somewhere in the middle of the middle classes' [16]. In the affluent post-war society, certainly from the late 1950s onwards, the middle classes operated considerable power in respect of public libraries. They exercised a mighty leverage over both the type and standard of service provided (Jordan, 1972). As one of our sources recalled, in the middle class suburban branch library he worked at in the 1950s 'the clientele was critical and vocal ... they were quite demanding; they appreciated good service but they pretty soon made their complaints known if complaints there were'. The middle classes also dominated even in less leafy suburbs. In Tottenham in 1947 it was found that: 'Compared with the general population [of the area] ... the library members, like the bookreaders, are predominantly young, middle class and well educated ... Analysis by social class shows how little, compared with the middle class, the working class has been penetrated by consciousness of the public library' [17].

The post-war middle class bias was confirmed with academic credibility, in 1971, with the publication of Bryan Luckham's *The Library in Society: a Study of the Public Library in an Urban Setting*, which showed that working class groups used libraries in proportions lower than their representation in the population as a whole. Moreover, Luckham's study reflected a growing reaction of some public librarians, unaware as they were of the historic middle class heritage of the public library, to what they saw as a lurch towards an elitist position. Cracks began to appear in the public library's universalist facade, in the same way as the efficacy of the welfare state itself came to be questioned as a result of the 'rediscovery' of poverty in the 1960s and the gradual dissemination of that rediscovery thereafter. For the first time since the public library's earliest decades, librarians and commentators on libraries began to engage purposefully with the class issue (Devereux, 1972), not least in the context of race relations and services for ethnic minority groups (Jordan, 1972). Contrary to the spirit of paternalism and benefaction that had imbued so much early public library activity, the modern institution was said to be abandoning its working class roots. This was certainly the historical line followed by a seminal source for the community librarianship movement, *The Libraries' Choice* (Department of Education and Science, 1978), which was noticeably eager to quote from Charles Dickens' famous speech at the opening of the Manchester Public Library in 1852, when he expressed the hope that the library would 'prove to be a source of pleasure and improvement in the cottages, the garrets and the cellars of the poorest of our people'. Public libraries, the report continued, 'retained a working class image at least until the 1930s ... The well-to-do preferred the allegedly cleaner books and more reputable customers of the private subscriptions libraries like Boots'. It was only after 1945, it was argued, that middle class users were to any significant degree attracted by the institution. Hence the need, inferred in the report, to revive an essentially working class past.

It is in the misreading of the public library's history by librarians in the late 1960s and early 1970s that community librarianship drew much of its impetus. In viewing modern public library development against the backdrop of a proletarian past, professionals were in effect echoing claims made elsewhere that the welfare state was essentially *for* the middle classes. This appeared always to have been the case in respect of the respectable suburban public library. What was more worrying for some librarians (though confusing may be a better description of their state of mind) was the loss of a working class feel to branch libraries in the inner cities and industrial towns. Here, whereas at one time an artisan elite had typified public library use (the skilled worker providing almost a caricature of the average public library patron), this particular class, as Gorz (1982) has argued, was slowly absorbed into the lower reaches of middle class society. When public libraries in such areas failed to change and to reflect this social transformation, they naturally began to look anachronistic, appearing both historic and irrelevant. Unable to take account of cultural shifts, many public libraries found themselves marooned in a Carnegie time-warp, in an age when class relations had moved on and communities had fragmented away from the Coronation Street model. In short, many librarians felt that they had lost, inexplicably and suddenly, a whole social class of reader.

In the 1970s, therefore, it became fashionable for librarians to try and reclaim the working classes. This entailed a re-statement of the need to work primarily according to a social, as opposed to a purely professional-bureaucratic, model of service. Librarians thus sought to play down their technical and administrative inheritance, which had proved to be beneficial in the 'furnace of planning' that had characterized the era of the classical welfare state, and reinvigorate their ethical purpose. To do this they would at least be able to draw on the ideological commitment that had carried the profession through the post-war years. However, the community librarianship approach that was to emerge from this episode of soul searching paid less attention to the universalism of the post-war settlement and the 'social service state', and owed considerably more to the idea of discriminating in favour of the disadvantaged; although not, as shall be argued, the very poorest sections of society labelled earlier in this chapter as the 'undeserving' poor.

In forging a new social mission out of the ideological credentials of the welfare state, librarians also found helpful the new outward-looking stance adopted in the 1950s and, especially, the 1960s. Making libraries more open, accessible and user-conscious was part and parcel of the mature 'welfare state' public library's personality, and formed one of the main planks of the community librarianship philosophy (although some, it is true, have interpreted, wrongly, an improved image and a healthier interaction with the public as its *essential* principle). After the war the public library gradually became a more open institution. The new attitude of the public library was to carry its message, in a missionary fashion, out to the people (Murison, 1988, p. 147). Victorian-style restrictions could not, of course, be eradicated overnight. Recalling her use of a public library as a child in the 1950s one reader recalled that:

> I was allowed only two tickets, one for fiction the other non-fiction. And exchanges were not permitted until the third day. The Dragon sternly sent me back if I tried to take out a book from the Adult section. But she had a soft heart and after a while suggested my mother should have two tickets and empower me to choose books for her! But there was still a benevolent censorship exercised by 'I don't think your mother will like this' if I tried to take a book the Dragon considered unsuitable for juvenile eyes. [18]

However, such evidence should not detract from the argument that the 'welfare state' public library, for all its officiousness and its interest in bureaucracy and technical procedures, evolved slowly towards a professed goal of increased user-friendliness. The perspective adopted was one of 'the library in society' [19]. Engagement by librarians *in* society intensified. The groundwork for this social engagement appears to have been done in the 1930s which one of our respondents, a former chief librarian, recalled as a turning point for public libraries: 'During the 1930s there seemed to be a lot of good librarians about, very active people who were determined ... to pull libraries out of their Victorian image and give them a twentieth century image. It was the 1930s before the twentieth century arrived ... You talk about community librarianship but there's always been community librarianship in my experience really ... art exhibitions, lecture programmes, bulletins for users, story hours, visits to schools. There was a lot of community work but it wasn't called that' [20]. The depth of some librarians' social involvement was detailed by W.C.B. Sayers in 1947:

They have established reading circles, library talks, exhibitions, story hours for children, musical recitals, and have also encouraged to meet in the libraries - or at least to work in complete harmony with them - such organizations as the National Home Reading Union, the Workers' Educational Association, the University Extension movement, and similar bodies. In Croydon your Chief Librarian holds the view that he should endeavour to link every noteworthy society in the town with the library, in the effort to make it the centre of the cultural activities, especially the non-formal ones, of the borough. He holds (unsought) the offices of President of The Croydon Contemporary Arts Group, and of The South Norwood Social Centre; Chairman of the Writers' Circle, The Croydon Music Club, The Croydon Players; Vice-President of The Croydon Philharmonic Society, The Croydon Symphony Orchestra, The Croydon Workers' Educational Association; and is a member of The Chamber of Commerce, The Croydon Rotary Club and the Council of The Surrey Archaeological Society; he is also Librarian of The Croydon Natural History and Scientific Society. [21]

Extension activities boomed in the post-war ear. Luckham (1971, p. 13) reported how most non-book cultural services like lectures, film shows, gramophone recitals and poetry readings doubled or even quadrupled in their frequency in the 1960s. Public libraries sought to extend their expertise into new and dynamic areas, such as occurred in Cambridge in the late 1960s when plans were put forward for the public library to house or run the local tourist information kiosk [22]. Similarly, outreach was extended and refined. Novel and interesting models of service were evident even during the war, when libraries began to operate in tube shelters (Snaith, 1942; Russell, 1995, pp. 40-47). In 1948 Westminster inaugurated a 'personal delivery service', where the old and infirm were visited once a fortnight, the first housebound service to be set up in Britain. Westminster also visited a number of Darby and Joan clubs [23]. The number of mobile librarians in operation throughout the country escalated rapidly, initially as replacements for bombed library premises, but later as a helpmate to expanding county services, and also to urban library authorities faced with the problem of vast new housing estates having been constructed at breakneck speed without due attention being paid to the supply of supporting social and cultural facilities. Improving outreach also entailed the identification and targeting of groups with 'special needs', although the use of this term differed considerably from the meaning that community librarianship proponents were later to attach to it. Thus, in 1950 the Library Association identified rather loosely such groups, organizations and institutions as hospitals, old people's clubs, the housebound, prisons, adult education centres, technical schools, youth clubs and community centres as being in the 'special needs' category (Library Association, 1950, p. 20).

To promote its new 'public' image, the institution's professionals began, albeit slowly, to develop public relations skills (Harrison, 1973), although this was accompanied by the realisation that 'librarians must stop acting as their own public relations officers' and enlist help, to complement their developing publicity skills, of newspaper editors, journalists, public relations experts and other media professionals [24]. Only in this way, it began to be said, could justice be done to the splendid new extension and outreach activities that were being put in place. Aside from accessing the promotional techniques of the commercial world, librarians also paid close attention to the latest ideas in design, especially modern styles imported from Scandinavia. The post-war years witnessed what Berriman and Harrison (1966, p. 18) referred to as a 'renaissance' in British library buildings, particularly after 1958 when wartime building restrictions were finally lifted. Included in the *Library Association Record* of 1960 was a special supplement on public library buildings which were said to be 'reclothing the library service in this country' [25]. Moreover, with regard to the new Holborn Public Library in London it was the editor's opinion that: 'This library puts British design on the level of all that is best in post-war continental library building ... From the moment one sets foot inside the door, one progresses through a sequence of dreams-come-true ... The final impressions were of a friendly and stimulating library' [26]. Inside buildings, both new and old, attention also began to be paid to brightening and improving the experience of public library use. To meet an expanding educational demand, reference and study facilities were quickly developed. Displays of materials were enlivened. Finally, there was considerable exploitation of the explosion in paperback publishing, much of it educational [27], which, because of the vivid designs involved, dramatically changed the general internal appearance of libraries; similarly, the introduction of transparent plastic sheaths for hardback books allowed brightly coloured dust jackets to be retained and the dull mono-coloured bindings of old to be phased out. Together these developments - in design, promotion, extension and outreach -

amounted to a determined desire to improve significantly 'library assistance to readers' (Collision, 1950), this being the title of a popular librarianship text which, by 1963, had run through four editions.

A further manifestation of the public library's widening interest in the satisfaction of its users was the increasing time and energy devoted to researching needs and patterns of use. Informal, background research had always been a feature of public library planning. Even in the nineteenth century a degree of investigative enthusiasm was in evidence in the form of fact-finding, descriptive surveys of the public library scene by local authorities seeking either to establish a library or to improve the existing service by taking note of new buildings and procedures established elsewhere (Relton, 1887; Johnman and Kendall, 1885). In the inter-war years, to a large extent motivated by work done in the United States, in particular that of the Graduate Library School in Chicago, there appeared the first acknowledgement of the importance of systematically appraising user requirements (Kelly, 1977, pp. 285-6). However, such appraisals were usually conceptualized as studies of reading habits. Such research was advocated, partly, in the tradition of the librarian as moral adviser: it was the librarian's aim, remarked W.C.B. Sayers (1935-6, p. 233), to match 'the right reader with the right book'. However, most research in the post-war era was concerned not with users but with the organization and supply of materials. Research projects remained, like the Library Association's *Survey of Libraries* (1938), essentially library not customer oriented, and descriptive rather than theoretical. Not until the 1960s did the emphasis shift to analysing the information and reading needs of users, a trend illustrated in the publication of a steady flow of works either on the methodology of library research (Line, 1967) or as the result of particular projects aimed at a deeper understanding of library use, through both the exploration of user attitudes and the recognition of a variety of pertinent variables. Local government reorganisation in the 1960s and 1970s gave a boost to such research. The larger library authorities that ensued meant that dedicated research officers could be appointed; and many public libraries, in fact, 'accepted the challenge of reorganisation with eager anticipation and chose to plan their new library service on a sociological basis rather than historical (Barnett, 1977, p. 302). More and more library authorities were anxious to tap into the deepening expertise in social science methods, as in the case of Westminster Libraries in 1967 when it co-operated with an Office of Scientific and Technical Information survey of reference library activity which employed a rich combination of administered, telephone and postal questionnaires eliciting answers from thousands of users [28]. Such exercises prepared the way for the later enthusiasm for community profiling (Ritchie, 1982, pp. 39-43; Beal, 1985), as well as for the general insistence that defining customer requirements is a central feature of planning library services (McKee,

1989, pp. 54-7). Library research was but one element in the public library's drive for greater responsiveness. Awareness of the need to study both users and the characteristics of a community in a purposeful and scientific way was a significant forerunner of community librarianship (Redfern, 1989, p. 3) - to the extent that in some minds such market research, and the operational changes made as a result, are seen as virtually synonymous with it.

The modern outward-looking stance that public libraries took up in the post-war years, especially from the 1960s onwards, was by no means a universal phenomenon. It should be emphasised that the pace of change varied wildly from place to place. Even today some public libraries appear still to be languishing in a Victorian landscape. Nonetheless, over the past forty years public libraries have, generally speaking, endeavoured to display a closer interest in their users, attempting to do so by becoming more user-responsive, partly through the undertaking of user studies; and also by appearing less formal in the image they broadcast to the public, particularly in the use made of new building, decorative and display styles: designs such as those employed for the central libraries of Bradford (1968) and Croydon (1993), in modern and post-modern styles respectively, have attracted, genuine praise. At times, however, it appears that for public and professional alike publicity, user-friendliness, user needs/satisfaction research and the modernisation (or in some cases postmodernisation) of the built-form - each of these key features of the post-war public library - constitute the *essence* of a new community approach to the provision of services, expressive of a *fundamental* shift towards greater cohesion between librarian and user. Indeed it might not be an exaggeration to argue that community librarianship is widely viewed as merely the achievement of a closer interaction between provider and customer engendered by an ambience of modernity, often associated with new electronic technologies devoted to catalogue searching and the issue/return of stock [29]. The community librarianship which emerged from the era of the 'welfare state' public library sought to throw aside the bureaucratic straightjacket that planning sometimes provided, yet at the same time looked to draw on the social commitment to people and to greater access which the post-war ideological climate engendered. But this was to be achieved not simply through intensified user-friendliness and an aping of good practice in the world of retailing, but via a realignment of priorities in favour of the poor. Community librarianship was to amount to much more than the replacement of linoleum and light bulbs with bright carpets and fluorescent lighting. In fact it came to constitute a radical social engagement which, because of the historic exclusion of society's severely disadvantaged, largely occurred outside the library built-form, and owed only *something* to the publicity and promotion drives and image-building that the public library undertook after the Second World War.

The post-Fordist public library

Whereas the modern, Fordist, 'welfare state' public library, reaching a peak of development in the late-1960s and early-1970s, displayed an unqualified concern for greater equality and social justice in keeping with the general ethos of the post-war politico-social settlement, it did not set out in any significant fashion to *target* socially disadvantaged users and non-users. That particular policy departure, one of the key elements of community librarianship, was not undertaken first in Britain, nor in any other European 'welfare state' society [30]. Like so many public library initiatives of the past - one could cite here the turn-of-the-century emphasis on good services to users, or late-nineteenth century systematic classification, or early twentieth century commercial and technical libraries - it originated in the United States. It was there, against the backdrop of social tensions in the 1960s, that public librarians began to talk about prioritizing service objectives in respect of the 'unserved', a social grouping described by one writer as being made up of: 'Negroes, Indians, Spanish Americans, Appalachian poor Whites, migratory workers, slum-dwellers - the twenty five percent of our population who live in or on the outskirts of poverty - who constitute a distinct subculture with values different from the prevailing values of the majority middle class culture' (Golighty, 1970, p. 12). As part of the general strategy to arrest urban decay, in particular the economic and cultural emaciation of the inner city, American public librarians broke new ground in the resourcing of services to the socially deprived. The term 'information poor' was coined: a concept designed to describe in an emotive yet precise way the deficiency in information-seeking skills, or information aptitude, which could be suffered by anyone in society - including obvious groups like the elderly, the handicapped, the imprisoned, the ethnically oppressed - but mostly, to employ the best demographic descriptor, by the economic poor (Childers, 1975). Numerous library programmes were set in motion on the basis that the public library could assist in the quest for urban renewal [31].

One contemporary commentator, whose words are worth quoting at length as an illustration of the social determination and optimism of the American public library profession at the time, asserted that:

> Not enough librarians realize that they can no longer preside over institutions or agencies in splendid isolation ... in this day of interlocking complexity, when we seem to find only half-solutions to the problems of our own human aggregation, let us be firmly committed to providing a lateral outreach to the poor and to the disadvantaged, to involving them in a shared responsibility for planning and implementing community action programs. Too long we have either ignored the poor or else have provided

39

welfare services to the poor and the disadvantaged on the basis of superior-inferior authority relationships ... The excitement, the cutting edge of things in education today, is in the dusty streets of urban areas, the large cities and in the slums. That is where the action is. That is where we need the boldest, the most creative, and the best of our educators and librarians, if we are to fill out the mosaic of a still distant Great Society. It is in these areas that the disadvantaged are and where one can most truly become an innovator ... libraries of all kinds have an essential role to play in putting those disadvantaged by poverty and prejudice on an equal footing with those who are more familiar with abundance and social success. (Nyquist, 1968, pp. 78, 81, 83)

He goes on to give a vivid example of the innovative work in which some American librarians engaged in the 1960s:

Administrators of public libraries in the major cities of New York State knew that their services were being used very little by the poor, the illiterate, and those disadvantaged by prejudice. There were language barriers, educational deficiencies, and limited mobility, to name a few deterrents. Most of these libraries have now set up special programs in an attempt to reach the disadvantaged. The Brooklyn Public Library established a position in 1961 called Community Coordinator to work with individuals and organizations to help them become more aware of the very existence of the library and the many services it has to offer. When in 1964 federal funds under the reconstituted LSCA became available for urban areas - and, incidentally, this is another recognizable admission of the financial plight of the cities - the Brooklyn Public Library added three more community co-ordinators and some supporting staff to the program. Approaches are tailored to the communities served so that an honest attempt is made first to determine and then to meet needs. If the section comprises many Spanish-speaking people, the community co-ordinator learns enough Spanish to converse with the residents and the local civic, educational and political leadership. Books are brought to meetings or social hours at which these people are in attendance and a description of the pertinent services offered is made. The goal of the project is to widen awareness of the library as an information centre and a source of continuing education in low-income, low-education communities, to find new ways of reaching those unreached who have most to gain from a library's services. The co-ordinators work out in the community rather than within the library building. They operate as 'salesmen', working with individuals, institutions, and organizations in disadvantaged areas to interpret the library's resources and to promote greater use of its services.

The co-ordinators have taken different approaches to reaching people. They even ring doorbells in housing projects to acquaint residents with the library's services. One co-ordinator established a Career and College Club to raise the aspirations of promising teenagers, to encourage them to go on with their education. They have established community dialogues to attack the problems of crime and juvenile delinquency, an activity that involves many official and community agencies. They have taken basic informational paperbacks into bars, beauty and barber shops in an experimental project to encourage people to turn to books for answers to their daily problems. The newest project is the operation of a Sidewalk Service - an 'autovan' - (a type of bookmobile) that will permit the co-ordinators actually to take books, book displays, records, and films to the street corners, parks and gathering places of the various neighborhoods, actually going to the people not just with words but with materials to show these 'disadvantaged' citizens what the library can do to aid them in improving their lives - to help each individual to 'read your way up'. (Nyquist, 1968, pp. 84-5)

Such library work *in* the community resembles closely some of the imaginative community librarianship that began to appear in Britain a decade or so later. Another contemporary American commentator referred to this type of work as 'ghetto services' undertaken in what he called the 'disorganized districts' of larger cities (Martin, 1969). It was acknowledged in the United States at the time that reaching down into the depths of society, into 'disorganised' cultures, was a difficult thing for librarians to do, accustomed as they were to dealing with an articulate, educated and informed middle class clientele. British librarians, while some have relished the opportunity of radical social engagement, have similarly been uneasy with the prospect of taking their services and professional expertise deep into the 'disorganised' layers of society. As discussed above, the public library in its formative period never really intended that its services would be taken up by the 'undeserving' poor, those with little intention of helping *themselves* to live a respectable and rewarding life. This tradition appears to have continued into the late-twentieth century. Public librarians, with some exceptions of course, appear to be happier in dealing with 'settled' and 'rehabilitated' communities where even those on modest incomes seek to better themselves materially or enrich their lives in a spiritual-recreational sense through using cultural institutions like public libraries, rather than dealing with social groups that have no inclination towards respectability or cultural enlightenment.

Yet this is a constituency that will not go away. On the contrary, social commentary over the last decade or so has been rich with the concepts of the new poor and the burgeoning underclass. Although in the quarter-of-a-century after the Second World War poverty never quite disappeared as a social issue (unlike in Germany, Denmark or Holland, for example, where social security benefits were set at a higher level), it did seem to be fast becoming a thing of the past. The rediscovery of residual poverty in the 1980s thus came as something of a shock to social planners and professionals who had got used to the idea of the material advance experienced in the 1950s and 1960s being the natural state of affairs [32]. From the economic downturn of the mid-1970s onwards, therefore, public library professionals found themselves confronted with a *relatively* new social problem and constituency. Some responded quickly, in the form of a new service mode called community librarianship, to the increasingly 'disorganised' (to use the American term) communities that emerged as a common feature of urban life in Britain. Others, the majority, have been content to remain within the traditional, mainstream operations and rationale of the public library.

Addressing the need of poor, 'disorganized' communities is not at the heart of the inherited rationale of public library work in Britain. In postmodern society, however, social institutions are faced, at every turn, with the problems of social disorganization - but of a kind which are not confined to the lower orders but permeate the entire social fabric. As discussed in Chapter 1, in the postmodern world, societies are de-massifying and fragmenting, whether in respect of cultural, economic or political life. For example, leisure - a major service area for public libraries - is fast losing the uniformity that characterized it under modernity. Whereas the modern project brought with it 'organized' leisure where, to a large extent, activities were predictable (often according to social class) and directed (often in a paternalistic way), in the postmodern age tastes are infinitely more varied, are decoupled from social class and can now not be dictated to the degree they were in the past. Moreover, leisure goods and services are no longer merely commodities with a price-tag, but icons, used by individuals and groups to symbolize the cultural niche they wish to occupy at any particular moment in any particular social circumstance among the bewildering array of changing lifestyles that characterize the postmodern era (Bramham and Spink, 1994; Rojek, 1993).

The disorganised nature of postmodernity is something which the public library - certainly in the realms of leisure - cannot afford to ignore. Under modernity, as we have seen, the public library developed a Fordist response to the needs of a society seeking to heal its rifts and build a lasting consensus. Planning, universality and social justice were the orders of the day, in public library policy as in social policy generally. Arguably, it was from this modernist post-war project that community librarianship emerged. It is true that community librarianship bears many of the credentials of postmodernity - certainly, it is a service mode that acknowledges difference and diversity, and the need to respond to them in a bottom-up, flexible way. However, it is important to identify the core element of an authentic community librarianship philosophy as the *prioritizing* of services to the disadvantaged, an objective which draws heavily on the ethical project of modernity. Tom Featherstone (1992, p. 147) thus defines community librarianship in the following way: 'There are a number of definitions of community librarianship but in general terms it can be said to concern itself with the needs of communities and the giving of priority to those least able to help themselves'. Earlier, in 1981, one of the leading exponents of community librarianship, Barry Totterdell (1981, pp. 39-40), explained that behind the practice lay 'a recognition that public library services are for all, not only for the better educated, more affluent 'middle class' minority from whom the service has tended to draw its clientele, but also for the less literate, the disadvantaged, those who are perhaps less book-orientated but whose needs for information and for life-enrichment may be greater'.

However, also in circulation are definitions of community librarianship which display less explicit references to serving the disadvantaged. For example, Bob McKee (1982, p. 72) sees community librarianship as something that replaces 'a passive, buildings-based approach to service with a more pro-active, developmental approach which gets much closer to the customer community and seeks to meet 'need' as well as expressed 'demands'. Such recent, more acceptable definitions of community librarianship, though urging that services be community-based, tend to avoid the word 'disadvantaged', reflecting a movement away from ideological thinking and policymaking in the postmodern age. The age of the grand idea appears, for the moment, to have passed. In its place has arrived a multifarious array of socio-political groupings, each with its own agenda which at times may connect with the agendas of others, but rarely in a way that constitutes an ideological platform of universal ideas. If the public library is to flourish it must, of course, address the postmodern, pluralist constellation of lifestyles and communities. Consequently the tendency among strategists nowadays is to frame policy objectives in the broadest way possible. In the language of post-Fordism the aim is to serve all social groupings and communities in a *flexible* and *responsive* fashion. Reflexivity and responsiveness set the post-Fordist library apart from its Fordist predecessor which, like other 'welfare state' social agencies, looked to centralization and massification rather than to devolution of managerial and operational responsibility and to niche marketing.

But the Fordist and post-Fordist public library diverge in a much more significant way than in the simple matter of providing an adaptable, community-oriented, 'listening', market approach. For in respect of ideological commitment, specifically the redistributive ethic, they are worlds apart. Whereas inherent in the modern, Fordist public library, as in social policy generally (Lowe, 1994, p. 3), was the desire to *redistribute* opportunity, if not

43

wealth - even if in reality the welfare state often worked in favour of the middle classes - the postmodern, post-Fordist public library avoids the idealistic, crusading, prioritizing language that characterised earlier rationale, part of which was the community librarianship initiative of the later 1970s and early 1980s, moulded in the image of the 'Great Society' civil rights movement of 1960's America. Postmodern community librarians, including many we spoke to, believe it is appropriate to dilute vocabulary that smacks of targeting the poor, reforming society or making judgements about social priorities, preferring instead - admittedly sometimes not genuinely but merely in order to deflect political hostility - to emphasise traditional, professional expertise in collecting and organizing information and disseminating it efficiently to the whole community. In short, community librarianship is now conceived of in a 'safer' way, as 'librarianship for the community', in its entirety [33].

In some respects this apolitical post-Fordist orientation rediscovers the ethos of the proto-modern, 'civic' public library which sought - as truly 'town' libraries, to repeat Edward Edwards' exhortation - to incorporate, with the exception of the 'undeserving' residuum, the entire citizenry. It certainly replicates the social neutrality that early public library protagonists trumpeted as a prime feature of their institution. On the other hand, the utilitarian and idealist pioneers of the public library at least displayed a virile ideological commitment to an infant universal democracy and to an emergent, open, industrial capitalism; promoters nearly always spoke of grand ideals, such as the mission to civilize society. Community librarianship should be located within that tradition of public library provision which stresses the importance of an ideological undergirding to practice, although in seeking a *radical* reordering of social relations it stands, of course, in stark contrast to the essentially conservative ideologies of utilitarianism and idealism that propelled it into the twentieth-century.

Yet community librarianship also draws on certain utilitarian and idealist prescriptions for *practice*. For example, in respect of utilitarianism, community librarianship emphasises the teleological function of information for improving life chances [34]. Of even greater relevance is the idealist trait of the teacher/professional going *to* the pupil/client. Indeed, the community librarianship fraternity continues to stress, as did their Victorian progenitors, the importance of 'reaching for outreach' [35]; whereas many of the practical 'outreach' elements of community librarianship - Vincent (1986, pp. 9-11), for example, notes such activities as storytelling, talks about materials and use, booklists and information aimed at target groups, and a new approachability of staff - were in evidence before the First World War [36].

In the final analysis, however, what stands out is the *discontinuity*, in terms of ideological content, which community librarianship represents in the history of the public library. Unlike either the 'civic' or post-Fordist public library, community librarianship's ideological foothold - notwithstanding its endorsement of postmodern pluralism in respect of its servicing of alternative, 'questioning' social groups and movements - lies in the ethical, social justice thrust of the modernist welfare state. It is perhaps for this reason that many public librarians, perhaps sensing the passing of an age of ideological commitment, do not see community librarianship as a service ethos which has been, or can be, fitted into the historic, socially conservative and neutral objectives of the public library. As one chief librarian told us: 'community librarianship always appeared to us to be something that was bolted onto the general library services'. The roots of community librarianship in the history of the public library are manifold and identifiable. Its status as a discontinuous phase in that history, however, is more credible. It has largely been an 'appendage', an 'encrustation', in the history of an institution which, in its current post-Fordist orientation, has returned to an apolitical, neutral past.

Notes

1. Wilson (1977, pp. 54-5) outlines three types of voluntary association which arise out of social dislocation: groups which seek a revolutionary rewriting of social values; people who are apathetic to either new or established values; and those who wish to reestablish or rework values, in a way which takes account of the social change that has occurred, and who might therefore be termed reformist.
2. *Manchester Examiner and Times*, 14 August 1852.
3. *Manchester Spectator*, 11 January 1851, quoted in Munford (1951, pp. 60-61).
4. Communication from Sir John Potter, printed in *Manchester Council Proceedings*, 4 August 1852. Manchester Public Library Archives.
5. South London Chronicle, 28 May 1887.
6. As listed and discussed by Harris (1995) and Marriot (1996).
7. A change of status first noted formally in the United States. See Martin (1937).
8. 'Our readers' views: unemployed's home from home', *Liverpool Evening Express*, 9 May 1933. *Library Association Newscuttings: Libraries*, March 1933-June 1933. British Library Information Science Service.
9. Quoted in Hebbert (1980, p. 33).
10. The 'cycle of deprivation' is discussed in a community librarianship context by McIntosh (1979, p. 12).
11. *Pictorial*, 31 May 1968.
12. 'Crisis what crisis', *The Bookseller*, 6 March 1992, p. 611.

13 McColvin was responsible for important reports on the public library services of Australia, Germany and the Middle East.

14 The title chosen by Kelly and Kelly (1977) for the final chapter of their book.

15 Broadcast 11 March 1957, 10.45 pm. Transcript in Westminster PL Archives.

16 Quoted in Devereux (1972, p. 170).

17 'Reading in Tottenham', File Report 2537, November 1947, pp. 19-20. Mass Observation Archive, University of Sussex.

18 Directive on 'Regular Pastimes', Autumn 1988, Mass Observation Archive, University of Sussex, volunteer P715.

19 Title of ch. 1 of Harrison (1963a).

20 Interviewed January 1995. The talk given by this librarian to schools and other local organisations in the 1940s and 1950s was called 'The Library in the Community'.

21 Newscutting, Croydon Public Library Local Studies Department.

22 'City information kiosk idea turned down', *Cambridge News*, 28 January 1965; 'Tourist kiosk should be in library says report', *Cambridge News*, 29 August 1969.

23 City of Westminster Public Libraries, *Annual Report*, 1948-9.

24 'Librarians not publicity men', *Westminster and Marylebone Chronicle*, 6 May 1966.

25 Vol. 62, p. 345.

26 Vol. 62, pp. 360-61.

27 'New status in paperbacks', *Cambridge News*, 12 November 1965.

28 *Westminster and Pimlico News*, 20 October 1967.

29 Many of the volunteers for the directive on 'Regular Pastimes', op. cit. displayed a fascination with new technology in public libraries.

30 Brown (1981) offers evidence of a style of community librarianship operating elsewhere in Europe.

31 Grundt (1972) provides an extensive list of writings on such subjects. See also Bendix (1969) which contains five essays on the urban public library and its response to lower class disaffection.

32 See Room (1990), especially ch. 2, for a discussion of the recent reappearance of poverty as a social issue and for a description and definition of the new poverty. For a discussion of the 'new' underclass in Britain, see Murray (1990) and Mann (1992).

33 Coleman (1992, p. 301) draws the distinction between, on the one hand, the term 'community information/arts' which carries the radical inference of empowerment and people themselves taking control, and on the other, 'information/arts *for* the community', a transposition which delivers a different semantic connotation which has less to do

with community development understood in terms of supporting marginal communities and more to do with traditional professional public service.

34 Of interest in this regard is the current reseach project 'Social Audit of Public Library and Information Services' being undertaken by the Department of Information Studies, University of Sheffield, which aims to establish criteria for measuring the social effects of services provided.

35 Term borrowed from the 'Reaching for Outreach' Study Day, 27 June 1990, organized by the Library Association's Information Services Group (South-East) and Community Services Group (South-East).

36 Black (1991) discusses the long history of the so-called 'new' departures offered by community librarianship.

3 The emergence of community librarianship

The end of consensus and the 'community' approach

The literature of public librarianship tends to see the 'community' approach as timeless and inevitable: libraries self evidently serve 'communities'. However, it is clear that contemporary community librarianship, on the contrary, developed under a specific set of historical conditions and pressures which shaped its ideology and practice. These conditions prevailed in the 1970s, a decade which Arthur Marwick (1982, p.188) describes as signalling 'the break up of the optimistic consensus ... which had, according to one point of view, successfully served Britain through the difficult post-war years into the affluence of the sixties'. They resulted in the radicalisation of a significant minority of librarians, who came to adopt a particular critique of the modern public library, and who sought (and in some cases still seek) to transform its purpose and character. The ideas associated with this movement coalesced under the label 'community librarianship'.

Marwick's decade of discontinuity provided the seedbed for many of the ideas underpinning community librarianship. It marked the end of the social stability and solidarity which had characterised post-war Britain. Economic weakness became real decline, as British heavy industry contracted under the impact of the 1973 oil crisis and the emergence of global competition. Unemployment rose from 2.6% in 1970 to 6.1% in 1978 (Marwick, 1982, p.189). Industrial and political polarisation accompanied decline in the shape of the divisive miners' strike of 1973-4 and increasing industrial militancy in the late seventies. At the same time, rises in welfare spending, which might have alleviated some of these problems, were reversed and libraries, like other local services, began to take their share of 'the cuts'. There began to be talk of a 'North South divide'. Decline, division and 'disadvantage' - obvious again for the first time since the thirties - began to characterise British perceptions of themselves. And in the general election of 1979, politicians divided radically - again more so than at any time since the thirties - in the medicine they proposed.

It was not only Britain's 'Fordist' industrial base which was undergoing rapid disintegration. 'British' culture too - a discourse of class, family, empire, locality and civic solidarity - was diversifying as individuals became conscious of 'other' allegiances and identities. Bernice Martin (1981) had noted that Britain in the late sixties had already moved towards more libertarian moral and sexual codes, signalling a break up of the family centred puritanism of mid century. The seventies accelerated these processes, as alternatives to conventional life (such as feminism, ecology and 'new age' religion) became increasingly popular 'new social movements'. Britain's ethnic minorities, too, emerged from the shadows, to campaign, with some success, for civil and cultural equality [1]. National identity resurfaced in England's oldest colonies, Wales and Scotland, presaging according to some a 'break up of Britain' (Nairn, 1977). By the end of the decade, it could be argued that Britain was becoming 'multicultural' in the broadest sense of the word. But it was characteristic of the time that there was little consensus about this and that the English would elect, in 1979, a prime minister set on reversing many of these trends.

One particular aspect of these discontinuities which deserves attention is the perceived 'crisis', from the late 1970s onwards, of the British welfare state and public services. For at precisely the point in the 1970s when spending on 'universal' welfare provision had to be curtailed, a consciousness emerged of the limitations of the social wage. Women, ethnic minorities, people with disabilities and others who had been denied equal access to services began to demand change, encouraged by race and sex equality legislation passed in 1976. As Williams (1994, p.61) notes, 'the 'universality' of many post war services and benefits was based on the norm of white, British, heterosexual, able bodied, fordist men'. With increasing consciousness and confidence 'other' identities began to demand a share. For public service professionals like librarians, the pressure was thus to restructure services to account for multiple facets of disadvantage - physical, economic, social, educational, cultural - and thus *redistribute* social welfare in a climate of retrenchment.

Cynthia Cockburn (1977) argued that one way in which local authorities began to respond to such demand was through the development of a 'community' approach which sought to manage localities by incorporating interest groups into the machinery of the state. In the Britain of 1980 such an approach was far from straightforward. 'Communities' could no longer be seen as simply territorial or geographical [2]. Communities of 'attachment', such as ethnic or racial groups intersected with communities of 'interest' such as pressure groups and communities of 'need' such as the ill and disabled. Some of these communities adopted strategies of protest and conflict, others had great difficulty in finding a voice of their own. Some localities were a hive of community activity, others a void. But, as the Gulbenkian Report of 1973 noted, 'community groups have been making it clear that they can and will hold authority directly to account and expect a proper hearing and a reasoned response'. The community approach was thus a 'tiger, which conventional councils are unlikely to mount without some hesitation and a bit of prodding' (Cockburn, 1977, pp. 119-20). So it proved in the case of libraries.

Nevertheless, the climate of local government in the late seventies and early eighties at least began to favour change. The period was characterised by intensifying attempts from Whitehall to control and limit local expenditure, and by a 'rationalisation' of local government, culminating in the abolition of the GLC, the ILEA and metropolitan counties. Local politicians and professionals (predominantly, but not exclusively those on the Left) saw these developments as an attack on the autonomy of local government and hence on local democracy [3]. Resistance to such manoeuvres involved enlisting the support of the local population and local government professionals in a series of campaigns led by radical councils in London and some of the larger conurbations. Concern for 'community', for a time, involved the building of a local populist coalition against a bureaucratic and managerial centre and this provided encouragement and space for those interested in radicalising and decentralising local services. A few of the most 'radical' councils such as Lambeth, Brent, Manchester and Sunderland so provided a testing ground for community librarianship in its most developed forms where council policy encouraged 'community' approaches. However, as we shall see, in the closed and professionally dominated world of the public library, such responses to the times often proved the exception rather than the rule.

The critique of the traditional public library

From the perspective of the 'information age', it is all too easy to imagine the public library of 30 or so years ago in nostalgic terms: 'a lost world of silence and furniture polish' (Greenhalgh et al, 1995, p.140). Such visions are perhaps more myth than reality, but for many advocates of the public library service in the 1970s they represented a stigma which contained more than a grain of truth. Progressive librarians were uneasy about a conservative service centred around the cloistered culture of the book. In a study of library use published in 1971, sociologist Bryan Luckham had questioned the traditional ideology of 'openness and non exclusivity' of the public library, arguing that it inevitably favoured upper and middle class users at the expense of the less privileged. He concluded that the public library had 'an obligation to discard its traditional reluctance to play a dynamic role' and that it should look outwards and create a 'new public' for itself (Luckham, 1971, p.126). Increasingly, many in the profession - especially a new cadre of young graduates - concurred. Displaying little of the complacency with which librarians are commonly charged, they began to develop a comprehensive critique of McColvin's 'modern' public library as it had developed since 1945. This critique, in its turn, formed the basis of community librarianship.

The dimensions of the critique were essentially fourfold. First of all, libraries were perceived to be elitist and exclusive, in contrast to their claimed universality. They had become middle class institutions, according to Joe Hendry in an article in *Assistant Librarian* in 1973. Most librarians 'tend to provide their best services in areas where demand is coherent and vociferous ... libraries are apt to give their best to the middle class community because librarians often identify with this community and see tangible appreciation of their efforts there' (Hendry, 1973, p.174). According to other writers like Devereux (1972), public libraries made little effort to understand working class culture, and the impact upon it of television and the rest of the mass media. Problems like literacy were shunned: 'librarians do not tend to see the role of libraries in reading development as a strong or active one' (Jackaman, 1972, p. 102). As a result, it was not surprising that studies like those of Luckham showed alarmingly low levels of working class take up of public library services - as low as 8% membership for unskilled manual workers and their families in Luckham's sample (1971, p. 26).

For the influential American librarian, Mary Lee Bundy, reflecting on similar trends in the United States, the reasons for this situation were clear. Libraries indulged in an 'inhumane liberalism' which treated all comers 'equally'. As a result 'the deprived make next to no use of libraries and libraries do next to nothing to reach them' (Bundy, 1978, p.109). Influenced by writers such as Bundy, British librarians began to see exclusion and disadvantage as a function not simply of class or disability. Peter Jordan (1972) drew attention to the need for public libraries to develop collections which met the cultural needs of ethnic minorities as opposed to simply treating them as 'immigrants' to be assimilated. For black writers themselves, waking up to the potential of the public library, the solution was not so simple. Len Dawes saw public libraries as part of an imperial culture which perpetuated the 'process of everyday racialism'. Libraries as they stood were 'trivial and irrelevant' to the needs of Britain's black communities, who felt excluded from them not only because of their eurocentric bookstock, but also by their bureaucratic practices and the paternalistic and patronising attitudes of staff (Dawes, 1973).

51

Such specific observations connected more generally with a questioning of the contemporary relevance of traditional *librarianship*. Throughout the 1970s a growing sense of unease about the adequacy of the values, culture and practices of the profession began to manifest itself among progressive librarians. Most directly, younger staff complained about the *passivity* of the profession: 'everything you did seemed to be in spite of rather than because of the line manager' [4]. Children's librarians in particular, often motivated by the ethos of the active educator, began to rebel against this culture. Janet Hill, a leading children's librarian from Lambeth, claimed in 1973 that many of her colleagues were crushed in 'dinosaur-like library systems' where the dominant ethos was of buildings, organisation of materials and technology. 'Too many librarians', she wrote 'are not very interested in books and don't read much ... many are dazzled by computers, though probably more by audio visual aids and resource centres' (Hill, 1973, pp.24-25). Pat Coleman, in a blistering attack in a similar vein, characterised public librarians as conservative minded bureaucrats with 'an orientation towards the past and an overwhelming interest in the acquisition and organisation of materials, and, in many cases, their conservation' (Coleman, 1981, p.58). Libraries were, as a result, static rather than dynamic organisations, staff were obsessed with problems, self-criticism and professional job demarcation. For both Hill and Coleman, librarianship had lost its humanism: librarians were 'confused about the basic purpose of public libraries ... aims which are verbalised are diverse and many of them related to materials and systems rather than people' (Coleman, 1981, p.59). The philosophy of public librarianship typical of the McColvin period - stressing as it did neutrality and public service - had thus vaporised and become little more than a smokescreen for inaction, bureaucracy and muddle.

Such criticism was at the time dismissed by the professional establishment as extreme and unbalanced. However, as the seventies progressed it was supplemented by evidence which made it increasingly clear that the effectiveness and responsiveness of public libraries left much to be desired. Of particular note was an influential study of public library effectiveness carried out in Hillingdon in 1976 [5] which was highly critical of the extent to which public libraries identified and satisfied user and community needs. Its authors argued that libraries were 'supplier rather than user oriented' and 'supplier effective, user ineffective'. Claims that libraries were 'local' services were simply not shared by the public: 'overwhelmingly all public libraries were seen as essentially similar and, even when favourable local exceptions were made, stereotypes were strongly adhered to'. Overall, public libraries 'operated on a minimum level of user satisfaction surviving largely on the goodwill, low expectations and relatively easy demands of users' (Totterdell and Bird, 1976, p.130). Libraries failed to promote themselves adequately and readily dismissed unmet needs as beyond their remit. They lacked detailed knowledge about the communities they served; these communities in turn lacked detailed knowledge about the range of potential services available.

For most progressive librarians, such arguments pointed towards the need for a new culture of public librarianship focused around a more 'community oriented' service. However, according to a number of more radical critics, such a goal was a near impossibility without a change in the structure of provision. The problem was posed as follows: how could a buildings based service, run by educated professionals as part of a state/government apparatus, possibly respond to the needs of often disadvantaged communities? Libraries were remote, bureaucratic, and in a term coined later by Martin (1989), 'institutionalised'. In the view of writers such as Peter Stokes (1978), libraries were located *in* communities but not part *of* them: in contrast they were part of a governmental structure dedicated to the efficient management and control of localities. Libraries played their part in such 'management' by acting as a gatekeeper determining in part the kinds of information that local people might access, and the kinds they might not. Thus, libraries promoted 'business' information but neglected services to trades unionists and the information needs of citizens. Professionals colluded in this process, entering into a bargain with the state which traded the protection of the status quo for occupational control of the workplace - in this case public libraries. Thus, for Stokes, 'only the professional librarian is so well equipped to recognise a worthwhile book that he can exclude all those (often) shabby, ill produced publications of fringe groups which might disturb the sober, octavo volumes lining his walls' (Stokes, 1978, p.135). The logic of this analysis suggested drastic medicine. Some sort of inroad had to be made into the structure of public library services and their 'distance' from local people, either through a decentralisation of services, an element of community control or both. Further, there seemed to be a need for what Stokes termed a 'post professional ethos' of public librarianship which was non-managerial and encouraged public librarians to get very close to the culture of local communities. All of this amounted to a call for the 'deinstitutionalisation' of the public library which, had it happened, might well have revolutionised the service. As we shall see, community librarianship as it emerged had a rather different character and rather more limited impact on public libraries than that.

The emergence of mainstream community librarianship: the public library and the disadvantaged

Despite this discourse of 'community', it was the issue of disadvantage and inequality which animated the movement for public library reform in the 1970s.

Bill Martin, in a landmark publication entitled *Library Services to the Disadvantaged*, proclaimed that 'the time of the disadvantaged is now upon us'. He argued that the way to break the inaction, passivity and neutrality which bedevilled the public library was through an appeal to the 'tradition of social involvement in the profession'. Socially conscious librarians would then recognise that it was their duty to 'add their expertise to the struggle against those social evils which beset society: the evils of poverty, discrimination, inequality and crime' (Martin, 1975, pp.7-10).

In response to this kind of professional concern, the Library Advisory Council of England commissioned in 1975 a report on library services to the disadvantaged which appeared in 1978 with the title *The Libraries' Choice* (Department of Education and Science, 1978). The terms of reference of the working party charged with producing the report were broad: in particular its working definition of disadvantage incorporated any group of people who appeared to experience difficulty in accessing conventional library services. Thus hospital patients, housebound and handicapped people and prisoners were dealt with under the same umbrella as ethnic minorities and 'deprived areas'. This eclecticism proved to be both a strength and weakness. Because of its scope, the report was able to review and recommend the development of a whole raft of 'special' services targeted at the identified groups and advocate a significant expansion of 'outreach' services outside library buildings. But as Hennessey (1979) pointed out, the approach resulted in a perception of disadvantage almost purely in terms of access to existing library services, and an avoidance of the discussion of possibilities of more fundamental change. The conclusions of the report were thus in the end rather weak and open ended, recommending a series of pilot schemes and extensions of existing practices. For more radical librarians, this seemed a fudge. The public library was 'failing to provide a service for the whole of society, as it is legally bound to do' (Coleman, 1981, p.10). In fact, radicals argued, libraries had *no choice* but to change.

Such criticism of *The Libraries' Choice* became a focus for those public librarians who wanted to see more rapid change. Pat Coleman's *Whose Problem? The Public Library and the Disadvantaged*, which appeared in 1981, argued for much more fundamental changes to the structure and culture of library services, and crucially, called for a refocusing of priorities and a targeting of resources towards disadvantaged localities and 'client groups'. Its publication was important because, for the first time, it presented a reasonably complete alternative vision of the public library as part of an active and interventionist welfare state. This vision utilised the concept of 'community' as a metaphor for social inclusion. For Coleman, community was the social whole, and the priority in service provision was to improve service to malfunctioning parts of that whole. Social improvement depended on a partnership between

54

state, civil society and locality: 'the success of a library service depends upon the support and willing involvement of the community and corporate action with other agencies and community groups' (Coleman, 1981, p.60).

Such ideas gained widespread support. Within the profession socially committed librarians argued for the formation of a professional group dedicated to the development of services to the disadvantaged and, at a meeting in Leicester in 1982, the 'Community Services Group' of the Library Association was formed. From the outset, the focus of the group was disadvantage although, as its title suggests, it sometimes adopted the more ambivalent language of 'community'. Nevertheless, its 'primary concern', adopted as part of its original constitution, makes clear its priorities and emphasises again the notion of 'the community' as social solidarity:

> The primary concern of the group shall be the development of appropriate library and information provision in deprived areas and the encouragement of the use of those services. It will pay special attention to the needs of those groups within the community, such as the elderly, the unemployed, adult basic education students, and people of ethnic minority origin, whose needs are not met by traditional library services. [6]

The mainstream model of community librarianship was thus born. In spite of the disagreements between advocates of far reaching change such as Coleman and the more moderate advocates of the developments recommended by *The Libraries' Choice*, we can see in hindsight a broad degree of commonality between them. Both accepted the notion of 'disadvantage' as the starting point for an analysis of society; both accepted that the public library had to intervene to improve the lot of the deprived; both argued that by thus doing they would serve the whole 'community'. Some argued that such a shift in focus would involve the fundamental restructuring of public library services, whereas others hoped that a more piecemeal approach would suffice and that 'community services' could be added to the traditional library service rather than replacing it. In practice, however, these differences were often forgotten in the drive to be practical for, in contrast to the often heated strategic debate, there was widespread agreement about the operational initiatives involved in developing services to the disadvantaged.

Mainstream community librarianship, as it had evolved by around 1983, was thus fertile with ideas for a new public library service. What were the elements of this approach? Among reformers there seemed to be common agreement on the following points:

- Libraries needed to investigate and profile localities in order to gather detailed data about both users and non-users. Such community profiling needed to focus on the socio-economic and the cultural make up of library catchment areas.

- Libraries could as a result adopt a client group approach to service provision, targeting services particularly at disadvantaged sections of the community. Such services might be special or additional to the 'basic' library service, or involve, according to some advocates of this approach, a major re-orientation of existing services.

- Libraries needed to embrace multiculturalism in response to the settlement of ethnic minorities in Britain and the fact of cultural difference. Such multiculturalism would involve a major rethink of stock selection and staffing policies [7].

- Outreach as a mode of service provision needed to be expanded in order to bring library services to those who could not or would not use them. Deposit collections, mobile services and associated 'extension' activities such as children's storytelling all had a part to play in service development. Outreach could, it was argued, dramatically improve feedback from users about the relevance of service offered and help to publicise and encourage use of existing services [8].

- Public library reference and information services needed rethinking. They needed to be supplemented, and some argued, replaced, by community information services more relevant to the everyday needs of disadvantaged groups. Libraries needed to follow the lead of information and referral services in the United States and the voluntary sector in the United Kingdom in expanding its involvement in the provision of welfare information [9]. In 1980, a Library Association consultative document concluded that services needed to be developed 'which assist individuals and groups with daily problem solving and participation in the democratic process. The services concentrate on the needs of those who do not have ready access to other sources of information and the most important problems that people have to face, problems to do with their homes, their jobs and their rights' (Library Association, 1980, p.12).

- Libraries needed to become community oriented services and involve local people as much as possible in service initiatives and developments. Libraries needed to work with other local government departments and the voluntary sector in order to avoid duplication of services and to maximise co-ordination of provision.

Such a programme seemed sweeping at the time. In hindsight, however, what seems paramount is the *welfarism* of this approach. Mainstream community librarianship was committed to the project of the post 1945 welfare state: to eliminate what Beveridge called the 'five giants': want, disease, ignorance, squalor and idleness. Like other moves in the seventies towards a 'community' approach (community education, community social work and so on) it sought to modernise public service by focusing on 'disadvantaged' groups that had been previously neglected or overlooked. But it continued to assume, like other forms of librarianship before it, that the problems of the disadvantaged could be addressed by an allocation of resources by professionals acting on behalf of the state. For Coleman, therefore, the voice of locality had its limits: 'although the stated requirements of the local community must form an important part in designing a library service, they must be supplemented by ... professional judgement about what is required' (1981, p.60). And the core of professional judgement was a belief about need, a belief in public librarianship that needs were not simply wants, but that people had common needs which provided a passport to education, culture and citizenship itself. Community librarianship of this sort, contrary to later criticism of it, was never about populism or cultural and educational relativism: the purpose of the public library was to *improve* the lot of the disadvantaged and not simply respond to impulse. In the grand tradition of the welfare state, the object of the public library remained that of 'creating a better society ... you can in the end incorporate a professional approach to needs as long as you consult with the community' [10].

Philosophically, mainstream community librarianship aspired towards the social solidarity of the post war era. It sought to ensure that the disadvantaged obtained a fair allocation of the social wage in the shape of, in this case, access to and use of library services. It was prepared to countenance the major reform of public library services to achieve this end, although most public librarians hoped simply to be able to develop additional initiatives based on it in order to make services more comprehensive. By 1982, however, when the Library Association Community Services group was formed, some of these ideas were already beginning to seem behind the times. From both political directions, critics were beginning to attack the 'outdated' paternalism of welfarism, its professional arbitration of need, its insistence on the priority of 'service' and its reluctance to listen to what diversifying 'communities' actually said they wanted. If communities were now something more than passive localities which received state services, why not adopt a more active view of community and a more dynamic model of community librarianship to match?

A radical alternative? 'Working with people and not for them'

For some radical librarians, these questions linked naturally with the critique of the public library which focused on its role as a cultural institution of the state. According to librarians like John Vincent in Lambeth [11], the mainstream/welfarist approach could never approximate to 'true community librarianship' because it maintained the central role of the library as a service controlled by the state and professionals rather than local people. 'Real' community librarianship, on the contrary, would involve a 'radical redefinition of the library service' (Vincent, 1986, p.2). Such a redefinition would mean abandoning the notion of a service focused on buildings, seen by Vincent as a symbol and embodiment of the distance between public libraries and communities. Instead, the public library was envisaged as a deinstitutionalised service embedded very deeply in the structures of the local community. Its purpose would be to assist local people in making their own culture on their own terms rather than the provision of an elite or uniform mass culture for them. This would involve recognising the impossibility of serving 'the community' as if it were a solidaristic whole and accepting a multifaceted conception of communities of interest with multiple cultures and needs. Practically, it involved focusing on outreach as a mode of operation 'for its own sake'. Community librarianship would effectively be about supporting local groups with materials and resources in natural settings as opposed to the institutionally structured world of the library. It was about encouraging all elements of the community - but especially the disadvantaged non-users of buildings - to utilise resources on their own terms and for their own purposes. The 'library' would become an agency of animation and development, rather than an institutional bureaucracy, working very closely with all kinds of local organisations and groups.

The impetus for these ideas came from a number of directions. Specifically (and perhaps surprisingly given the critique of the role of the professional inherent in this approach), a number of librarians were experimenting in the field with ways of working which fell outside the accepted norms of public library services. In Lambeth itself, Janet Hill and others had for years been developing innovative ways of taking books to people in a deprived, inner city community where many barriers - physical, social and cultural - militated against public library use. Hill's direct and common-sense philosophy that 'books should be where people are' (Hill, 1973, p.45) had its roots in her work as a children's librarian, but her ideas, encapsulated in her widely acclaimed book *Children are People: the Librarian in the Community*, had a wider influence throughout the 1970s. She called for an end to the focus of librarianship on systems and structures and instead a dynamic and flexible organisation of staff in area teams which could develop provision outside library buildings. A number of inner city library authorities, like Lambeth, adopted these ideas and attracted radical and socially committed librarians. An atmosphere of innovation and experimentation often developed. One of our interviewees, who worked in inner city Manchester in the late seventies and early eighties, described things as follows: 'it was a totally different way of doing things ... we were encouraged to try one offs and I spent most of my time outside the library, taking books to groups, getting information for them, reading stories to kids ... nobody thought about measuring what we were doing ... we were given so much freedom, it was really good fun' [12].

From a more general perspective, however, these ideas were associated with the growth in importance of a 'community approach' to local governance in Britain in the late 1970s. Such an approach involved the partial deinstitutionalisation of welfare justified by philosophies of community development, which stressed participation, local self determination, self help and education as opposed to traditional paternalistic state welfarism. Community work as an activity was often placed at the sharp end of such approaches. In spite of the supposed 'failure' of experiments such as the Home Office sponsored Community Development projects of the early 1970s [13], community work as local practice became increasingly pervasive in Britain in the late seventies and early eighties. Funded by various forms of central government urban aid and local authority grant aid for the community and voluntary sector, community workers were employed to support local communities in a variety of ways. Activities included sectoral initiatives such as community arts work; work with client groups such as youth and ethnic minorities; anti poverty and welfare rights work; work with the homeless and groups of tenants. Community work developed an eclectic range of philosophies, ideologies and methods of working. However a central distinction developed between those who focused on *community development* - 'the participation of the people themselves in efforts to improve their level of living' - and *community action* - 'communities making demands of policy makers to acknowledge their interests and be responsive to their demands' (Glen, 1993, pp.24-28). Cockburn (1977, p.120) labelled these approaches the *social planning approach* and the *conflict method* respectively.

Most interestingly from our point of view there is evidence that community workers in the late 1970s began to see the potential of the public library as a way of supporting community development and (occasionally) stimulating community action. On one level, this was because community workers were especially conscious of the importance of informal adult education as a means towards consciousness raising and self help, and this concern linked naturally with the traditional educational purpose of the library. In other, less traditional ways, however, community workers saw libraries as an indispensable provider of information to local groups engaged in community action. For writers like Tony Gibson (1979, p.121), in *People Power*, 'the facts, like the professionals, must be on tap, but not on top'. In 1978 two community workers, Barbara Darcy and Ashok Ohri, published a pamphlet entitled *Libraries are Ours* which argued that libraries should 'confront the politics of information by collecting information from all standpoints and for all sections of the population' (Darcy and Ohri, 1978, p.8). For them, libraries had the potential to offer free and open access to increasingly complex official information systems and channels and hence to act as a counterbalance to the increasingly visible divide between information rich and information poor. Not only could they support directly the information needs of community organisations, but they could also offer an important backup service for the growing numbers of rights, advice and independent resource centres which were increasingly a feature of community activity in Britain [14].

Throughout the seventies and early eighties a growing number of initiatives and experiments based on this cluster of relatively radical ideas began to be reported. In 1974 Bill Martin had claimed much potential for a new kind of radical librarianship where conventional provision had broken down. His account of a 'community library' operated by volunteers from a terraced house on the Highfield estate of West Belfast testified to the fact that a thirst for books and information could be tapped even in Britain's most scarred and battered communities. The key, according to Martin (1974, p.242) was a sense of local ownership and involvement 'working with people and not for them'. The London Borough of Lambeth, developing many of Janet Hill's ideas, began to extend outreach services to a very large number of community groups (over 500 in 1977) and to radically devolve the library service to community spaces and locations [15]. The commitment to outreach by others library authorities was never as sweeping, but some followed suit with innovative and imaginative schemes. Bradford, for example, purchased and refurbished a double decker bus which carried children's materials, books in Asian languages and rights and advice workers to some of the city's most deprived estates. In other locations the cue was taken from demand for local resource centres in library buildings. Manchester took the decision to run down traditional reference services in a number of inner city branches and develop instead advice services in conjunction with local agencies as well as community meeting places and publishing and resource centres. In Peterborough libraries worked in tandem with community workers from the new town development corporation to establish similar centres in neighbourhood libraries at Bretton and Orton [16].

By about 1983, as a result of these developments and the debates surrounding them, it seemed possible to identify a radical alternative philosophy of community librarianship and a loose grouping of radical librarians who advocated it. Its elements comprised:

- a focus on working very closely with users and communities - particularly the deprived and disadvantaged - and obtaining feedback about needs through constant work and contact *in* the community. Users should and would participate in stock selection and resource allocation.

- an adoption of outreach as an end in itself: in some cases it would be the preferred mode of delivery of library services. The library would become a community resource agency providing materials and information in all kinds of community settings.
- library buildings would become 'community libraries' or decentralised community resource centres rather than 'branch' libraries, although central services would remain to provide specialised backup. Such community centres would provide information backup for local organisations, community information services, meeting and publishing facilities and cultural and educational materials and facilities. They would serve as a focus for local activity and culture.
- community services could not simply be organised around a fixed notion of 'special' or 'client' groups such as the elderly, youth or ethnic minorities. Libraries had to respond more flexibly to communities of interest and especially those emerging in importance such as the unemployed, the homeless, lesbians and gay men, women, 'black' groups and numerous emerging 'issue' based groups.
- information provision and cultural provision could not be the exclusive preserve of the library. Libraries had to work with independent community agencies of all kinds and especially the voluntary sector in the development and operation of services and local networks. Interest groups should be able to argue for and obtain grant aid in developing and operating their own information and cultural services.
- the role of the librarian would radically change, and the drift of librarianship towards systems, technology and expert 'professionalism' would have to be reversed. 'Community' librarians would operate as educators, facilitators and advocates for local culture. They would use their 'expertise' to enable local people to make sense of and utilise the increasingly complex and systematic global information environment.

Bill Martin (1989) later identified 'deinstitutionalisation' as the key concept underpinning this somewhat eclectic and idealistic programme. Certainly it was this which differentiated radical from mainstream community librarianship. The radical alternative effectively sought to fragment and decentralise the public library as an institutional force, with the objective of embedding the idea of the library very deeply in local community. Mainstream community librarianship never went this far: it sought predominantly to reform and improve the public library as an institution in order to sharpen its response to the facts of inequality and disadvantage. Because of this implicit threat to the public library as an institution, the radical model was always marginalised in the profession: a former President of the Library Association and a leading advocate of the mainstream approach told us that he felt it had 'threatened mainstream librarianship' [17] and for that reason and its equivocation about 'professionalism', it was always resisted by the professional establishment. Moreover, a number of our other informants recalled how local radical initiatives in the early eighties had been 'suppressed by the Labour Party establishment' [18], unhappy about the apparent loss of control of resources, the lack of financial accountability inherent in some outreach and experimental projects, and the politics of conflict with local authorities which emanated from community groups benefiting from these approaches.

Nevertheless, radical community librarianship was to leave a legacy which the public library movement would find it difficult to completely erase. For unlike mainstream community librarianship, it looked forward to a period when public services provided by monolithic, professionally dominated bureaucracies would be regarded as ineffective, remote and unresponsive. It raised the possibility, instead, that community development might become the widely recognised responsibility of all kinds of local service providers and that the public library might potentially hold 'a unique pivotal position between the community and the machinery of statutory and voluntary agencies' (Liddle, 1980). It was to open the door, perhaps, to a reconceptualisation of public library purpose in a 'post-Fordist' welfare state.

Towards an 'effective' public library: community librarianship as responsive librarianship

For many public librarians of the time, such ideas were little more than a utopian deviation. For them the real problems of the public library centred around a long decline in public library book issue figures which had begun in the early 1970s. Libraries had to compete increasingly with the mass media and other providers of leisure and information, and political pressure to justify services was growing in an era of local authority spending cuts. Moreover, the public seemed indifferent to the decline of the public library. John Saunders, Chief Librarian of Surrey, noted that in 1976 his staff had expected an outcry after a 10% reduction in the library service budget resulting in cuts in opening hours, bookfund and special services, but that nothing had happened (Saunders, 1981, pp.36-43). For Saunders and librarians like him, such public indifference was worrying because it indicated that maybe libraries were no longer effectively meeting the demands of their core, existing clientele. As a result, he reasoned, the priority was to develop a service with a more dynamic and appealing public image. Such a service would need to be flexible, popular and above all able to respond to the demands of its users and (the words were often used loosely and interchangeably) communities.

The impetus towards such a responsive service was underpinned in the seventies by a growing number of library surveys which investigated user and community preferences [19]. However, although these surveys provided a wealth of information about user behaviour, they were limited in two main respects: they said little about non library users, and seldom were their conclusions translated into effective action. Totterdell and Bird (1976) argued that the reason for this was because libraries were 'supplier' rather than 'user' focused. Libraries should not try, they argued, 'to separate real needs from mere wants or desires' but should adopt 'user satisfaction' as their core purpose and rationale. A major effort was also needed to improve public knowledge about the library service and to overcome evident misconceptions and ignorance - especially about services other than the lending of books. For Totterdell and Bird, the public library did not require 'particularly new functions to attract more people ... a very good start could be made by *effectively* carrying out accepted and quite traditional functions' (Totterdell and Bird, 1976, pp.128-133).

In many respects, surveys like the *Effective Library* empirically laid the foundations for a third approach to community librarianship: one based on redefining the public library as a responsive public service organisation. However, such an approach, seen in embryonic form in the 1960s, had already begun to acquire a broader intellectual justification as part of a general attempt to apply commercial ideas to public service organisations. As we have noted at the beginning of this chapter, the rationale of the Keynesian welfare state, based on the provision of universal services to cater for common human needs, was beginning to be questioned and undermined during the seventies. Professionals who claimed to be able to define and determine needs were condemned as paternalistic at best and dictatorial at worst [20]. Instead, users of public services began to be reconceptualised as customers, with rights of choice and satisfaction broadly parallel to those enjoyed by consumers in the marketplace. As early as 1973, Yorke and Colley attempted to apply these arguments to the public library. They claimed that 'there is no intrinsic difference between the problems faced by a manufacturer seeking increased profits through consumer satisfaction in the use of his product or service and those faced by government or local government pursuing an increased subvention through public satisfaction in its end product'. Thus libraries needed to adopt a 'consumer orientation' - a service geared towards customer and community choice - to supplant the existing 'product orientation' based on 'professional' judgement about universal needs. In order to achieve this, libraries had to accept they were 'in competition for the potential consumers' money and time' (Yorke and Colley, 1973, pp.203-4). They had to accept they were in a marketplace.

The key ideas associated with 'responsive' librarianship thus came to be those associated with marketing. Influenced by Kotler's *Marketing for Non-Profit Organisations* (1976), a number of writers began to argue that libraries needed to adopt a fully fledged market-oriented approach to service. Tinkering with incomplete community profiles and surveys would not suffice. For Yorke (1977, p.47), marketing was a 'fundamental approach to determining the needs of the community in the fields of knowledge and leisure, and to meeting those needs by the provision of the required services and by the communication of their existence to the required market or market segments'. For Cronin (1984, p.34), the core of marketing involved 'the opening up of effective two way communication between service providers and the users (actual and potential) of those services'. According to Smith (1983) this would incorporate not only conventional market research, but also analysing market opportunities, changing priorities in decision making, constant 'product' development and review, and the implementation of new communication strategies based on marketing principles. Yorke further argued (1977, p.47) that this would mean limiting the exercise of traditional 'professional expertise' and replacing it 'with the ability to manage and control resources to the greater benefit of the total community'.

For many librarians, one of the key marketing issues to be addressed seemed to be that associated with the 'image' of libraries and librarians. The Hillingdon surveys had suggested that the public had numerous misconceptions about libraries and their services: Usherwood (1981, p.13) summed this up for community librarians when he noted that 'there are many people whose perception is such that they do not see them as being relevant to their everyday lives'. In a popular book of the time - *The Visible Library* (1981) - Usherwood set out to detail the ways in which a considered approach to library public relations might overcome negative and misconceived public images. He emphasised in particular the importance of a librarian who looked outwards to the community rather than inwards to stock and systems. Such community orientation needed to be fostered through numerous library related community activities, librarian contacts with local groups and organisations and professional library publicity that was in tune with local culture. The role of the professional librarian had, in this view, to become a proactive one involving constant liaison, contact and awareness raising.

In spite of muted traditionalist criticism, this 'responsive' approach quickly became popular in many public libraries in the late seventies: according to several of our informants working in a range of authorities at the time, it was 'especially attractive to younger staff who wanted to get outside traditional procedures and routines and show they could do things' [21]. The ideas underpinning it loosely brought together various trends of the time which perhaps looked forward to the new social and political climate of the eighties. Overall, its key facets seem to have comprised:

- an identification of communities as predominantly collections of individuals with tastes and preferences.
- an attempt to develop a service responsive to users and communities predominantly on the basis of demand and expressed need, and an expectation that this would lead to marked variations in levels and types of library services provided in different areas.
- the use of market research techniques and community liaison and feedback as methods of determining appropriate services.
- an attempt to reform the static management hierarchies characteristic of public libraries, and to develop a more dynamic culture based on user orientation and marketing principles.
- an attempt to develop an image conscious 'visible library' which might compete with other leisure and knowledge providers. 'Locality' was often seen as a particular strength of the public library in this regard.
- a willingness to extend the range of products and services provided by the public library in response to latent and expressed demand, with a focus particularly on electronic leisure and information services.
- a proactive conception of the role of the professional librarian, incorporating a public relations/market research/communicator paradigm. The community librarian would form networks and links with local organisations of all kinds and would promote library services as well as trying to tailor them to local needs.

The extent to which this populist programme of public library reform can be called 'community' librarianship is perhaps questionable. Contemporaries tended to identify it as a shift in management strategy rather than a change in fundamental rationale and purpose. It tended to conceive 'communities' as little more than aggregations of individual users with common needs, and it lacked the fundamental commitment to the disadvantaged that underpinned both the mainstream and radical models of community librarianship. Moreover, its populism arguably deflected from the basically educational vision of the public library that still remained at the centre of many ideas about community librarianship. Nevertheless, it did propose community orientation as a management philosophy in a way that other visions of community librarianship did not, and its advocates, like John Saunders (1986), were to argue that it forced librarians to listen to the views of customers and communities. These arguments were persuasive, and for this reason many writers on mainstream (and sometimes radical) community librarianship tended to assume that responsive approaches could be unproblematically bolted on to other developments [22]. The difficulties and conflicts inherent in such attempts were, of course, to become apparent as the eighties wore on.

Table 3.1
Philosophies of community librarianship circa 1980

	Mainstream (Welfarist)	Radical	Responsive (Consumerist)
Conception of community	Solidaristic Interdependent	Group identity and culture	Atomistic, individualistic
Orientation to users	Paternalistic	Participative, developmental	Market driven
Characteristic modes of service	Special services to client groups; welfare information	Outreach, support for community groups	Satisfaction of demand; popular leisure, local information
Mode of management	Administrative planning	Participative, teamwork	Entrepreneurial, proactive
Institutional culture	Bureaucratic, buildings based, professional	Decentralised, diffused, locality based	Managerial: efficiency and image conscious
Political rationale	Disadvantage	Inequality, liberation	Value for money, consumer choice

Perhaps, in hindsight, the emergence of 'responsive' librarianship is best seen as a result of the increase in social diversity and the crisis of the Keynesian welfare state which characterised the late seventies. Universal, uniform standards and services were no longer enough, and in some senses each of the models of community librarianship we have described (see Table 3.1) can be seen as a proposal to restructure public library services in the light of this new historical reality. The mainstream model proposed reform of services and their extension to the 'new' disadvantaged, but with little change in professional and institutional cultures. The radical model proposed a deinstitutionalisation of

66

services along with deprofessionalisation and elements of 'community' control. The responsive model envisaged community orientation fundamentally along consumerist lines, alongside a move to a new managerial and market based professional ideology of librarianship. Of course in practice, the restructuring of public library services was to become (and is) a much more complex process than any of these models or 'ideal types' would suggest. Throughout the eighties, policies and practices were forced on public library authorities by both central government and local authorities who constantly changed both political priorities, funding levels and criteria. The trajectory of public library policy was to be determined by a complex set of social, political and economic imperatives. No library authority would ever 'adopt' a model of community librarianship pure and simple, and a not insignificant number would virtually ignore these ideas altogether.

Nevertheless, perhaps more than in any other decade of the twentieth century, public libraries in the 1980s embarked upon experimentation with new initiatives and services. Many of these developments drew their inspiration from the ideas and models of community librarianship which we have examined in this chapter. It is thus to a discussion and assessment of this period of innovation that we can now turn.

Notes

1 Although note the long history of black struggle for recognition in Britain as detailed in Fryer (1984).

2 See Dolan (1989). Dolan's chapter has an interesting discussion of libraries in relation to the 'new' communities.

3 See Blunkett and Jackson (1987) for a politicians' account of this period.

4 Interview with Principal Librarian, Community Services, Midland County, April 1994. The interviewee was reflecting on his first professional post during the period 1978-1982 with (another) Midland county.

5 See Totterdell and Bird (1976). Although the study was limited to the London Borough of Hillingdon it claimed general applicability by seeing Hillingdon as a 'typical' case. Moreover, it to some extent broke new ground in public library studies by surveying a large sample of users and non-users and using qualitative methods very successfully. No other study had reported user perceptions of public library services in such graphic detail.

6   The quotation is taken from the constitution of the Library Association Community Services Group adopted at that time. See Library Association Community Services Group (1986, pp.18-19).

7   See Clough and Quarmby (1978) for an argument for an incrementalist approach to multiculturalism. Alexander (1982) argued for more radical change.

8   See Armour (1975) for an example of the early advocacy of outreach.

9   See Bunch (1982) for a summary of these trends.

10 Interview with Senior Children's Librarian, Inner London Borough, October, 1993.

11 See Vincent, *An Introduction to Community Librarianship* (1986). The quotations in this paragraph are taken from pages 2-6 of Vincent's pamphlet. It is interesting that, as part of his argument, Vincent recognises that it is doubtful, 'given public libraries' place within the state machinery, whether real community librarianship will ever occur'. Such doubts mirror contemporary discussions in community work about working 'in and against the state', although Vincent's conclusion, that all we can do is 'work in the direction' of community librarianship, is characteristically pragmatic.

12 Interview with Principal Librarian, Community Services, Northern Metropolitan District, April 1994.

13 There are numerous accounts of the various conflicts and ideological debates surrounding UK community work in the late sixties and seventies including one in Cockburn (1977) pp. 120-131. The debates are interesting because they mirror some of the theoretical concerns about the possibility of 'real community librarianship' within a state bureaucratic apparatus raised by Vincent. Darcy and Ohri (1978, p.9) also usefully reproduce some of the findings of the final report of the Coventry Community Development Project concerning poverty, inequality and community work strategies.

14 See Bunch (1982) Chapter 3 for an account of the expansion of rights and advice work in Britain in the seventies.

15 See London Borough of Lambeth, Libraries Working Party (1992), *Community Based Library Services.*

16 See Bunch (1982) Chapter 4 for details of these developments.

17 Interview, August 1994.

18 Interview with County Librarian, Northern County, November 1995.

19 See Yorke (1977) Chapter 2 for a review of public library user surveys of the period.

20 See Illich et al (1977).

21 Interview with Principal Librarian, Information Services, Midland County, April 1994. Several informants who had worked for county

authorities in the late seventies described their perceptions of community librarianship largely in terms of a 'proactive' approach.

22　See, for example, Coleman (1981, pp.65-67).

4   The limits of community librarianship

'Community' in crisis and the zenith of community librarianship

If British society in the seventies was characterised, as Marwick suggests, by discord and discontinuity, the period 1979-86 undoubtedly marked a hardening of these tendencies. For most commentators, the period is one of crisis and division, signposted by flashpoints such as the Brixton Riots (1981); the Falklands War (1982); the local government crisis (1984-5) and the Miners' strike (1984-5). Directly or indirectly much of this social division stemmed from the election in 1979 of a radical Conservative government under Margaret Thatcher: a government determined to restructure not only Britain's ailing economy but also its political, social and cultural character. The Conservatives adopted economic policies based on monetarism and free market principles which exposed British industry to the full force of global competition and led to the demise of much of its heavy manufacturing base, prefiguring a transition to a 'post-Fordist' regime of accumulation based on services, information and industrial flexibility [1]. According to commentators such as Jessop (1994), their accompanying political project stressed a rolling back of the Keynesian welfare state and an assertion of tighter central control over those elements of the public sphere which remained. Culturally, the Conservatives sought to balance social fragmentation and individualism with a renewal of the faith in national cohesion and traditional family values (Hall and Jacques, 1983). Such 'Thatcherism', as it became known, devastated many of Britain's industrial communities, and, because of the social dislocation it caused, for a time seemed to threaten the very notion of 'community' as social solidarity. Unemployment rose to 3.5 million in 1986; poverty indices of many kinds spiralled downwards; class and geographical inequalities widened. Politics inevitably polarised. Resistance to Thatcherism, given a weak and divided Labour Party in parliament, took numerous extra-parliamentary forms.

Trades unionists, whose jobs were under threat, took industrial action against closures and cuts. Some local authorities, whose services and powers were curtailed, engaged in popular resistance. Young people, many of them unemployed, took to the streets. The 'liberal' establishment, whose values were threatened by the Thatcherite blend of free market economics and nationalistic cultural politics, took to the quality broadsheets. But in spite of the depth of such opposition, the Conservatives maintained majority popular support during this period: in 1983 Labour, riven by factions and depleted by defections, suffered its heaviest election defeat since 1929.

Paradoxically, it was against this backdrop of social strife and consolidation of right wing power that community librarianship reached its peak. But for public libraries the most immediate consequences of Thatcherism were financial. The long expansion of the public library service, halted in the seventies, was now reversed. In their determination to cut back on local government expenditure and also to more directly control *how* local authorities spent money, the Conservatives embarked on a series of legislative manoeuvres which ultimately led to 'rate-capping' [2]. These manoeuvres effectively imposed maximum levels on the amount any local authority could spend, and such levels were set centrally. Local authorities were not permitted to raise extra amounts through rates or other forms of local taxation without incurring a corresponding deduction of central government grant. In such a climate, local authorities of all political shades tended to prioritise spending on 'essentials', such as education or social services, and penalise non-vital activities like libraries. In 1984 the *Library Association Record* noted that expenditure on public libraries had risen in cash (not real) terms over the previous decade by only 5.3%; this compared with a rise of 9% for local authority expenditure as a whole [3]. Cuts were inevitable. The Library Campaign, a pressure group established in 1984 to campaign against cuts in public libraries, noted widespread reductions in bookfunds and trimming of staff [4]. High profile library closures began to create headlines: St Pancras Reference Library in Camden was closed, and even Manchester Central Library was put out of commission for one day per week.

However, in spite of budget cuts and the generally unfavourable political climate, it is clear that this period marks a high water mark for the practice of community librarianship. The literature of the time is full of local accounts of innovation in public library services and of new initiatives directed at groups such as unemployed people, ethnic minorities, older adults, teenagers and other 'disadvantaged' groups. Libraries also appear to have been more willing than at any time before or since to experiment with methods of service delivery. Outreach and community information services of various kinds flourished and a willingness to work with the voluntary sector and community groups in joint service provision became apparent. Nationally, this activity seemed to be accompanied by a shift to a more interventionist and socially responsive conception of the librarian's profession. The formation of the Library Association Community Services Group in 1982 was one result of this process, but the Library Association as a whole issued progressive policy statements concerned with Community Information (1980); Services to Unemployed People (1983); and Services to Ethnic Minorities (1986) [5].

Partly as a result of this activity and the growing national visibility of some of its main advocates, the ideas associated with community librarianship were widely disseminated. In particular, they seemed to link at local government level with alternative thinking on the left about the changing role of public services and the need for a more flexible and proactive welfare state. The 1985 Labour Party election manifesto for Nottinghamshire - not a county renowned for innovation in the community librarianship field - makes explicit this thinking, and the influence of community librarianship:

> under Labour every local library will become a community resource and information point. Staff will be trained to provide information vital to the needs of particular communities and especially their least well off members ... Priority will be given to the development of services for the disabled ...; special services to ethnic minorities and the provision of balanced multicultural books and materials in all libraries. Collections will be organised at unemployed centres, community centres and elderly people's centres. (Nottinghamshire County Labour Party, 1985, pp. 16-17)

Such adoption of community librarianship by sections of the left in the early eighties undoubtedly provides some explanation of its growth. It became part of the widespread resistance to the attempts of Thatcherism to radically restructure British society and culture. Along with other initiatives led by Labour controlled local authorities, 'community' initiatives in libraries often had the objective of mitigating the social effects of monetarist economic policies. By prioritising library services to groups such as unemployed people or focusing services on areas of crisis such as inner cities, Labour authorities hoped that the local state might compensate where central government had stepped aside. Library authorities such as those in Renfrew, Strathclyde and Sunderland, Tyne and Wear, stand out as particularly active in this respect. In other localities, such as Manchester, such welfarism became infused with the more radical cultural politics of the period [6]. Community librarianship in London boroughs such as Brent, Lambeth and Camden took on many of the ideas associated with the doomed Greater London Council, and the development of services to controversial minority groups such as gays and lesbians attracted occasional notoriety in the right wing press [7]. Nevertheless, as we shall see, some of these boroughs undoubtedly became centres of innovation and excellence in community librarianship: in particular the development of 'multicultural' approaches to library provision and 'outreach' services of various kinds.

It would be a mistake, however, to simply associate community librarianship with radicalism in Labour local government. For one thing, councillors of other political affiliations - especially Liberals - were sympathetic to 'community' approaches and indeed were very active in the development of varieties of community politics. Moreover, as a number of our informants have noted, traditional socialist councillors often had a strongly institutional conception of the library service and could be at the forefront of attempts to 'close down outreach' [8] or 'stamp on agitation' [9]. As a result, the development of community librarianship was above all an 'uneven' phenomenon. It flourished in particular ways in Leicestershire, Devon, Cambridgeshire and Derbyshire: all of them less than 'radical' in their own way. Often development in these areas can be explained by the particular interests and drive of senior managers or groups of library professionals, or sometimes by particular circumstances such as the location of new towns and new libraries. In other cases, it was the availability of non-mainstream funding for the pursuit of innovation which proved crucial.

In particular, central government programmes of special financial support proved crucial for community librarianship. Although hostile to the principles of public intervention, the Thatcher government in the early eighties recognised the expediency of targeting funding at urban areas threatened by acute social disruption and occasional disorder. Thus, the Urban Programme of the Department of the Environment, expanded in 1977 to cover 41 urban areas in England and Wales, was continued (Blackman, 1993). Equivalent arrangements for Scotland were maintained. Home Office grants under Section 11 of the 1966 Local Government Act, targeting support funding at areas of high Asian and Afro-Caribbean settlement, were untouched. Such money was increasingly used to develop 'community' based library services in the early eighties and seems to have acted as a spur to innovation. In Gateshead, Inner Area Programme funding was used between 1980 and 1983 to develop a ground breaking 'library promotions team' which attempted to initiate a community development role for the library (Liddle, 1980). Bradford's library bus (see ch. 3) and innovative community information projects in Sunderland and Devon all utilised central government money (Barugh, 1984; Venner and Cotton, 1986). Manchester developed a Community Reprographics Unit, an Immigrant Language Community Information Service, and a street festival equipment pool (Godwin, 1981). Neville Price (1989) noted that, by the end of the eighties, librarians employed under Section 11 still formed the mainstay of a specialist and largely separate public library service to ethnic minorities. By 1985, urban library authorities ignoring central government supplementary funding of one kind or another were rare. Opportunism dominated urban aid. In retrospect, the projects it supported look like a patchwork of fragmentary schemes based on local conditions and personalities. But many, like the examples noted above, pushed back the boundaries of what it was thought acceptable for libraries to do. As Martin (1989, p.66) concludes, 'there can be little doubt that without the existence of urban aid, there would have been instances when innovative new developments simply would not have got off the ground'.

Because of this eclecticism, and the variety of influences which shaped community librarianship, it is easy to dismiss it as simply a series of initiatives and practices unevenly implemented at local level. However, as we have shown, the ideas associated with the new librarianship marked a significant disjuncture with traditional conceptions of public library purpose. As the practice of community librarianship developed in the eighties, so new ways of defining and delivering public library services emerged. Public libraries on the whole accepted responsibility for *cultural pluralism*: the complexities of providing a multicultural rather than an ethnocentric service. They accepted, sometimes reluctantly, the responsibility for *information provision* to the whole range of social classes and interests. Moreover, libraries began to adopt a much more *active* stance towards their publics, developing services and systems targeted at particular social groupings and moving literally and metaphorically 'outside' the library in order to operate as part of a network of public, private and voluntary provision. The permanence of these changes and the extent to which they fundamentally redefined public library practice remain, however, a matter of debate. What follows in this chapter will explore these questions through an analysis of three key facets of the community librarianship of this period: the development of services to unemployed people, community information services, and 'multicultural' library services.

The public library and the new disadvantaged: the case of services to the unemployed

One of the major challenges facing the 'new' librarianship of the eighties was that of developing an effective response to unemployment. If libraries were to be seen as relevant to disadvantage and social deprivation, they had to assist in efforts to alleviate the most visible social evil of the new decade. Aggregate unemployment in the UK rose from 0.5 million in 1976 to 3.5 million in 1986 and became a permanent, structural feature of the economy. Unemployment affected social groups and localities unevenly: the unskilled, the young, ethnic minorities and inner city residents were among those groups particularly in danger of being, or becoming, out of work. Spectacular examples of industrial decline plunged particular communities, many of them in Britain's heavy industrial heartlands, into crisis. As the eighties wore on, new, unstable labour markets emerged with as much as 60% of the labour force in temporary or part-time employment in some localities. In others, unemployment rates of 50% and above were quite common by 1986 [10].

What could public libraries do? Libraries had, of course, a tradition of providing assistance to the working class: as long ago as 1927 McColvin had written of various forms of 'extension' work with the unemployed, and especially the desirability of a 'spare room set aside for them which they will use as a social room for reading etc., with occasional lectures' (Redfern, 1989, p.2). But would a limited focus on the book as a pastime suffice for the more shifting and complex clientele of the eighties? It appeared not. Libraries in areas of high, sudden unemployment often noted a surge in usage of the library, but not in book borrowing which sometimes perplexingly went down [11]. A study of unemployed library users in Cheshire found that, instead, they seemed to look to the library for a range of enhanced services: newspapers; magazines to borrow; local information; careers and job information; cassettes; videos and so on. Even then, only 'about half' of the Cheshire unemployed regularly used the public library (Cheshire County Council, 1985). As a result, some argued that more radical initiatives had to be developed to reach those most in need, and that 'the needs of the unemployed may not be for traditional library services and may lie in the area of information in the form of advice' (Barugh and Woodhouse, 1987, p.7).

The public library response was in general far from radical, although worthy and perhaps symptomatic of the welfare professionalism of a passing age. The profession organised a special conference at Loughborough in 1982 out of which a volume of papers stimulating good practice emerged (Astbury, 1983). It was followed by the adoption of a wide ranging policy statement entitled *Public Libraries' Duty to the Unemployed* [12]. This stressed to need for public libraries to be proactive in their response, and noted the need to focus services on non-traditional library users such as young people, ethnic minorities, the disabled and the unskilled. It identified five key tasks for the public library in the areas of public awareness of unemployment; welfare information; leisure and free time; retraining and reemployment; and economic regeneration. In a good number of library authorities it stimulated a review of services and strategic planning alongside other local authority service providers such as education, social services and economic development.

At street level, however, the pattern of initiatives which emerged was more limited than many would have liked. In the only evaluative study of responses in the eighties, covering eight local authority areas in the North East of England, Barugh and Woodhouse (1987) noted that the most widespread development had been that of 'self-help' community information collections in libraries, which included information about welfare benefits and other topics relevant to unemployed people. 'Job boards', where libraries in areas without local job centres displayed details of opportunities and vacancies, were also widespread. Libraries also tended to upgrade their business and technical information services, focusing them in some cases on local economic development and new employment issues. Beyond this, activity was patchy. In some cases libraries had even utilised grant aid of various kinds to finance *general* library development such as refurbishment, computerisation and extension of mobile services (Dean, 1981). These developments were often undertaken on the contentious assumption that heavy unemployment would simply lead to greater demand for existing services: predominantly book borrowing. And such demand did not automatically emerge.

Of course, there were imaginative experiments that pointed to the possibilities of a more proactive approach. In one well documented case - Clwyd - the library service operated as the focus of a coordinated local authority approach to the problem, serving as a multifaceted provider of information and advice following the closure of steelworks and other heavy industries on Deeside. Williams (1983) describes how this approach had the effect of breaking down barriers between 'information' and 'advice' providers in both the social welfare and business start-up spheres. Clwyd Libraries became involved in producing focused and locally relevant welfare rights material, employing full time welfare rights officers who supported the voluntary sector, and in developing a business information service targeted at redundant workers in conjunction with Industrial Development and Business Advice agencies. Crucially, in Clwyd, the library service had shown its potential by placing itself at the centre of a network of local information providers, rather than on the margins.

In other cases, local authorities were beginning to adopt community development strategies as a response to unemployment, and in a small number of these the public library began to occupy a pivotal role as a focus of local resources. Renfrew, in Strathclyde, was one example of this approach: the authority opened two neighbourhood centres at Linwood (1981) and Johnstone (1984) which integrated public library services with a wide range of support functions for unemployed people. The Johnstone Information and Leisure Centre, for example, provided not only information and advice services but facilities and activities targeted at local teenagers (youth unemployment in the area was especially high) and resources and meeting space for local community organisations. As well as this, it was still a traditional public library (Hendry, 1986).

But initiatives such as this, with consistent, long term financial support, were the exception. Many others were supported only by temporary urban aid or similar funding, and thus had a limited or problematic lifespan. According to

Woodhouse (1983), many were poorly evaluated and discontinued after an initial term. By 1987, Barugh and Woodhouse would conclude that most librarians had 'little substantial communication with those working with the unemployed' and that the 'provision of library services to organisations working with the unemployed appears to be in many cases underdeveloped and in many cases unexplored' (p.93). Initiatives seemed to take off, it seemed, only in exceptional circumstances where a combination of the drive and interest of senior library management linked with political will and vision and the availability of 'additional' funding from outside the mainstream library budget.

This is not to say that public libraries did nothing. Most studies found that librarians, and indeed the profession as a whole, were very sympathetic to the plight of the unemployed, and they were prepared to adapt and focus existing services to meet what they thought were new needs. Thus, community information 'packs' of various kinds, job boards, focused business information: all proved popular. But these were all services easy to provide within a traditional range of roles and functions and within library buildings. Beyond this there lay professional and institutional resistance to a change of role. Woodhouse (1983) notes that radical service initiatives, sometimes promoted by senior managers, often floundered because of an unwillingness of library staff to take on flexible work roles and develop involved relationships with users. Resistance to 'advice work' or 'youth work' was common. Demarcation disputes and uneasy relationships with other local authority departments and the voluntary sector were additional problems. In all, it seems that public libraries found it difficult to respond to the social problem of unemployment in ways other than those associated with institutionalised welfare. Librarians were still, it seemed, uneasy about more radical 'community' approaches, uneasy about a new professional role.

Citizenship in the 'information' society: community information and the public library

Unlike initiatives focused on the unemployed, which were seen by many at the time to be a response to a short term problem, community information services were claimed to represent a more permanent transformation of public library purpose. Fundamentally, community information came to be seen as the 'fourth right of citizenship' in a burgeoning 'information' society. As the National Consumer Council (1977, p.1) noted:

> people will not be able to get their due as citizens of present day society unless they have continuous access to information which will guide them through it, and where necessary, the advice to help them translate that

information into effective action; and unless they get their due they are unlikely to recognise the reciprocal obligation that all citizens have to society.

Advocates of community librarianship linked such statements with the traditional aspirations of British and American welfare programmes. Bunch (1982, p.43) noted how Beveridge had proposed in the forties a network of advice bureaux aimed at providing information for everyday problem solving as a way of mitigating the bureaucratic tendencies of the new national insurance system. Tracing the later development of community information to American information and referral services developed as part of Lyndon Johnson's 'Great Society' programmes, Bunch argued that the key objectives of community information services involved the development of harmonious communities through the amelioration of disadvantage. For him

the term *community information* has two key aspects. One is concerned with the nature of the information provided, that is information in the community to help people with daily problem solving or in raising the quality of their lives; the other is concerned with the nature of the clientele served, namely those who belong to the lower socio-economic groups or are disadvantaged through an inability to obtain, understand or act on information that affects their lives. (Bunch, 1982, p. 4)

Underpinning this definition was the perception of an evolving information intensive society, complex and sophisticated, in which the vulnerable and deprived were ill equipped to claim their rights of citizenship. It was clearly the business of the public library to help.

Such welfarist ideas - which we have already linked closely with mainstream community librarianship - attracted a good deal of support among public librarians. In 1978 the Library Association set up a working party on community information which produced a widely disseminated consultative document: *Community Information: What Libraries Can Do* (Library Association, 1980). The working party drew together examples of innovation and good practice and developed a working definition of Community Information very similar to the one used by Bunch [13]. The British Library also funded a number of action research projects in the field and helped develop the Community Information Project, which was to become for a time a central resource centre, clearing house and centre for bibliographical projects in the field (Community Information Project, 1987). At local level community information became an issue in perhaps the majority of public library authorities. The Library Association working party reported in 1980 on detailed developments in 11 local authorities, many of them by no means radical in political orientation. Watson, Bowen and Walley (1980) similarly undertook detailed case studies of seven library authorities, all involved in the development of community information in some way. They identified three characteristic 'models' of service:

- *back up*, which concentrated on providing information support for advice agencies and other voluntary and community groups.
- *direct service*, which offered an enquiry service providing mainly local information.
- *self help*, where librarians had organised and repackaged often ephemeral materials for borrowing, take away or reference purposes.

Not surprisingly, the researchers found that library staff were most comfortable when they could apply traditional skills to each of these models, especially regarding the acquisition, organisation and repackaging of documents, however ephemeral. Nevertheless, libraries were beginning to acquire a much wider range of information sources in this field and beginning to engage more actively in gathering and organising local information. As one interviewee noted, the idea that library staff should be 'the information officers for their community' was becoming a popular one (Watson, Bowen and Walley, 1980, p.78).

The *back up* service model perhaps became the most successful and permanent element of public library participation in community information. Community librarians quickly realised that, in order to effectively provide services of this sort targeted at disadvantaged groups, the co-operation of advice agencies of all kinds was necessary. Advice, community and welfare workers similarly began to wake up to the potential of the library as a source of information and in some cases grant aid, premises and other kinds of support (Darcy and Ohri, 1978). Inter-professional and bureaucratic barriers gradually began to melt. Libraries shared premises with advice centres and other agencies, sometimes, as in the cases of Bretton Aid Centre in Peterborough and the South Moulton Community Project in Devon, sharing information resources and staffing as well [14]. Coleman (1986, p.310) notes how, by 1986, Sheffield library staff were regularly involved in joint information projects with local voluntary and welfare groups and that over half the neighbourhood libraries in the city accommodated Citizens Advice Bureaux and independent advice centres. Many other library authorities were involved in local community information and networking groups: some librarians indeed co-ordinated these. Librarians often could offer special assistance in improving systems of information provision and control in this field. At both local and national level classification schemes for community information were developed, pressure was put on bodies like the DHSS to improve leaflet organisation and supply, and some library authorities produced specialist guides, bibliographies and directories [15].

Predominantly, however, these developments took place within the existing institutional and professional framework of the public library system. For those like John Barugh, who advocated a more radical approach based on a committed attack on information poverty, they were clearly not enough. Barugh (1989, p.41) argued for an emphasis on 'community education and information dissemination ... people are needed to decode, explain and interpret information on behalf of those unable to do it themselves'. The majority of librarians, however, shunned this role. In the study by Watson, Bowen and Walley, library staff overwhelmingly expressed a fear of the consequences of becoming involved in advice work, many commenting that it was beyond their skills and training and, more significantly, beyond their professional responsibility. Librarians also felt constrained by their position as local government officers and uneasy as a result about supporting local campaigning groups with a radical political agenda (Watson, Bowen and Walley, 1980, ch.3). Instead, co-operation flourished with the organised and 'formal' voluntary sector, even though many of these agencies, like the Citizen's Advice Bureaux, often had well developed information resources of their own. In practice, librarians pursued those initiatives they felt comfortable with, justifying these by arguments about skills and professional demarcation. Thus 'self help' collections which maintained an arms length relationship with users were common. Thus 'enquiry' services tended to focus on local information rather than matters of rights.

As the eighties unfolded, the welfarist focus of community information in libraries began to weaken. In many local authorities the emphasis reverted to the business of providing local information enquiry services together with a more wide ranging 'public' information service which included information about local authority activities and services. In some cases, 'community' information was redefined in this way; in others, the label was dropped altogether [16]. In some ways such shifts reflected the times and the growing influence of a consumerist approach to community librarianship. Coleman, reflecting on the political pressures and changes of the period, concedes that these general services would have 'far wider appeal' than those targeted at predominantly disadvantaged groups (1986, p.312). But the changes were also a symptom of the growing interest in and influence of information technology in public libraries. A survey in 1987 by Chris Batt of information technology applications in public libraries reported that 41% of British public libraries claimed to be providing some form of technology based 'community information' service. Some authorities like Sheffield and Berkshire were in the process of developing in house viewdata systems; others like Hertfordshire and Northamptonshire, were experimenting with use of PRESTEL. Some, like

Devon and Bedfordshire, used stand alone microcomputers, floppy disks and databases. These systems predominantly provided what Batt called 'signposting' information: details of local clubs, societies, community groups, council services and in some cases tourist information (Batt, 1988). Bill Martin, concerned about disadvantage and community involvement, was to protest, predictably, that 'this is not community information at all' (Martin, 1989, p.155).

But such relabelling of 'community' information was, of course, very significant. It signified an uncontentious category of information that libraries as public institutions could package and purvey, and it was attuned to conventional expectations about their purpose held by a clear majority of both their workforce and users. From the mid-eighties onwards community information, as far as many librarians were concerned, was increasingly seen as a broad spectrum of information services provided for localities [17]. The concern with disadvantage and information poverty was to be diluted, if not ditched. The institutional and professional limits to welfare were clear.

The public library and cultural pluralism: towards a 'multicultural' library service?

As the pace of social change quickened in the late seventies, the institutions of the British welfare state were forced increasingly to face the fact of a society characterised by cultural, ethnic and racial difference. By 1985, Britain had a population of over 3 million people who were post-war immigrants or their descendants [18]. The majority of migrants had come to Britain in response to labour shortages, and most originated from the West Indies or South Asia (India, Pakistan, Bangladesh). Other significant groups had settled from nations as diverse as Hong Kong, Cyprus, Poland, Italy and Somalia. Most migrants were granted formal citizenship rights including, of course, the right to make use of public services like libraries. But many, especially African/Caribbean and Asian migrants, suffered from a racism which had its roots in British colonialism and from subsequent discrimination, especially in employment, housing and access to public services. Partly as a result, many migrants (and indeed their sons, daughters, grandsons and granddaughters) resisted an unproblematic 'assimilation' into the British way of life. Instead, they formed distinct 'communities' of their own based on shared identities of language, culture, religion and sometimes 'race'. By the mid seventies, as a result of the persistence and development of such identities, commentators were claiming that Britain was a plural 'multicultural' society. Such 'multiculturalism', in tune with the liberal orthodoxies of the time, replaced assimilation as the goal of much of British public policy [19].

As we have already observed in Chapter 3, the public library had been characteristically leaden footed in response to these developments. In 1969, research indicated that around 30 local authorities were making some sort of provision of Indic language materials in public libraries, but noted that collections were small and limited and that few other activities or plans for ethnic minority services were in evidence (Lambert, 1969). Norman (1972) reported a wider range of initiatives in Lambeth which included, importantly, a realisation that issues of service provision were not simply those of language. However, it soon became clear that the accusation of a 'poverty of thinking' in multicultural library provision, made in 1974 by Waters and Wilkinson, had more than a grain of truth. Waters and Wilkinson accused libraries of both *specific* failings - such as low levels of stock, few attempts to employ black or minority ethnic staff and little effort at community liaison - and, more importantly, the general failing of cultural exclusivity. Libraries as institutions were, according to them, hostile to and ignorant of African, Asian, Caribbean and Black British culture:

> not until librarians question their own assumptions, examine their own role as intermediaries and the function of libraries for the propagation of certain ways of thinking, can they even begin to provide a real service for the community (Waters and Wilkinson, 1974).

Waters and Wilkinson's article provoked a furious response in the correspondence columns of the *Library Association Record* of the time [20], but it paved the way for the widespread adoption of multiculturalism as a service philosophy in public libraries. At policy level it was followed by a flurry of official concern. In 1976 a joint working party set up by the Library Advisory Council and the Community Relations Commission produced a report entitled *Public Library Service for a Multicultural Society* (Community Relations Commision, 1976). Accepting the basic tenets of multiculturalism and the desirability of its continuance, it went on to recommend action in the areas of library stock provision; community links; interagency co-operation; and staff recruitment and training. A similar statement followed from the Library Association (1977). Occasionally, groups of librarians adopted a more radical stance: the Association of Assistant Librarians, in a statement entitled 'Libraries and racialism', explicitly recognised racism as a major problem in a way that some other official documents shunned (Association of Assistant Librarians, 1981). Significantly, many of these policy documents recommended action based on the principles and practices of community librarianship. Multiculturalism became an integral part of the 'community' approach to librarianship and vice-versa. Many of the personalities involved in the foundation of the Library Association Community Services Group in 1982 were heavily involved in the development of multicultural services, and the group attracted many 'ethnic minority' librarians as members. As a result, for a time in the early eighties, the debates concerning multiculturalism particularly animated all 'community' librarians (Price, 1989, p.652).

The extent to which such rhetoric was reflected in real changes to service provision remains an issue of contention. Gundara and Warwick (1980, p.69) argued that there was a danger that many multicultural initiatives might turn out to be tokenistic and that 'simply to extend services to minority communities from within an essentially Eurocentric library structure does not in our view constitute a multicultural library service'. But in many ways it looks as though this is precisely what happened. The predominant strategy adopted by public library authorities was the appointment of an 'ethnic minority' librarian under Section 11 of the 1966 Local Government Act, which enabled part payment of salary from central government funding. Provision for black and minority ethnic communities as a result often developed as a separate entity having only a marginal impact on mainstream library services, despite the many valuable and creative initiatives undertaken.

Nevertheless, there were some fundamental changes. By 1980 60% of public library authorities were reported as making specialist stock provision for ethnic minorities (Cooke, 1980). By the mid-eighties co-operative schemes of stock exchange through LASER and other organisations were well developed. Moreover, children's librarians in public libraries and educational services were becoming especially sensitised to issues relating to multiculturalism and racism in children's materials, encouraged by the popularity and currency of ideas associated with multicultural education. Many children's library services developed quite sophisticated and sensitive stock selection guidelines which grappled with many of the complex issues relating to the nature of 'multicultural' provision. However, only in a very small number of cases were such criteria extended to adult materials, although many local authorities did develop some sort of policy for general multicultural provision and commit specific elements of the bookfund to developing it [21].

As well as general change, there were real examples of excellence and innovation. London boroughs such as Brent, Lambeth and Camden, stimulated by the cultural and political climate of London in the early eighties, attempted much more thoroughgoing approaches to multicultural provision. Brent took a particular interest in researching, sourcing and acquiring multicultural materials of many kinds and gained national recognition for its resource lists and a 'Roots in Britain' exhibition about black history. The local authority as a whole took a lead in developing racism awareness training and other equal opportunities initiatives (Alexander, 1982, ch. 4). Lambeth developed similar initiatives and particularly linked multiculturalism with its expanding outreach collections in a large number of community meeting places. Lambeth librarians also came to pride themselves on the great care they took in selecting resources according to multicultural and non-racist criteria and they became well known for the feedback they gave to the publishing industry on multicultural matters [22]. Camden developed innovative community information resources and services targeted at ethnic minority groups (Thompson, 1989). Elsewhere in Britain, such innovation was occasionally repeated. Leicestershire, concerned about low numbers of Asian and Afro-Caribbean librarians, developed a much needed and for a time highly successful, graduate recruitment scheme (Cooke, 1987). Bradford, in conjunction with the local university, experimented with a unique local history, oral history and archive project.

By mid-decade, however, it was becoming clear that such initiatives were exceptional and indeed running out of critical mass. Multiculturalism was still seen by many as relevant only to special services directed at 'ethnic minorities' and these services were often marginalised and under resourced [23]. A Library Association survey of the ethnic identity of members in 1987 indicated that only 1.96% of members had African, Afro Caribbean, Asian or Oriental ethnic origins (Talbot, 1990, p.502) and there was much concern about the lack of recruitment of ethnic minority library staff. The Library Association issued another policy statement in 1986 - 'The recruitment and training of library and information workers of ethnic minority background' - but it received only a cautious and sceptical reaction (Raddon, 1987). Evidence also began to emerge that general activity on the ground was thinner than the literature of initiatives seemed to suggest. Elliot's research into the links between public libraries and ethnic minority community groups in London found a 'remarkable lack of interest and assistance' on the part of libraries in those organisations developing library and resource centres of their own (Elliot, 1984, p.102). Similar doubts began to be raised about the extent of multicultural materials provision in libraries. A stock survey undertaken in North West England by Talbot in 1987 found poor levels of penetration of key works representative of South Asian and Afro Caribbean culture. She noted also that 'where there are examples of good practice, this does not appear to be consistently exercised throughout the whole of the library authority'. Her conclusion, that 'most library authorities in the North West of England are not providing a truly multicultural library service' (Talbot, 1991, p.53), seemed to bear out Alexander's earlier observation that 'there remains the normal library service, and stuck haphazardly onto it, this wart of multiculturalism' (Alexander, 1982, p.53). By 1986, the same could perhaps be said of many of the other 'warts' associated with community librarianship.

The public library as professional bureaucracy: the limits of community librarianship

What common themes emerge from this analysis of key initiatives? Was community librarianship 'changing the face of public libraries' in the eighties, as Bill Martin (1989) hoped? In some locations, initiatives seemed to amount to more than wishful thinking. Dolan (1989, p.16) suggested that developments in Manchester amounted to a 'new deal' in terms of the conversion of buildings for community use, the development of community liaison and the establishment of new services for disadvantaged groups. Lathrope (1989), reporting on developments in Derbyshire, noted that the number of centres receiving outreach services in the form of deposit collections and/or support services had leapt from 179 in 1980 to 564 in 1986-7. In Lambeth, 'outreach' had been developed as a whole philosophy of service where library buildings were held to be less important in themselves than the use of resources in the community. By 1982 this small and poor London borough was serving 'over 550' [24] community organisations. Hendry (1979) disliked the notion of 'outreach' and used the idea of 'community service' as a basic philosophy. But his authority, Renfrew, adopted similar practices renaming 'branches' as 'community libraries' and boosting the use of library materials by over 1 million issues per annum over a three year period.

Perhaps more importantly, there is undoubtedly evidence of something of a general movement in attitudes and practices. Some services like local information, community information self help and ethnic minority services became commonplace in perhaps the majority of public library authorities. In many too, librarians became less insular and worked with professionals in other agencies and leaders of community organisations to develop joint projects. Equal opportunity developed as a core philosophy of service provision and was applied not only to ethnic minority groups but to a broad range of client groups and service areas. There were numerous initiatives in areas we lack space to examine in detail here, and services and access arrangements were undoubtedly improved for people with disabilities, the elderly and people with visual and mental handicaps (Ryder, 1987; Bowen and Dee, 1986). At the general level it was, perhaps, possible to note that by 1986 the public library movement as a whole had become much more conscious of the need for equality of access and community orientation than a decade earlier.

However, most contemporary writers on public libraries recognised the limitations and in some senses the fragility of these developments. In particular, the notion of the basic, institutionalised library service and of 'community librarianship' as something extra, special or marginal to it, was one that proved resilient and very difficult to break down. As part of our own research in 1993, we circulated to all English and Welsh library authorities a request for information about policies, practices or initiatives associated with community librarianship. The Head of Library Services in one London borough replied that 'the library service is structured on traditional lines of a major central library with supporting branches. Our branches could be regarded as 'community' service points and we have links with other council organisations such as schools, playgroups etc. but no formalised devolvement of services' [25]. Such concerns with institution and system were commonplace. Even into the 1990s they resulted in the structural and often financial isolation of many community services and initiatives which were still, in the case of around 50% of our respondents, labelled as or grouped with 'special' or 'extension' activities like mobile, housebound and prison services. Even these traditional extension services were 'cinderellas' (Lewis, 1987), compared with mainstream reference and lending services. For the newer initiatives associated with community approaches, such marginal status came as standard and was reflected commonly in poor staffing levels, accommodation, transport facilities and equipment.

All of this points to the power of the traditional public library *as an institution* and its reluctance to adopt community approaches as part of its basic business. Such resistance set real limits on the development and expansion of community librarianship. A debate in the mid-eighties about outreach illustrates this resistance very well. In July 1987 a working party of the Association of London Authorities (ALA) reported on a range of issues affecting service delivery in inner city libraries. The ALA was a relatively radical body, composed of mainly Labour controlled London boroughs in the wake of the abolition of the Greater London Council in 1986, and the working party on libraries, not surprisingly, endorsed many of the principles of community librarianship. Its definition of outreach was comprehensive and apparently uncontentious. Following the lead of the *Libraries Choice* (Department of Education and Science, 1978), it conceptualised outreach as 'any library service which fulfils a need of and provides a service to the local community beyond the confines of library buildings' [26]. However, this attracted criticism, the borough of Lambeth commenting in the following terms:

> ... outreach, in fact, requires a more major reorientation of the whole service than is implied ... it is simply not the case that a library authority which runs, for example, a housebound service is actually taking a 'community librarianship' or 'outreach' approach. 'Community librarianship' in fact means a fairly radical change, whereby the library service recognises the needs of its local community (most specifically the communities which are traditionally excluded from council services rather than being 'disadvantaged' ...) and targets its services to begin to meet

those groups' needs both in library buildings and in the community. It is absolutely vital that these two elements of the service are integrated and that, for example, feedback from community groups is actually taken into account in providing building based services, and that 'outreach' is not seen as an addendum to a continuing 'traditional' buildings service, which, in effect is often little more than a cop-out. [27]

The real issue here is not simply that of outreach and definitions of it. Lambeth was contending that community librarianship (of which outreach is indeed a crucial element) cannot flourish *without* a major restructuring and reorientation of the whole library service. Such a redefinition must, according to them, involve a diffusion of the institution into the community which the library serves. Such diffusion, such *deinstitutionalisation* (to use Bill Martin's term), was precisely what even comparatively progressive library authorities, like those in the majority in the ALA, were unwilling to concede. Hence, for most, community librarianship involved the retention of the 'traditional' service and the development of new or 'special' initiatives outside this institutional core. In most public library authorities, the advocates of community librarianship never gained the confidence, or the power, to challenge and change this core.

Why was there such reluctance to refocus the basic public library service? Undoubtedly part of the problem lay in the essentially bureaucratic nature of the library function. This inevitably involves the subjection of chaotic cultural records to bibliographic organisation and control and the standardisation and maximisation of their use through cataloguing and indexing systems and other techniques of administration. In consequence, as Jones (1984) argued convincingly, libraries developed as rule bound, hierarchical and conservative institutions bearing close affinity to Max Weber's definition of a classical bureaucracy. Recent efforts to modify this model have had only mixed success. Moves towards automation of systems and services reduce hierarchy, but increase the power and pervasiveness of set rules and functions, leading to the development of what Jones defines as 'machine' bureaucracies. The 'professionalisation' of the workforce in the sixties was in theory supposed to tame bureaucracy and create institutions led by ideals of education and public service and characterised by the exercise of variation and professional discretion. But as we have seen, the institutional preoccupation of librarians dies hard, for the demands of the library as machine, or system, are ever present and in some ways expanding. Arguably, 'librarianship is perhaps closer to full bureaucracy along the continuum than are most professions, and as a form of professional bureaucracy it has closer affinities than most with machine bureaucracy' (Jones, 1984, p.15).

Of course, as we have seen in chapter 3, some of the protagonists of community librarianship were only too aware of this state of affairs and throughout the seventies and early eighties made significant attempts to improve things. In particular *team librarianship* was developed as a management strategy for encouraging a community oriented approach [28]. Pioneered in Leicestershire in the 1960s, 'team' structures in public library systems sought to overcome the bureaucratic preoccupation of the service by curtailing the administrative functions of the average professional librarian. Instead, buildings and systems were to be run by administrative/clerical specialists and librarians freed for 'professional' work in the community. Thus, in a typical team structure like that implemented in Tameside, Greater Manchester, small libraries were run by Senior Library Assistants and were organised into area groups under 'Principal Assistant Librarians'. In each area this left a team of three other professional staff who focused on children's and other community services, bookstock work, and various other special services like audio visual materials, exhibitions and services to industry. In the case of these latter specialisms, further cross area 'teams' were formed to co-ordinate services on a 'matrix' basis. These librarians had little managerial responsibility and were notionally free to pursue community librarianship. In Tameside, this evidently led to increases in work with children, community profiling improvements in services to industry, and development of exhibitions work with the arts and museums service (Featherstone, 1979).

Team librarianship had obvious advantages. In county areas like Leicestershire and Cambridgeshire, where professional staffing could be thinly spread, it brought some enhanced services and expertise to small and isolated service points. Many librarians liked it, especially the young. One of our informants, who worked in a county authority team structure in the late seventies and early eighties, commented that 'you had intellectual freedom, but you had to deliver, you were monitored ... we changed a lot of things, a group of us were sharp, young, quite dynamic people ... a nice little mafia I suppose!' [29]. But at the same time, others resisted and change could often be slow, superficial or transient. The same informant commented on sullen inertia 'refusal to play the game' from an area librarian and other experienced librarians and library assistants. Inertia could take other forms too - in Tameside a lot of the new work focused on children because community oriented work with this group 'had been a professional tradition'. Nevertheless some librarians found it difficult to come to terms with 'the idea that there is more to librarianship than ferreting out bibliographical enquiries' (Featherstone, 1979, p.9).

From the perspective of community librarianship, the benefits of team approaches were mixed. Many librarians utilised their freedom to practise a proactive librarianship and develop community oriented innovations. But they were often structurally - and culturally - marginalised within library systems. Responsibility for 'outreach', client services and special initiatives of many kinds had been given to 'junior' professionals who often had a great deal of freedom but little responsibility for or control over resources and staffing. Such control usually remained vested in an often traditionalist middle management and at street level it was passed to senior library assistants, newly enhanced in power and status. These were both groups who, as a result of both background and function, were likely to reinforce the continuance of a traditional bureaucratic culture. As a result, there could often be little link between 'community' services operated by 'community' librarians and the 'basic' reference and lending service that underpinned the public library as an institution. In some authorities, community librarianship might thus have been marginalised three times over: in terms of funding; in terms of its labelling as 'special' service provision; and in terms of the group of relatively powerless staff expected to deliver it.

In the end, team librarianship seems to have compounded the marginalisation of community librarianship within the public library. As Barlow (1989, p.153) noted, tampering with structures in the end did little to alter the fundamental *organisational culture* of the public library. By the mid 1980s the basic character of the public library as an institutional professional bureaucracy remained largely unchanged, and this seems to have been a major obstacle to attempts to reform the public library as a community oriented service. Nevertheless, some of the ideas associated with community librarianship were well known but, with some justification, there was confusion about its coherence as a total philosophy of service. Except in a minority of local authorities, community librarianship as *practice* remained confined to certain sectors and levels of the library service. Librarians, in the main, seemed to prefer a role which focused on 'helping people without getting too involved' [30] and the bureaucratic imperative of library operations could offer a continuing and deadening brake on change. By the mid-eighties, community librarianship had gained some acceptance, but it remained marginal in the public library community. Its roots were in many ways shallow, and as the ideological landscape of Britain changed still further, 'community' library services looked to be vulnerable. How community librarianship responded to this challenge of a new set of ideas about public library provision - this time from the political right - is the focus of Chapter 5.

Notes

1   For the important argument that economic changes in the early eighties amounted to much more than 'recession' see Newby (1985).

2   See Cochrane (1989) for a good account of the local government politics of this period. Broady and Usherwood (1985) investigate the effects of rate capping on the public library service.

3   'Government statement on libraries is complacent', *Library Association Record* (1984), vol. 86, no. 12, p. 501.

4   See Lambert (1985). The Library Campaign newsletter *Campaigner* (1984 - current) also provides a blow by blow account of expenditure reductions in the eighties and their effects on the public library service.

5   Library Association (1980), *Community Information: What Libraries Can Do. A Consultative Document*; Library Association (1983), *Public Libraries Duty to the Unemployed*; Library Association (1985), *Library and Information Services for Our Multicultural Society*. Note that this latter policy statement expanded and superseded a previous statement - *Public Libraries in a Multicultural Britain* - issued in January 1977.

6   See Godwin (1981). On Renfrew, see Hendry (1981). On Sunderland, Barugh (1984).

7   Indeed, community librarianship as a whole has from time to time been stereotyped and associated with the supposed excesses of political correctness and the 'loony left' in local government. Keith Waterhouse, in the *Daily Mail* of 28th June 1993, links the supposed 'decline' of the public library firmly to 'community' approaches: 'nowadays the local library is likely to be a cultural slum, festooned with reams of print out paper and leaflets offering information on the nearest gypsy encampment, its tattered books being gradually edged out by videos and compact discs, its be-jeaned, earring sporting assistants treating their 'customers' to the self righteous evangelical smile of the Politically Correct and whining for more resources ...' Cited in Greenhalgh, Worpole and Landry (1985), p. 140.

8   Interview with Principal Librarian, Inner London Borough, October 1993.

9   Interview with County Librarian, Northern County, November 1995.

10 See White (1992) for a comprehensive review of these trends and issues.

11 See Fryer and Payne (1983) for a discussion and limited investigation of this phenomenon.

12 Library Association (1983). Martin (1989, pp.98-99) contains a detailed discussion of the document.

13 Library Association (1980, pp.11-12) for the definition. Allan Bunch was indeed a leading member of the working party.

14 For details of Peterborough see Bunch (1982), pp.77-84. For Devon see Venner and Cotton (1986).

15 See for example London Borough of Camden, *Free Information Leaflet Suppliers* produced in a number of editions 1983 - current. A number of librarians - including the Classification Research Group - began to devote expertise around this time to the problems of organising community information materials, and some of their ideas were subsequently taken up by producers of materials such as the National Association of Citizen's Advice Bureaux. See Bunch (1982) for a discussion.

16 See Usherwood (1992a) p.20 for examples.

17 This was the predominant finding of our own field research. See Chapters 5 and 6.

18 According to the 1991 census just over 3 million people (5.5%) of the UK population described themselves as belonging to a 'non white' ethnic group. Most experts agree that this is almost certainly an underestimate. See Central Office of Information (1994), *Britain 1995: an Official Handbook* .

19 There is, of course, a vast literature covering these matters. For an introduction see Parekh (1991).

20 See the 'letters' column of the *Library Association Record* from February - April, 1974.

21 Klein (1985) provides an excellent overview of some of these issues. In our own investigation a few local authorities, notably Lambeth, Sandwell (West Midlands) and Gloucestershire, provided us with examples of detailed and impressive multicultural selection criteria.

22 See, for example, Lambeth Libraries, *Children's Book Selection Guidelines* (1982).

23 See, for example, the discussion of Birmingham in Dolan (1992).

24 See London Borough of Lambeth, Libraries Working Party (1992) *Community Based Library Services*, p.3. Our special thanks to Lambeth Libraries who made numerous detailed working documents available to us.

25 Correspondence from Borough Librarian, Outer London Borough, February, 1993.

26 See Association of London Authorities, Arts and Recreation Committee (1987), *Library Services in ALA Boroughs*. Document provided by Lambeth Libraries.

27 Letter from H. Gilby, Director of Amenity Services, London Borough of Lambeth, to David McCollum. The letter is attached as an appendix to the *ALA Officers Working Group on Libraries, Draft Report* 5th June 1987. Document provided by Lambeth Libraries.

28 For a detailed study of the implementation of team structures see Barlow (1989).

29 Interview with Principal Librarian, Reference and Information Services, Midland County, April, 1994.

30 Taken from an informant's response in Slater (1980). Quoted in Jones (1984), p.12.

5 Community librarianship in retreat: The impact of the market

Third term Thatcherism and the restructuring of the British welfare state

In the late 1980s British public life came to be dominated by right wing politics and ideas perhaps more than at any time since the nineteen thirties. The Conservative election victory of 1987 cemented this dominance and allowed the Thatcher government - its opponents weakened and neutralised by the conflicts of the earlier part of the decade - to turn its attention to a radical restructuring of public institutions. Such restructuring was based on ideas associated with *public choice* - a set of theories developed initially in the USA concerned with the role of state bureaucracy in free market democracies. Public choice theorists [1] argued that the public sector was characterised by *oversupply*, primarily because it was run by bureaucrats and professionals who pursued budget maximisation strategies in their *own interest* rather than those of consumers. Public services thus were riddled with inefficiency and waste. The remedy lay in a range of policy options from wholesale privatisation of public services (as in UK public utilities) to the development of quasi or internal markets within public institutions (as in the National Health Service). Where such change was organisationally or politically impossible the introduction of 'business' management techniques - such as performance measurement, total quality management and customer care - were recommended. Such changes, it was claimed, would bring about improved efficiency in public services coupled with improved customer satisfaction at the expense only of the vested interests of complacent professional/bureaucratic public employees.

It would be misleading, however, to claim that restructuring is driven exclusively by politics and political choice. For writers like Paul Hoggett (1990), the politics of the new right represent a relatively superficial attempt to shape a modernisation process which   at root is technologically and

93

economically driven. The foundations of modernisation, in Hoggett's view, lay in the development of 'post-Fordist' economies characterised by flexibility of production, deregulated labour markets and the sovereignty of the consumer. Information technology makes possible the 'flexible accumulation' of capital in an organisation whilst at the same time enabling 'centralisation of command'. Its impact on organisational form is to simultaneously enable centralised strategic planning and devolved and decentralised delivery - what Peters and Waterman recommended as 'tight/loose' systems of organisation (Hoggett, 1990, pp. 4-5). For public service bureaucracies like libraries, such modes of regulation signalled the incipient decline of paternalistic/bureaucratic methods of working characteristic of the mid-century welfare state. From all sides they began to be seen as inefficient, inflexible and unable to respond to diversifying client demands. In their place, as we have seen, the right was to advocate a strategy of efficiency, public choice and marketisation. For the left, according to Hoggett, 'the strategy of decentralisation and democratisation should also be considered as an attempt to harness the new logic of capitalist development' (1990, p.15).

Such a strategy, of course, has close affinities with the radical versions of community librarianship examined in chapter 3. But in 1986-7 radical conservatives, not the left, were in the driving seat, and they became interested in the activities of all kinds of public institution - including, as we shall see, the public library [2]. Stewart and Stoker (1995, p. 2) note that after 1985 Conservative concern about the local state 'became wider in its focus and far reaching in its implications ... it moved beyond public expenditure restraint to a more far reaching attempt to restructure local government'. Although this process was and is uneven in its application and uncertain in its outcomes, some have claimed it amounts to a 'revolution' in local governance. Its elements include:

- financial constraint
- the fragmentation of local government
- a commitment to competition
- a shift towards local authorities as 'enablers' of services rather than direct providers
- a closer relationship for consumers between paying for and receiving services
- a greater emphasis on customer choice
- the development of voluntary and private sector provision of public services
- the challenging of 'producer' and professional interests in public services
- a commitment to more business like management

94

- the development of new providers of services at local level often accountable to central government
- the development of new mechanisms of local accountability which bypass the elected authority [3].

Some of these elements have, of course, impinged on the public library community less than others. Unlike in the education sector, there have been few changes in formal arrangements for public accountability of library services. As of yet, too, there has been little formal 'privatisation' of library services, although pilot studies have been conducted and the recent Department of National Heritage study *Contracting-Out in Public Libraries* (KPMG and Capital Planning Information, 1995) has not ruled this possibility out. However, in tandem with other local authority services, it is arguable that libraries are experiencing something of a revolution in the way they are managed and in the way they relate to and provide services for their public. For public libraries, this organisational revolution is undoubtedly the most important aspect of the restructuring of the period.

Managerialism and subsequently consumerism were, and are, the ideologies of this organisational shift. Local government in general and libraries in particular were increasingly seen as 'big business' in the late eighties, and exhorted to change their character and culture and adopt competitive structures, practices and rhetoric characteristic of the private sector. Managerialism posited the replacement of professional control of public services by managerial direction based on the principles of business efficiency. At its core was a 'generic model of management, which minimised the difference between private sector business management and the running of public services' (Pollitt, 1993, p. 27). Pollitt's research in the civil service, the NHS and local education authorities carried out in the mid eighties revealed the following common managerial strategies:

- tight cash limits and cash planning
- staff cuts
- the introduction of performance indicators stressing economy and efficiency
- the extensive introduction of staff appraisal
- 'devolved' budgetary systems giving greater responsibility to line managers
- planning systems (including management by objectives) which stress concrete, short term targets
- rhetorical emphasis on responsibility to the consumer, although consumers were often only hazily conceptualised [4].

Pollitt labels such managerialism *neo-Taylorian* because of its emphasis on staff control, performance measurement, central planning and efficiency. Its concern with the consumption of services was weak and rhetorical only. Rather, it sought efficiency and economy of provision, often using the analogy of the 'lean and fit' organisation.

Around 1990, however, it is arguable that the focus on the consumer began to take on a more serious character, signalled by John Major's inauguration of the 'Citizen's Charter' in 1991. A concern with service 'quality' and guarantees of minimum service standards were underpinned by a new interest in management alternatives to neo-Taylorism. These alternatives, such as the 'public service orientation' (Stewart and Clarke, 1987) and a growing interest in 'cultural' approaches to organisational change, popularised by writers such as Peters and Waterman (1982) and Handy (1976), promised something of a new direction in the public services. Typically, they stressed the importance of getting closer to the consumer, citizen or customer and developing consumer focused organisational cultures and practices. However, the extent to which such a 'new public management' (NPM) based on consumerism has succeeded remains uncertain. Its 'customer' focus has been criticised because of its individualism, as has its concentration on existing rather than potential users of services. It is primarily concerned with wants and demands rather than unarticulated need - a focus which particularly affects disadvantaged consumers who may have difficulty speaking for themselves and little power in the marketplace. Pollitt observes that it accords a mainly passive role to citizens: their participation is chiefly 'one of feeding back via questionnaires and other market research their (dissatisfaction) levels with what managements have designed and delivered'. Perhaps aptly, he concludes that 'NPM is not so much a charter for citizen empowerment as managerialism with a human face' (Pollitt, 1993, p.187).

The impact of the restructuring of the British welfare state on public libraries, and community librarianship in particular, is the concern of this chapter. An account of this process is far from straightforward because, as we have seen, restructuring has many facets: public choice theory and policy; post-Fordism; and managerial and consumerist organisational change. Moreover, because the process of restructuring public libraries is mediated though the institutions and practices of local government in general, its impact on differing library services is inevitably uneven. Local authorities, as Stoker and Mossberger (1995) argue, adopted markedly differing policies and organisational strategies in response to the dynamic of change, and this is undoubtedly reflected in the specifics of public library development in the eighties. Nevertheless, if we are to chart the trajectory of community librarianship since its high point in 1985, it is important to assess the impact of these 'new times' on public library policies, services and the organisational structure and culture of public librarianship. More specifically, it will be crucial to look at empirical evidence. How did the advocates of community librarianship, as well as its practitioners and indeed its critics, react to this new philosophy of public provision which seemed to constitute a threat to the very idea of the community itself?

The public library, restructuring and the new politics of the right

Perhaps one obscure but significant indicator of the 'new times' of the late 1980s was the politicisation of the public library. In spite of some nuances of emphasis, the post-war UK public library service was, as we have noted in Chapter 2, predominantly a subject of party political consensus based on the principles of the Keynesian welfare state. Such consensus had been challenged to some extent from the left by radical community librarianship, but much of this criticism remained invisible to those outside the profession. However, the challenge of the 'new right', which paralleled its critique of other state institutions, was vociferous, outspoken and attained a high public profile in the broadsheet press [5].

For their ideas about libraries, however, the new right characteristically turned to the United States. In 1983, Lawrence White, an American economist, published *The Public Library in the 1980s: the Problems of Choice,* a work which specifically applied public choice theory to the library service (White, 1983). The book concluded that only those library services directed at children and students provided a 'justifiable public good'. Substantially, White argued, other aspects of the service would be better provided on market principles through a mix of public/private provision utilising fees and charges. This would lead, he argued, to improved efficiency, less wasteful provision, lower taxation and improved responsiveness to the demands of consumers. These ideas naturally proved attractive to radical conservatives in the UK. In 1986, the right-wing think tank, the Adam Smith Institute, published *Ex Libris,* a pamphlet which married them to a withering attack on the UK public library service. *Ex Libris* argued that libraries had become a 'system which largely supplies free pulp fiction to those who could well afford to pay for it' and recommended the extensive introduction of fees and charges except in those areas singled out by White. In such a way 'the range and standard of services would be determined by the consumer ... rather than by politicians and librarians ... services would have to be provided more efficiently or discontinued' (Adam Smith Institute, 1986, p. 42).

The publication of *Ex Libris* and the debate which followed it undoubtedly stimulated serious central government interest in libraries for the first time since 1964. However, unlike the Adam Smith Institute, traditional 'one nation'

Tories like Richard Luce and Peter Brooke were reluctant to attack the conventional public library service, noting both its popularity among the middle classes and its role as custodian of the nation's 'literary tradition' [6]. Nevertheless, in a policy green paper of 1988 entitled *Financing Our Public Library Service: Four Subjects for Debate* (Office of Arts and Libraries, 1988) central government signalled its unwillingness to fund any expansion of new services through public expenditure. The paper attempted to confine the definition of a 'free' and 'basic' library service to the borrowing and reference use of print materials only. As the Library Association response noted, this definition never embraced services aimed at specific groups in the community, 'including ethnic minorities, the housebound and disadvantaged groups' (Library Association, 1988, p. iv). Outside this limited free service, it was clear that public libraries were expected to fund any expansion on the basis of cost recovery. The green paper defined a whole host of services, old and new, for which it might be permissible to charge: IT, multimedia, audio-visual, premium fiction and 'value added' reference services among others. Moreover, it invited comment on a whole array of arrangements for developing, funding and operating these services: fees, charges, joint public/private investment, client contractor arrangements and compulsory competitive tendering itself. As the hostile reaction of the public library establishment illustrated, it was perhaps the most controversial official document affecting public libraries to emerge from central government since 1945, although of course it fell short of the demands of the Adam Smith radicals [7].

It is difficult to gauge the precise impact of the 1988 green paper proposals on public library services, partly because they took time to formally attain the status of legislation [8] and also because, as we have already seen, public library policy is always mediated by the general climate and circumstances of local government. Nevertheless, the green paper marked something of a turning point in the development of the public library service as a whole, for it forced library managers to confront and recognise the realities of survival in a market led environment. It was clear that central government had drawn a line under the further expansion of a public library service based on public taxation and that such control could be enforced through the mechanism of rate capping. It was also clear that new development would now have to be funded by a more open and entrepreneurial approach to service. As Peter Beauchamp, chief library advisor at the Office of Arts and Libraries, noted: 'in today's world libraries are a business and deserve a business like approach to make the most of them' (Beauchamp, 1992, p. 106). Moreover, the library profession tacitly recognised this fact. Although the Library Association responded with some hostility to some green paper proposals such as charges for reference services and 'premium' book subscription services, its response was perhaps in the end more notable for what it conceded: additional schemes for income generation; experiments with client/contractor service models and the principle of increased private sector involvement in service provision (Library Association, 1988). As we shall see, in local authorities increasingly short of money even for the purchase of basic bookstock and equipment, such schemes quickly became matters of priority discussion and action.

However, it is evident that many public library authorities responded to the policy imperatives inherent in the green paper by attempting to *rationalise* service provision. It became the general practice in the early 1990s to identify the *core* or free public library service in the fairly specific and traditionalist terms mooted by the green paper and accord this the highest priority in terms of maintenance of provision. Library authorities typically defined these services as 'book lending, reference services and associated study facilities' or a 'loan service of books and associated materials and a wide ranging information service' [9]. Organisational and financial pressures mounted to provide these services at levels of maximum efficiency, and the concept of 'tiered' services became widespread as a mechanism of establishing standards of basic provision for localities of different sizes. Indeed, one northern metropolitan district was forced to abandon its attempt to develop a network of 'community libraries ... where the size and nature of the collections, the range of materials and activities and opening hours were intended to reflect local library staffs' interpretation of community needs' in favour of a system based on 'key libraries, which will in future form the irreducible core of the service' [10]. 'Tiering' was much criticised because, as well as resulting in the closure of many small branch libraries, it tended to withdraw the full range of public library services into larger institutional bases. Such rationalisation was usually accompanied by a scaling down of outreach activity (by 1993 even Lambeth was serving only 350 groups compared with a high point of over 500 in the late 1970s) and by widespread dwindling of special services and new initiatives in the community librarianship field [11]. As we have seen, many of these initiatives were supported on the basis of non-mainstream finance, and such funding in the late eighties came to be in a decreasing state of supply. The gradual abandonment of Home Office 'Section 11' support for multicultural initiatives, begun in 1990, typified this scaling down, forcing local authorities either to integrate ethnic minority services and staffing into mainstream budgets or in some cases make cuts and redundancies [12].

Such attempts at rationalisation became increasingly difficult, however, because of the general demand for a diversification of public library services. These pressures for diversification were economic, technological and cultural and can be linked directly to the 'post-Fordist' modernisation processes discussed above, and the emergence of what Moore and Steele (1991) labelled 'information intensive' Britain. Information technology spurred the development of new information products and the demand for new modes and categories of information. Chris Batt (1994, p.16) found that 'between 1989 and 1991 there was a doubling of library authorities using CD ROM - back in 1987, just six years previously, there were only two'. In the same survey, Batt found that 107 authorities provided direct access to on-line databases and 113 provided local information utilising information technology: 38 had developed their own public access viewdata systems. Such general modernisation affected communication in business, education, leisure and social welfare and stimulated demand for services as diverse as 'value added' business information; 'open learning' support packages; audio visual loan services for entertainment in a variety of specific media and new services for people with disabilities such as Kurzweil reading machines. Many local authorities, unable to fund such innovative, labour intensive or expensive services, began to define them as outside the scope of 'core' librarianship and envisage their provision on the basis of either cost recovery/profit or through co-operation with partners in the private or voluntary sectors [13]. In such a manner, what McKee (1987, p. 22) saw as a 'new paradigm - information, technology, and commerce' began to erode the traditional public service ethos of the library service. Increasingly, libraries had to operate like a business.

For library managers, such change was supported, and in many cases justified, by the adoption of new managerial techniques and cultures. In order to control and plan both rationalisation and innovation, managers needed to replace the traditional service culture of professional librarianship with a more entrepreneurial and businesslike approach . Such 'managerial' approaches had much in common with parallel developments in other areas of public service. They incorporated:

- a resurgence of interest in management by objectives (MBO), a system of decision making emphasised setting objectives and identifying and appraising options. MBO, it was hoped, would improve organisational cohesion through a clear annual statement of measurable goals and targets. At national level the Library and Information Services Council sponsored a manual of good practice published in 1991, and our own survey of local authority policy documents in 1993 revealed extensive use of its guidelines and recommendations [14].

- a scramble of activity to develop performance indicators in public library services (Cope, 1990). Public library managers were anxious to develop quantifiable measures of public library activity in order to justify service provision, partly in response to increasing demands from the audit commission. Additionally, hard choices about service priorities seemed to demand 'objective' and 'scientifically' gathered data. Work in this field culminated in the publication, in 1990, of *Keys to Success,* a manual of performance indicators for public libraries which was extensively utilised in the service (Office of Arts and Libraries, 1990).

- the increasing use of management information and decision support systems in service planning and development. Technological developments, in particular the evolution of primitive computerised issuing systems into integrated library management packages incorporating bookstock, circulation, reader statistics and catalogues, provided an enabling technology which seemed to promise a technical fix to problems of planning and resource allocation (Kinnell Evans, 1990).

- the development of *financial devolution, cost centring* and ultimately *client /contractor* modes of service organisation. Financial devolution and cost centring, again enabled by sophisticated information systems, became relatively widespread in public library services in the late 1980s. They were claimed to empower service managers, who were now free to make detailed day to day resource decisions, whilst at the same time they enabled senior management to retain more precise strategic financial control. Client/contractor modes of service delivery as developed in Brent, Westminster, Lincolnshire and elsewhere formally embedded such devolution in a 'contract culture'. The client or council (in practice a senior officer group) developed service specifications and awarded contracts to 'business units' responsible for day to day service delivery. Such contracts specify that services have to be delivered to a certain standard or specification and within a given budget (Tyerman and Russell, 1992).

It is possible, of course, to mount a comprehensive critique of the effects of such concern with institutional efficiency and control on public sector organisations. In general, they marked a trend towards managerial as opposed to professional control of service development and such change has significant implications for the community approach. From the particular perspective of public library, it is important to note that they amounted to precisely the reverse of the trend towards *deinstitutionalisation* identified by Bill Martin, and seemed to harden the institutional boundaries and systems of the service. Such new, business like modes of management and control undoubtedly had the potential, if not handled carefully, to have an adverse effect on informal and organic relationships between libraries, their users and their communities [15].

Sensitive to such problems, public library managers were thus quick to seize on those emerging ideologies of management such as 'customer focus' which justified institutional efficiency and control only if they were centred around the demands and needs of customers, consumers or citizens. In 1991, the Public

Libraries Weekend School posed the question 'do we care for our customers?' and one speaker recommended the adoption of a complete package of customer care, which he defined as a 'total approach to service delivery, which takes as its starting point the needs and expectations of customers' [16]. In a contemporary article in *Public Library Journal*, John Pluse (1991) simultaneously identified and popularised the elements of the approach:

- a clear, customer focused, service strategy
- customer oriented front of house staff
- customer oriented systems.

The preconditions for the approach, according to Pluse, incorporated a clear marketing strategy dedicated to identifying customer needs and levels of satisfaction; a commitment to setting and maintaining standards and quality of service; and continuous innovation in training and development of staff. In essence customer focus applied to libraries the truism, popular in the commercial world, that businesses only survive if they put their customers first.

Such consumerist approaches appear now to represent a dominant paradigm of public library management and incorporate previous initiatives connected with marketing, total quality management and quality assurance, and customer care. Perhaps, indeed, in the long term, consumerism represents an opportunity for the rebirth of community librarianship of a kind. Our own field studies and analysis of policy documents revealed an almost universal commitment to this paradigm at the level of rhetoric among senior managers. At national level, the development of a *Public Library Charter* (Library Association, 1993) reflected this consensus. Moreover, as many librarians remarked to us, such concern with responsiveness towards consumers is a tradition within community librarianship itself, and to some extent the new consumerism simply restates the arguments of Totterdell, Bird, Yorke and others that libraries should become user rather than supplier oriented organisations [17]. However, in reality it was clear that the professional/bureaucratic traditions of the public library identified by Jones (1984) persisted and died hard. In a study in 1991 of marketing activity in public libraries, a team of researchers at Loughborough University found that only 25% of library authorities had a specific budget for marketing and concluded that 'generally there is a lack of awareness and understanding of the full implications of marketing strategies for service development' (Kinnell and MacDougall, 1992, p. 96). The 'responsive' approach, in the early nineties at least, still had some distance to go.

There were other problems too. As we shall see, many traditionalists agreed with Richard Hoggart that consumerism should never result in the public library becoming the 'MacDonalds or the Burger Kings of the printed word' (Hoggart, 1991b, p. 22). But if not, what was their purpose? In the late 1980s it became clear that, in common with other public institutions, libraries faced a problem of legitimacy. How could they reconcile the principle of free and universal public access with the burgeoning and expanding demands of a postmodern/information society? Would they break their attachment to the book and leap into the virtual world of electronic information and communication technologies? Could an organisation hitherto committed to principles of welfare and concern for the disadvantaged reconcile itself to an emerging entrepreneurial culture and the commodification of knowledge? The political and financial pressures of restructuring made it increasingly difficult for libraries to duck these issues: they were, as the important Comedia report was to indicate, on 'borrowed time' (Comedia, 1993). Consumerism seemed to lead to populism, and there ensued, as a result, perhaps the most wide ranging debate about public library purpose since the nineteenth century, drawing in cultural commentators, politicians and academics as well as the public library profession itself. The significance of this debate for the postmodern public library is the subject of Chapter 6.

Community librarianship and the new imperatives: compliance, innovation or decline?

How could community librarianship adapt to the erosion of the welfare principle in public libraries, and to the accelerating tendency for them to function 'like a business'? Professional commentators, library managers and indeed community librarians themselves were divided on this issue. Some saw no philosophical problem, and argued that the new consumerism in fact continued the original impulse of community librarianship towards a 'responsive' service. From this perspective, community librarianship had always basically been about tailoring service to user demand. Consumerism, and its allied techniques such as customer focus and total quality management, merely provided the tools with which to implement community based approaches effectively. One of our informants - a county librarian - criticised the community librarianship of the early eighties as failing to justify its use of resources and 'the almost complete failure of community librarians to come to terms with the evaluation and measurement of their work'. He argued that the new managerial climate provided a basis for a community librarianship that 'lived in the real world'. As a result of new techniques of quality control and performance evaluation, community initiatives could, he believed, be tested and refined in a way that made them genuinely, and not simply rhetorically, responsive to user needs [18]. Similarly Janet Hill, a children's librarian from Cheshire (not to be confused with her namesake, the author of *Children are People*), argued that the 'new management ethic' had many benefits: 'sharper planning; greater staff involvement; encouragement of new ideas and approaches; more two way communication with customers; emphasis on action; improved marketing'. In sum, an entrepreneurial approach encouraged customer focused change and innovation, and this could only be good news for user oriented approaches. Provided, Hill argued, that it was realised that customers included minorities whose 'voices might be lost', the new managerialism could be harnessed to develop a dynamic, assertive and community oriented library service (Hill, 1992, pp. 60-61).

Other commentators broadly supported the adoption of entrepreneurial techniques, but had reservations about business values and ideology. Bob Usherwood spoke for many in the public library profession who felt that aspects of the new managerialism had value, but that it needed, as John Stewart at INGOLOV had suggested, to develop a public sector orientation. Usherwood (1991,1992b) argued that public libraries had much to learn from the private sector in terms of marketing, planning and decision making, and user orientation. These techniques were essential, he claimed, if libraries were to remain popular and socially relevant - a 'visible library in the 1990s'. However, he found the accompanying ideologies of business, and the private sector model as a whole, an inappropriate one for public libraries. For one thing, Usherwood insisted, libraries cannot be simply demand led: public library collections embody recorded public knowledge and this exists independently of customer preferences. Moreover, library users are much more than customers; they are citizens with rights to education and access to information. The philosophy behind customer orientation thus holds dangers: it is founded on an exchange relationship based on price rather than one of freely given service. This consequently alters the relationship between the librarian and his or her community. Thus, library managers, in the end, need to be consumer 'aware' but in a sense much broader than that of the profitable business. They must comprehend 'need' as opposed to expressed demand, and address the whole 'community', not simply the library user. That accepted, TQM, performance measurement, marketing, and many other successful business techniques are, Usherwood argues, perfectly acceptable as a means of improving and focusing public service.

For pessimists, however, there could be no such compatibility. The new business ethic seemed to mark the end of community approaches. One of our informants maintained that, because of the 'enterprise culture', the community librarianship of the late seventies is on its last legs, really' [19]. Another felt that, as a whole, 'by 1989 community librarianship was very marginal within the profession' [20]. Indeed, in the same year Ray Astbury prefaced a book designed to disseminate good practice in community librarianship with a pessimistic note about the effects of the green paper. He claimed that it presaged a 'most significant deleterious impact on the future of community librarianship' (Astbury, 1989). For Astbury the sceptre of privatisation, of charges, and the growth of the commercial information industry seemed to prefigure the demise of public library concern for the disadvantaged and the information poor. In the consumerist marketplace, access to information was graded according to status and ability to pay. The moves to prioritise the traditional 'core' or 'basic' service and the new managerial imperatives of performance and efficiency seemed to tilt concern back to the demands of existing, vociferous and middle class library users. Joe Hendry called for 'caring libraries in a caring society', but noted that money for community projects was scarce and dwindling (Hendry, 1988). Some saw a hardening of the institutional identity of libraries and detected image changes designed to redefine them as 'the cultural supermarket' (Muddiman and Black, 1993). Others claimed that the benefits of consumerism - the promises of choice, standards of service, easy access and redress - were illusory. Consumerism offered users little real part in shaping and determining public services beyond the opportunity of limited feedback regarding satisfaction and 'demand'. Moreover, it was alleged, it ignored the idea of collective culture and identity at the heart of community approaches by treating customers as atomised individuals with aggregate tastes and preferences (Berry, 1988). As Hendry noted, the future of the local community library as 'the community's cultural catalyst ... bringing local people together as a wee intellectual hub' sat very uneasily with 'an enterprise culture and competitive society that has little need or desire for public services' (Hendry, 1988, p. 387). Philosophically, the two seemed worlds apart.

And yet, the empirical evidence suggests that, in name at least, community inspired approaches to public librarianship have survived into the 1990s. There are a number of explanations for their persistence: the popularity of community librarianship with a particular generation of committed public librarians; and the undoubted popularity of some services with users and with influential advocates such as local politicians, especially in urban and inner city areas. However, one crucial factor undoubtedly related to the relative autonomy of public library services. Unlike, for example, education authorities or social services, public libraries never experienced restructuring in the sense of a series of handed down policy directives from the centre - as we have already seen, central government interest in and control over the public library was relatively weak. Instead, as Oulton's research at the time indicated, restructuring was experienced primarily as a set of ever tightening 'environmental' pressures on library services, as a result of which management had to make increasingly difficult 'strategic' choices. Effectively, Oulton argues, managers picked differing routes between the options of lowering service performance, reducing costs, 'counterattacking' and 'redefining' services (Oulton, 1991). The results, depending upon a myriad of local factors and circumstances, were that

105

restructuring became an uneven phenomenon at local level. For community librarians, this could mean, at one extreme, a decision to protect community initiatives at all costs and accept consequent reductions in other kinds of services. At the other, it might involve a decision to abandon mainstream community librarianship altogether in favour of a customer focused consumerism [21].

Generally, however, things were less clear cut. In 1993 we obtained and analysed 74 public library authority policy and strategy documents from England and Wales which were relevant to community library services. Our analysis of these confirmed that the various pressures associated with local government reform and restructuring had indeed had a significant effect on how community library services were conceptualised, financed and operated. However that effect was uneven. Some library authorities appeared to be enthusiastic adopters of entrepreneurial and consumerist approaches, and they were busy developing what seemed to be a new 'community librarianship' based on them. A much larger number, however, were hesitant, pragmatic and much more uncertain about adopting the philosophies of the new right; their approaches often contained elements of consumerism, traditional public library professionalism and mainstream community librarianship. We labelled this group (the majority) 'uncertain compliers'. A smaller minority were much more critical of the new developments, often adopting change with reluctance and restating commitment to welfarist principles. These tended to include some of the most radical advocates of community librarianship in the early eighties. More latterly, however, many of this group had begun to attempt a reshaping of the managerial/consumerist ethos in order to adapt it to more radical aims. For this reason we have labelled this group 'critical compliers'. Finally, there were a large minority of local authorities who appeared to be reacting to the new imperatives by simply scaling down what little innovation or community oriented provision they had been involved in. Some of this group were evidently relieved that the early eighties had passed them by, and looked forward to a reassertion of the traditional, 'core' book based library service. These are the 'traditionalist rationalisers'.

Like all such typologies [22], this one needs to be treated with some caution. It is dangerous to generalise about large and complex organisations, and indeed in our field studies in 1993-4 we found elements of all these approaches in individual library authorities. Nevertheless, it is important to identify the dominant ideology of service within a particular library authority, and this approach does enable us to identify and explore in detail some of the key variations in contemporary community librarianship. In particular, we can examine how community library services are being affected by a changed policy environment in particular types of library authority. Moreover, we can ask how differing kinds of public library service now seem to view their relationship with their 'community', real or imagined.

Table 5.1

Categorisation of English and Welsh library authorities by type of response to the restructuring of local government, 1986-1993

	All library authorities (74)	London boroughs (17)	English counties (29)	Metropolitan districts (21)	Welsh library authorities (7)
Enthusiastic adopters	12 (16%)	6 (35%)	6 (14%)	2 (10%)	0
Uncertain compliers	30 (41%)	3 (18%)	14 (48%)	9 (43%)	4 (57%)
Critical compliers	16 (22%)	5 (29%)	5 (17%)	6 (29%)	0
Traditionalist rationalisers	16 (22%)	3 (18%)	4 (21%)	4 (19%)	3 (43%)

The concerns of the *traditionalist rationalisers* are perhaps most marginal to this study. Constituting approximately one fifth of our respondent library authorities (see Table 5.1), most were unable to provide us with any description of activity or policy relevant to community librarianship, broadly conceived. Some claimed not to understand or accept the appendage 'community' at all. Most stated that they provided a 'traditional' library service based on central libraries and their 'branches', together with 'special' services targeted at disadvantaged groups, who were usually defined exclusively as the elderly and disabled. Remarkably, these library authorities, apparently by-passed by community librarianship in the seventies and eighties, seemed to show little awareness of the 'consumer' revolution of the late eighties and nineties. In most the reaction to the restructuring of local government seemed to amount to a response to expenditure constraints through progressive savings in bookfund, library opening hours and staffing. A small number of these authorities proposed rather more drastic medicine through a clear definition of the 'core' service based on the traditional loan of books and printed materials. This provided a rationale for a limited 'free' service, and all other activities were to be based on cost recovery. Other members of this group were actively rationalising services by 'tiering' and effectively limiting the kinds of services which could be provided at branches of a particular size. Although this rationalisation was justified in terms of efficiency and the transparency of service standards, it often seemed to bear little relation to expressed community needs or user demands.

Enthusiastic adopters, on the contrary, claimed to be intensely concerned with their customers. For them [23], community librarianship is now predominantly conceptualised in terms of a library service which is innovative, popular, and responsive to customer demand. The elements of their approach to service include:

- a customer charter (in the case of some authorities a 'community' charter) laying out standards of service, service commitments, consumer rights and so on.
- a commitment to market research and the marketing of innovative services. In some cases, like that of Bromley's TALKBACK scheme [24], this might involve testing and action research focusing on new services.
- a linked commitment to customer satisfaction and feedback research incorporating focus groups and occasionally community liaison or library user groups [25].
- the continuous and rigorous use of performance measurement and evaluation to shape resourcing decisions.
- the enthusiastic expansion of 'popular' services including those outside the scope of the green paper definition of 'core' services. These might include loan of audio, video, computer software and provision of PC and Internet access in libraries, as well as the popularisation of local studies through 'heritage' initiatives.
- the development of a local information function for the library service through the expansion of 'community information' databases incorporating information about local organisations, council information and local events. In some cases authorities like Kent and Cambridgeshire have collaborated with other council departments in co-ordinating 'first stop' council information points based in libraries and other public buildings.
- involvement in community initiatives devised in collaboration with partners in government, the private sector and the local voluntary sector. Such partners include health authorities, the major charities, corporate

benefactors and the more established local organisations like the Citizen's Advice Bureaux.

In general, enthusiastic adopters stress change, flexibility and innovation as a solution to the conundrum of declining resources and multiplying demand. They are committed to 'customer care and a strong marketing approach' and concerned to deliver what customers want now rather than 'perpetuating historical patterns of provision' [26]. Services to disadvantaged people in general tend not to be a priority for these authorities, although all continue to make special provision for the elderly and disabled, and many extend their culture of innovation to the development of services in this sphere [27].

Uncertain compliers have characteristically taken on elements of this consumerist and popular model of library service, but in a much less thoroughgoing manner. In the main this is because this group - around a half of all our respondents [28] - seems reluctant to abandon a broad and multifaceted approach to public library purpose. In many cases this incorporated a keen sense of the educative role of the public library and a concern for 'disadvantage' stemming from the previous adoption of many of the ideas we have associated with a 'mainstream' approach to community librarianship. Key characteristics of this group include:

- attempts to incorporate elements of consumerism/managerialism such as charters, performance measures and marketing initiatives. But these and other forms of entrepreneurial led activity are often isolated and incomplete, and never constitute a total philosophy of service.
- public library aims and objectives continue to be framed in very broad terms and often follow the I.F.L.A. model recommended by the Office of Arts and Libraries (1992). This model proposes a continuation of a wide range of public library activity in education, information, culture and leisure.
- a partial continuation of the prioritisation of services to a wide range of 'disadvantaged' users. Some authorities in this group, like Staffordshire and Northamptonshire, have attempted to continue to develop these services and have used equal opportunities policy as a basis for service decisions. Others, like Shropshire, have developed initiatives as a response to the move towards 'care in the community' in the nineties. These have included community care mobiles, improved deposit collections and targeted community information initiatives aimed at particular client groups [29]. All of these authorities have developed initiatives in partnership with other local authority departments, local quangos and national and local voluntary agencies.

- community information, especially the local information function of the public library, remains important in these library authorities. A number continue to try to systematise and improve both local and welfare information provision. Some, such as Cambridgeshire, Cheshire and Wiltshire, are attempting to expand public access IT provision.

Some managers in this group of local authorities would very much like to harness consumerism to the goals of the public service orientation, as advocated by Usherwood and Stewart. In these ways, some of our informants hoped, mainstream community librarianship might be modernised and updated. However, the key problem with this approach, and with uncertain compliance in general, lay in the contraction of the welfare state. As a result, many initiatives were often stifled or financially unrealistic while looking for partners, according to a number of managers, was becoming an increasingly difficult and competitive activity [30].

Uncertain compliance in Loamshire, one of our case study authorities, effectively seemed to amount to a process of negotiation between mainstream community librarianship, practised by a dedicated group of middle managers and community librarians in the field, and a new managerial and consumerist approach, advocated by senior management and other more recently appointed middle managers, librarians and 'library operations managers'. Such negotiation often manifested itself in the formation of managerial and workplace factions who engaged in disputes over priorities, staffing structures, duties and other matters. Some Assistant Librarians were bitter because they 'no longer had the time or resources to practice what we were taught at college', but other staff were excited by the enhanced opportunities for 'initiative and progression' on the part of junior staff. In the end, however, most hoped there could be an accommodation between the two approaches: that a 'focus on the customer is ultimately what community librarianship is all about, I suppose'. Like this assistant librarian, we are not so sure [31].

Most *critical compliers* shared this scepticism. Fewer in number, these authorities tended to include several who had developed community librarianship in a relatively radical direction in the late seventies and early eighties. At the level of policy and rhetoric, most of these authorities had initially embarked upon a strategy of resistance to the restructuring of the late eighties and many provided us with policy documents which still focused on disadvantage, outreach, equal opportunities and community involvement [32]. However, as much of this material and our field research in Inner, one of these authorities, made clear, it was obvious that a strategy of protecting mainstream and radical community approaches led to many pressures. Measuring and accounting for community initiatives and outreach were full of difficulties and staff in some authorities were now required to devote significant amounts of time to recording and analysing outreach activity [33]. Perhaps more importantly, because of cuts, financial pressures were brought to bear on traditional aspects of expenditure like building maintenance and bookfund, and a number of authorities in this group experienced severe difficulties in maintaining adequate purchases of new books in the period 1988-91. In the case of Sheffield, one of these authorities, subsequent pressure from the public and elected members resulted in a rethink about community librarianship [34].

Because of these pressures most critical compliers had similarly to rethink their strategy in the early 1990s. As a result, a number of attempts to rethink community librarianship began to become apparent. For critical compliers, such reconceptualisation might include some or all of the following elements:

- a refocusing of the consumerist agenda towards the 'community'. The London Borough of Sutton issued a 'community charter' which recognised that council services were aimed at social groups and the neighbourhoods as a whole as well as individuals. This was loosely linked to a strategy of community development which focused on 'building a community, in which all can take part and take pride' [35]. Most other critical compliers had evolved similar community development concerns.
- public library sponsorship of local networks and partnerships which enhance community access to information. For critical compliers, community based networks, as opposed to managerially inspired partnerships, were claimed to be of real importance. For example McDowell (1992) argued that they were perhaps the major way in which public libraries could support community development through enhancing the local information infrastructure and alleviating inequalities between information agencies and users. For many critical compliers IT based projects, such as the Manchester Community Information Network, were becoming increasingly important (Coleman, 1996).
- an adoption of the idea of equal opportunity as providing a wide ranging basis for service provision. In Birmingham, this has been adopted as an issue fundamental to the whole library service, the basic role of the library being defined as providing equality of access to knowledge for all members of society (Dolan, 1992). Some authorities, like Lambeth and Gloucestershire, have drawn up detailed service delivery and business plans based on the concept of equal opportunities and they attempt to embody the idea in statements of service standards and quality management.
- a new emphasis on buildings and books, and an acceptance of the importance of libraries as a public space and community resource. Even in authorities like Lambeth, the importance of the quality of buildings and bookstock has been re-emphasised, and in Birmingham the 'pre-eminence' of the book was revived. Many public library authorities designed library

111

buildings which incorporated 'community space'; for instance Waltham Forest proposed the development of a 'model library for the 1990s' which maximised this community role.

Of course it might be argued that many of these ideas are little more than old wine in new bottles. There is some truth in this: in many respects they embodied an attempt to adapt the principles of community librarianship to a more difficult political and social climate based on enterprise rather than welfare. However, more positively, one might speculate that they begin to lay the foundations of a 'new' community librarianship which recognises the limits of welfare but which nevertheless rejects the bland imperatives of the postmodern 'consumer' state.

Such questions about the future will preoccupy our final chapter. Here, it remains to reconsider the 'decline' of community librarianship. Clearly, its retreat was not absolute. Many public library authorities have attempted to retain the concern with social and economic disadvantage which so animated librarians in the 1970s. Most state a commitment to community involvement and orientation, and aim for responsive library services closely in touch with community needs. Moreover, as we have seen, the scope of the 'post-Fordist' restructuring of the public sector has been to some extent limited and its application has been uneven. Many community initiatives and other elements of the 'community approach' to librarianship remain. They flourish in some localities more so than others, but that indeed has always been the case.

And yet, we would want to insist, something has been lost. Community librarianship, by the early 1980s, had become more than simply a series of initiatives and service practices. It represented a whole philosophy of public librarianship which was based on the essentially idealistic conviction that libraries could initiate and support social change and improvement in a shifting and diversifying society. It held that such improvement might be achieved through a balance of public provision, professional commitment and communal involvement. For a short time, these ideas reinvigorated the public library profession and gave public libraries a renewed sense of purpose amid the confusions and conflicts of the late seventies and early eighties. But such purpose has, our study reveals, been dissipated and fragmented. Community librarianship has been challenged by managerialism, consumerism and other ideologies of the market. It is now one of a number of approaches to public librarianship; according to many librarians it has been redefined in lesser and more conservative terms as 'marketing', 'customer focus', 'networking' or 'community care'. Library services have been rationalised, reinstitutionalised and, like a 'business', required to demonstrate a degree of utilitarian efficiency. What looms as a result is a community librarianship with little sense of the communal, and a public librarianship with little sense of its ideals and a drift towards private provision and technological extinction. The alternatives, real and imagined, are assessed in the penultimate chapter.

Notes

1 Key strategists of the public choice school include Gordon Tullock, James Buchanan and William Niskanan. See Green (1987) for an introduction to the main ideas associated with public choice.
2 See, for example, White (1983). This book by an American economist developed a certain notoriety in public library circles in the eighties, but it was little recognised that it explicitly applied the principles of public choice theory to the public library.
3 The list is an edited and adapted version from Stewart and Stoker (1995, pp. 3-5).
4 This list is adapted from Pollitt (1993, p. 83).
5 For a summary of this see Rusbridger (1988).
6 Luce and Brooke were both Ministers with responsibility for the Office of Arts and Libraries in this period. Luce's concern about literary heritage is recorded in a speech to the AGM of the Library Association in 1987. The text is reprinted in *The Campaigner* (1987), no. 20, pp. 13-14.
7 Indeed, Douglas Mason is reported to have asked 'How long can a government committed to the virtue of a market economy make an exception of the library service?' See Coe and Parsons (1989, p. 531).
8 The Local Government and Housing Act, 1989, amended some provisions of the 1964 Public Libraries and Museums Act, regularising charges for certain library services. The Library Charges (England and Wales) Regulations of 1991 (Statutory Instrument number 2712) confirmed the scope of charges and the 'core' free service.
9 These illustrations are taken from Cambridgeshire Library and Information Service (1990), *Base Review,* and Bedfordshire County Leisure Services (1992), *The Public Library Service 1993-1998*.
10 See Sheffield Libraries and Information Services (1992), *Serving Communities: a Service Plan for the 1990s*.
11 See London Borough of Lambeth, Libraries Working Party (1992), *Community Based Library Services*.
12 Of course, many argued that the ending of Section 11 support and the 'integration' of multicultural services were, as ideals, extremely desirable. See Kendall (1992).
13 Our own field studies of local authorities in 1993-5 revealed numerous examples of such initiatives. For example 'Loamshire' was developing a

value added 'Information to Business' service on a cost recovery basis jointly with a local TEC; 'Northern' was developing a community arts strategy in partnership with the private and voluntary sector. Examples which relate specifically to the emerging practice of community librarianship will be discussed in more detail in Chapter 7.

14 See Office of Arts and Libraries (1991). Midwinter (1990) provides a more critical perspective.

15 Indeed, following the arguments of Jones (1984) utilised in Chapter 4, it seems that public libraries are engaged in a transition from professional to 'machine' bureaucracies where rules and procedures are embedded in systems and machines.

16 See the report in *Public Library Journal* (1991), vol.6, no.4, p.104.

17 See the section 'Community librarianship as responsive librarianship' in Chapter 3.

18 Correspondence from Head of Library Service, Eastern County, August 1993 and subsequent interview, December 1993.

19 Interview with Area Librarian, Northern Metropolitan District, April 1994.

20 Interview with County Librarian, Northern County, November 1995.

21 These extreme situations were encountered in two of our field case studies in 1993-4: 'Inner', an inner London borough battling to retain welfare based community librarianship, and 'Outer' an outer London borough enthusiastically redefining the meaning of community librarianship itself.

22 Our analysis and identification of ideal 'types' owe a debt to Stoker and Mossberger (1995). They develop a typology of general local government responses to restructuring, on which our particular analysis of libraries is to some degree based.

23 The analysis in this paragraph is based upon source material provided by Brent, Bromley, Kingston upon Thames, Solihull, Kent and Surrey. Our thanks to them for their assistance.

24 See Bromley Library Service (1992), *Issues: the Bromley Library Service Newsletter*, no.1, pp. 1-3.

25 Kingston upon Thames, for example, established a 'customer advisory group' at New Malden library in December 1991. See Kingston Libraries (1992), *Annual Report 91/92* p.10.

26 Kent County Council Arts and Libraries Department (1992), *Business Plan 1991-2*, pp. 1-3.

27 For example Kent collaborated with the Hi Kent association in a project funded under the public library development incentive scheme intended to improve access to library services for deaf and hearing impaired

people. See Kent County Council Arts and Libraries (c.1992), *Breaking Down the Barriers.*

28 This section is based on documents provided by a sample of these respondents: Cambridgeshire, Staffordshire, Shropshire, Wiltshire, Cheshire, Northamptonshire, Bolton, Rotherham, Leeds and Hounslow. Our thanks to them.

29 Shropshire Library Service (1993), *Community Care Business Plan.*

30 Group interview with senior management team, Midland County, April 1994.

31 Quotations are taken from the field diary compiled during fieldwork in Loamshire, November - December, 1993.

32 The following section is based predominantly on an analysis of policy and working documents provided by Lambeth, Sutton, Hammersmith and Fulham, Waltham Forest, Birmingham, Sheffield, Coventry, Derbyshire, Gloucestershire, Durham, Gateshead and North Tyneside. Our thanks to them.

33 Indeed in field research in Inner (October 1993) staff continually referred to an elaborate system of tracking and recording outreach activity on forms dubbed 'yellow perils'!

34 Sheffield Libraries and Information Services (1992), *Serving Communities: a Service Plan for the 1990s.*

35 Sutton Leisure Services (c.1992), *Sutton Leisure Guide.*

6 The heritage turn: Community librarianship subdued

It is our contention that community librarianship - and to a degree the public library's non-book and leisure-recreational functions which have so often been confused with that particular mode of service - has been subdued and has metamorphosed, in part, due to the recent reverence for heritage displayed by British society, including the profession of public librarianship. The link between heritage and public libraries is largely unexplored territory, despite the increased frequency in recent years of public library authorities adopting or annexing the label 'heritage services' (Jenkinson, 1995). The failure to view the public library through the lens of heritage is surprising since one of the main features of modern society, namely the rapidity with which a sense of continuity with the past can be lost, fits perfectly with the base, custodial rationale of the institution. If the past is disappearing fast, then the value of a 'recording' institution like the public library is at a premium. This would appear to be one of the reasons for the establishment of public libraries by the Victorians who were clearly conscious, as we at times seem to be now, of living through a new age, one characterised by unprecedented progress (Harris, 1993, pp. 32-3). Just as in the nineteenth century, when public libraries were promoted, to an extent, to help protect the elite cultural heritage in an era of unnerving cultural change and social threat, so also in the late twentieth century it has been proposed that they be appropriately mobilized in the battle to maintain moral standards and to protect the nation's cultural inheritance from the supposedly corrosive power of mass, popular society.

By virtue of its standing as a 'history' institution, as primarily an accumulator and preserver of knowledge, the public library is more suited than most other cultural agencies to fulfilling a heritage role. In effect libraries can, and do, serve as museums of literary culture. This custodial orthodoxy has ramifications for the public library's role in society; it explains why they are frequently awarded a neutral social function: institutions serving all-comers, safeguarding the cultural heritage of all and antithetical to the designs of any one faction. As Edward Edwards once wrote: 'They will never become schools of political agitation, but if they can be said to have any political tendency at all, it must need to be a "Conservative" one, since they plainly widen that public domain in which all classes have a common interest' (Thompson, 1977, p. 77). The public library's historic image as a socially neutral collector, preserver and disseminator of knowledge stands in stark contrast, quite obviously, to its flirting with the more radical forms of community librarianship which lay stress on active, participatory and social rather than passive, directing and technical preoccupations in service provision. Enthusiasm for a 'conservative', heritage mission for public libraries, involving a jettisoning of the more dangerous strains of community librarianship, has emanated from three distinct sources. First, from the political Right's determination to build a new cultural nationalism (viewed by some as a return to 'Little Englandism') and to compensate for continuing economic malfunction characterised by persistently high levels of unemployment. Second, from cultural commentators fearful of the drift of modern culture towards an abhorred relativism. And third, from librarians themselves, confused and at times ashamed by the perceived populist leanings of certain sections of the profession, and fearful perhaps of the effects of popularization on professional status and on the historic role of the public library as a rational cultural improver.

Heritage as a political tool

Public libraries' recent adoption of a heritage pose has been sparked by a revival in nostalgia culture in the 1980s. While societies of varying types are, and have been, prone to nostalgic thinking, the strain of nostalgia that swept through Britain in the 1980s, the remnants of which are still very much in evidence today, was particularly virulent. Its potency has been reflected in the establishment of a whole range of heritage enterprises (Hewison, 1987; Corner and Harvey, 1991), as well as in its use, particularly in its green manifestation, by industry and commerce as an effective marketing tool. In short, heritage has become big business. The origins and nature of the 1980's heritage boom are complex, and this is not the place to pursue that complexity; others have done so already (Samuel, 1994, pp. 306-7; Urry, 1996, pp. 52-3). Suffice to say at this point that the essence of heritage should be considered to be a loss of trust in the future, resulting in an overstrong desire to look backwards to more stable times, either real or imagined. Moreover, it is a tendency (some might say disease) experienced by all social groups. As Lowenthal writes: 'Once the menace of a small elite, nostalgia now attracts or affects most levels of society' [1]. The heritage rebellion against the past also crosses the political spectrum.

It owes as much to progressive as to reactionary tendencies (Samuel, 1994, p. 288). It is not only John Major who harbours a passion for Constable's England, warm beer and the sound of leather on willow; elements of the left, argue Mulgan and Worpole (1986, p. 103), are equally at home with 'a vision of maypoles and village greens, church and Sunday school, galas and choirs'. None the less, as far as 1980's Britain is concerned, the embracing of heritage by the Right appears to have been a highly comfortable, zealously pursued and strategically considered political project. As Samuel has argued, 'it fitted into, and could be seen as an expression of the dominant ideology, and the ruling politics of the time ... Heritage, in short, was Thatcherism in period dress' (Samuel, 1994, p. 290). Whether it be the perceived revival of world political and military influence in the wake of the Falklands War (Wright, 1985), of cherished Victorian values (Marsden, 1990) or of a gritty entrepreneurial spirit (Wiener, 1981; Rubinstein, 1993), a nostalgia for a golden British past was joyfully exploited by political ideologues who - backed enthusiastically, it should be emphasised, by popular sentiment - sought the refuge of past glory in the face of social strife and (post)modern uncertainty. Theirs was a nostalgia for a mythical lost world of order and stability, the aim being to impose this lost culture on the supposedly diseased culture of the present.

The slow pace of public library development over the past generation cannot be divorced from the general attack on the public sector commencing in the mid-1970s. Part of the intellectual armoury deployed by critics of the welfare state against the public library, we contend, is the heritage vision. Political ideologues have been extremely keen to depict public library services as extravagant and over-stretched, in terms of purpose, materials and services offered. This accusation rests, by definition, on a misconception of the public library's past mission as one confined almost exclusively to the dissemination of good literature, rational self-improvement and a social consensus orientation; as opposed to poor literature, recreational use and a questioning of existing social relations. Public libraries are often awarded a mythical, golden past, where self-helping, culture-hungry artisans and lower middle class clerks enriched society and their own lives through attentive and meaningful learning. In recent years, the argument continues, public libraries have lost sight of this focused and worthy role. As the former Minister of Arts and Libraries, Richard Luce (1993), asks, by over-extending themselves are public libraries not in danger of 'losing their identity and purpose by being all things to everybody?' Luce urges a more defined, residual role; and does so, moreover, with the almost obligatory heritage reference to Victorian beginnings: 'Nearly 150 years after the first public libraries were set up, there is a need for them to re-establish their role within the contemporary scene. The importance of books and information to educational self-improvement is as strong as ever, and needs to be fostered. I am absolutely clear in my mind that to value books and to enjoy reading them is one of the hallmarks of a civilized society, and that the welcome increase in book reading will enrich the lives of millions of people. This is so central to the advancement of this nation and to individual fulfilment that I believe we should return to the libraries' original roots and reassert this as the core of a modern library service. Libraries and librarians need to recognise that their primary role is to provide a book-based lending and reference service'.

The call for a new *core* service was formalised in the review of public libraries initiated by the Heritage Secretary, Peter Brooke, in 1993 [2]. The implications of a core service are clear: non-core, or marginal, services are by definition placed under pressure, if not threat. So also is innovation in service provision; for while the new core service may be facilitated by innovative information and communication technologies, *social* experimentation in service provision, of say the community librarianship type, is more likely to be criticized as wasteful compared to traditional activities and methods. As *The Times* commented in 1993 in respect of falling borrowing from public libraries in contrast to increasing sales in bookshops: 'libraries could do more themselves to reverse their declining trend and return to the high ground where they should be, as the cultural and educational centres of their communities. Today's weaker libraries seem stuck in a municipal time-warp of the fifties, acting as utility creches, out-stations of the social security offices and refuges from the cold' [3].

The notion of a core library service is driven, aside from the obvious economies to be made, by the desire for social safety and respectability. Such a desire, notwithstanding motives of social emancipation which the public library has always espoused, has been a persistent feature of the institution's rationale since its inception. Depending on the type of knowledge dispensed, and of methods used, libraries *can* be dangerous places (McCann, 1994, pp. 70-71). Generally speaking, political ideologues - of both Left and Right, though principally the latter - have never been entirely happy with socially interventionist/innovative roles for the public library.

Cultural commentators and rose tinted glasses

Recent research has revealed that this establishment view of the public library's past and its preferred contemporary role is widespread in the media and amongst cultural commentators, the general thrust of the commentary being that modernization and diversification - from CDs to information about gay rights - have gone too far and that, by comparison, past objectives and modes of service were rational and socially relevant (Greenhalgh, Worpole and Landry, 1995, pp. 139-41). A particularly vocal critic of the more populist public library thinking and practice of recent years is the cultural theorist Richard Hoggart, who looks back with pride at the educational environment provided for him as a schoolboy by Hunslet Public Library. Hoggart recalls how he haunted both the shelves and the study room and began to discover literature and learning for himself, 'beginning with Swinburne'. He, like many others who write and comment on the public libary's social role, is defensive in respect of past educational seriousness: 'If you say these things today you are likely to be accused of a rose-tinted nostalgia, which is nonsense. But the age is against all that such experiences stood for. It has downgraded the value of reading ... we need to be able to read now more than ever if we are to stand upright in what calls itself a democracy but is in reality a populist, uncritical, relativist, consumerist jungle' (Usherwood, 1993). Hoggart is vehemently opposed to the relativism - the notion that all culture and cultures command equal worth and that their value cannot be differentiated by objective judgement - which he believes has infected much public library provision (Hoggart, 1991a), a position supported by *The Times* in 1993 when it declared: 'To believe that they [books] are all equal and that all that matters is customer throughput is dotty relativism. A Library should be a ladder up which its readers can climb, not a playground of continual Mills and Boon and videos' [4]. In similar fashion, in lamenting the decline of public libraries, the late Brian Redhead (1988) declared: 'Nor was it any comfort to be told [by someone commenting on the local library service] that CDs and videotapes are increasingly popular'.

The depiction of public libraries as playgrounds rather than as workshops has struck a popular chord among cultural commentators. Few are prepared to back the popular tradition in public library provision as, for example, the historian Raphael Samuel (1992a) has attempted to do in writing about the value of popular literature and the public library's historic capacity to re-invent itself. Samuel (1992b) asserts that romantic fantasies of past public library provision - 'when all the world was a scholarship boy or supped on literature's beauties' - do no service to the planning and management of the institution today. Reference should be, he maintains, 'to the future not the past, to what is innovative in British cultural life'. Yet the greater part of cultural commentary on the public library is dominated by a 'retro' vision of an elite, self-improving past where provision for leisure and the consumption of literary trash counted for little in the planning of services - a view which recent work by Snape (1995) reveals to be wholly false.

The heritage path which many public library supporters outside the profession urge the institution to tread is founded not simply on an abhorrence of relativism, but also on a belief that a populist line is being encouraged by politically interested left-wing radicals. Hoggart's assertion that, despite a century of state education, the greater part of the citizenry remains sub-literate

120

(Usherwood, 1993) is supported by the historian W.J. West whose *The Strange Rise of Semi-literate England: the Dissolution of the Libraries* (1991) calls for the preservation of historic collections - the literary heritage of England - held by public libraries; as opposed to the policy of dispersal followed, he detects, by some library authorities, resulting in the worst cases in the ultimate philistine philosophy of 'if in doubt chuck it out'. West lays much of the fault for this policy at the door of politically correct 'loony left' librarians pandering to populism. By operating an 'inverted Nazism', he argues, such librarians are destroying the 'serious' educational role that public libraries once - supposedly almost exclusively - fulfilled. In short, the public library is in danger of losing its soul to radical demagogues [5].

Clearly, in an intellectual maelstrom of romantic visions of a past preoccupation with high culture, any movement towards alternative, radical democratic modes of service and collections of materials is open to criticism. Community librarianship has been forced to battle hard against traditional perceptions of the public library's stabilizing, neutral and 'high-minded' social functions. Central to this traditional social position is the notion of the public sphere as theorized by Jürgen Habermas in 1962, but not disseminated in English until the publication in 1989 of his *The Structural Transformation of the Public Sphere*. Briefly, Habermas argues that the bourgeois created public sphere is made up of non-interested, accessible and open 'citizen' arenas dedicated to rational debate and cultural enlightenment. It existed in its purest form, intellectually and in practice, in the mid-nineteenth century. Since then, the argument continues, the public sphere has declined, as collectivism has assumed an apparently irreversible downward trajectory (most notably the retreat from public service and the welfare state) and as the influence of a controlling mass media increases. A few commentators have been imaginative enough to locate the public library and its past in the context of Habermas' thesis (Mulgan, 1993). The information sociologist Frank Webster, for example, regards information as being at the core of the public sphere - whether in the form of *Hansard*, a free media, objective government statistics and reports or, indeed, the municipal public library. The latter, he says, features all the essential elements, theoretically, of the public sphere. But whereas public libraries were 'formed and developed on the basis of a notion that information was a resource which belonged to everyone' (Webster, 1995, p. 112), as authentic public sphere entities they are now fading fast, as the public sector shrinks and as ideas about charging for information take hold.

The argument that the future of the 'public sphere' public library is precarious is based, of course, on a belief that public libraries, at some time in the past, fulfilled the conditions of public sphere status. Yet such a premise is highly dubious, for it ignores historic aspects of the public library experience which might be termed bourgeois-directed, hegemonic, socially controlling, elitist, paternalistic or censorial - this despite the contribution made by an open, anti-exclusive utilitarian philosophy to the genesis of the public library cause (Black, 1996b). Taking account of such aspects reduces the impact that public sphere influences might be considered to have had on public library development, or on the contribution the latter may have made to the former. Consequently, in viewing the public library experience through the optic of the public sphere there is a danger, as is the case with many cultural commentaries on the institution, that too positive and too serious a picture of the public library's past social role is drawn. The public library has always been a multi-faceted institution, encompassing a wide range of social objectives and satisfying a variety of demands, often pulling in different directions. Running alongside its openness and its educational and 'high' cultural practices the public library has persistently responded to a popular market. Yet it has also, by virtue of its high-minded dimension, excluded certain social constituencies. Pushing to one side the marginal, the alternative, the radical and the different - these being the very focus of the community librarianship philosophy - is as visible in the public library tradition as its professed liberal desire to incorporate minority interests and its democratic impulse to address the mass reading and information market.

Librarians' quest for the core

Doubts about certain innovations like community librarianship in public library policy and practice expressed in a heritage vernacular by politicians and cultural commentators have been shared by librarians themselves. The professional reaction to cultural relativism and radical community oriented approaches, though not vitriolic, has been none the less hesitant. Librarians' reasons for hesitancy over the new social roles and values that have been asked of them in recent decades are complex, but probably include: a sincere belief in the superiority of quality over quantity; a traditional dislike of radicalism, of either left or right, in what is traditionally a conservative profession; the damage which populism has wrought on professional status; and the search for a *core* purpose in an age of change and confusion. But hesitancy there certainly has been. As one of our respondents explained, community librarianship was for many of her colleagues 'a fear of the unknown' [6]. Another explained how librarians had little enthusiasm for the idea of taking on interventionist social roles and becoming ultimately involved with people: 'they [librarians] didn't want to know about their problems ... you couldn't go about mixing it on the street out there, because that was hardly a professional role'; and, he added, he believed that for many public librarians professionalism in fact meant losing rather than adopting 'a street-level sense of mission' [7].

During the classical era of community librarianship, public librarians often seem to have found it difficult to live up to the radicalism inherent in the philosophy. In 1984, when Westminster Borough Council discussed the possibility of banning 'books with a political bias', arguing that libraries should not publicize, display or publish anything regarded by society as politically controversial (as well as suggesting the axing of 'amateurish' community noticeboards and their replacement by library wall space sold to advertisers), one librarian described how he thought 'libraries are becoming a political adjunct - we are being used as a noticeboard for a political controlling group' [8]. Librarians have often perceived a danger in radical initiatives like community librarianship in respect of the public library's overall standing in society. 'To some extent the community librarianship stuff is a useful rod with which to beat the public library's back', said one community librarian, 'because if they [opponents of the public library] can turn the perception from being a cherished resource for all the community, that everybody can use, into some sort of *Sun*-type image of nothing but books on black lesbianism and raving socialists behind the counter, then that makes it far easier to cut back on public libraries' [9]. Just how much mileage, if any, enemies of the public library have gained out of community librarianship is difficult to say; but many of the librarians we spoke to believed that it had resulted in some negative propaganda for the public library generally.

A leading librarian voice in the effort to repair the damage which community librarianship - or certain interpretations of it to be more precise - is perceived to have wrought is Pat Coleman. During the 1970s, she explains, librarians became 'patch' or community based, aiming to increase the relevance of their services to local communities, particularly in inner urban areas, by developing the public library as a focus for general community activity. As a result of this, Coleman argues, there was much criticism that such librarians were engaging in social work rather than performing a librarianship role; and, she adds: 'There is no doubt that some of the activities engaged in by librarians in the cause of community librarianship were not entirely appropriate' (Coleman, 1992, p. 301). Coleman's suspicion regarding community librarianship is echoed by another leading public librarian, Bob McKee, who believes that: 'Partly because of the misguided community librarianship movement, they [librarians] got into a curious mix of populism and political correctness which has nothing to do with literary value' (Van Riel, 1992, p. 38). The sense of having trod a wayward path out of keeping with the traditions of public library use was also conveyed to us by a current branch librarian, previously engaged in outreach work in inner London, who recalled that, at the height of the community librarianship era:

Most of us wanted to make libraries as successful as possible to everyone in the community; and particularly to people who would not come into libraries or had a perception of libraries as being quiet places, and I think we were trying to go out and change that. To an extent we achieved it. But some of the things we did had consequences that we did not think of at the time, such as losing control of the stock and allowing people to join without proof of identity. People came to see libraries and librarians as an easy touch.

As a result of community librarianship practices, it is now widely argued, the image of the public library has suffered and its identify has become blurred. The project of making the public library 'much more than books', it is said, has gone too far. Librarians are seen to have lost sight of what they do best: the promotion of good literature and the guiding of people's reading development; this being 'one of the most obvious areas in which public libraries can provide information', says Coleman, 'but for many years no really purposive attempts have been made to do so' (Coleman, 1992, p. 307). Public libraries' support for literature, the argument continues, is too *passive*, to the extent that they have almost stopped noticing that they do it, concentrating instead on newer things (Van Riel, 1992, p. 32) - whether they be materials like video, or service modes like community librarianship. Instead of diversifying into new areas librarians should concentrate their resources on 'our core product', advises McKee (Van Riel, 1992, p. 39). Diversification, according to one of our field sources, was unmistakably a negative influence, 'turning the library into a fairground' [10].

The notion of core services and purpose is central to the 'heritage turn' thesis. Our review of public library policy documents has revealed a keen desire to retrieve core practices. However, the core professionalism described is often defined in terms of materials and services rather than ethical ends. The idea is being put forward that what libraries should be providing is, in Coleman's (Van Riel, 1992, p. 33) words, 'what is least accessible'; that is to say, according to McKee, 'the full range of reading, including hardbacks, out-of-print material, classic material, esoteric material, giving the opportunity for people to extend their reading and to take risks' (Van Riel, 1992, p. 39). In this way, librarians would be able to demonstrate to the wider world that 'the core of their professional role is books' (Van Riel, 1992, p. 34). Moreover, in promoting books there would be a heavy emphasis on 'good' books and the classic writing of all generations: our 'literary heritage' (Van Riel, 1992, p. 33). Such a strategy clearly finds favour among some library users, one of whom stated: 'I believe I am somewhat against my local library, it appears to be stocked with nothing but Mills and Boon' [11].

There would also be a rejuvenation in lending services, with librarians returning to the paternalistic role they had once occupied with ease, in the form of the reader's adviser. The latter function appears attractive to some members of the library public. One reader related her affection for a traditional librarian, now retired, who had advised her on reading since she was a child: 'she used to point out books to me which she thought I would like and she was usually right. The present librarian who has been there about 4 years is much more non-committal when I ask her advice' [12]. In the new core library service, lending would strike a traditional pose. One of our interviewees, unhappy with some of the community approaches taken up in the 1980s, was especially critical of the adoption of a trendy categorization of lending stock in his community library, and urged a return to more traditional methods of ordering and presenting materials which he believed confused readers less [13]. In fact hesitancy concerning categorization appears to have been widespread in recent years. The staff magazine of one library authority, indeed, was forced to support categorization in the following defensive tone: 'It isn't a gimmick; it isn't a plot to undermine the library service; it isn't further proof of the decline of civilisation' [14]. Interestingly, the idea of retro-reformed lending services being placed at the forefront of the quest for core purpose fits neatly with the theory that community librarianship is in decline. Many of the best community librarianship initiatives have been driven by reference librarians: witness the expansion of community information services. Arguably, lending librarians, although it is dangerous to generalise, have been often less enthusiastic. In support of this theory one community librarian likened the lending-reference divide among librarians on the community librarianship issue, which he witnessed very visibly in his own library, to Churchill's adventurous Admiralty in the Great War developing tanks as 'landships', with the more cautious British Army initially having nothing to do with the idea [15].

Finally, no heritage picture of the public library would be complete without mention of what is perhaps the institution's most celebrated historic, traditional, core role: that of the people's university. In an age when educational and economic under-performance are seen as inextricably linked, much has been said about how public libraries can return to their role as 'temples of learning' for the manufacturing of rational and productive citizens. This would entail reviving the concept of the people's university (Smith, 1987, pp. 576-8), with librarians once again taking on a quasi-teaching role, especially in respect of adult learners (Dale, 1980). In short, the vision is one of the public library restoring its image as a supplier of serious reading for students, school pupils and autodidacts, this being a pathway that has attracted the support of library historians, some of whom have sought to extract from the public library's past the celebrated role of librarian as mentor rather than marketeer (Allred, 1990).

Promoting the public library as a temple of learning and dispenser of quality literature is not in itself, of course, an unworthy objective. But the economic reality is that choices in service provision have to be made and it is plainly possible that, if 'retro' core services are prioritized, then newer, experimental methods, including community librarianship, run the risk of being marginalized. It would be wholly wrong to suggest, however, that librarians who favour the heritage approach are unswervingly hostile to the community librarianship experiment. Coleman argues that, generally speaking, community librarianship has been very good for public libraries: 'For the first time concern was expressed about non-users and a pro-active approach developed to identify and provide for a greater range of needs than hitherto, with a particular emphasis on those people from socially, educationally, physically and mentally disadvantaged groups' (Coleman, 1991, p. 20). In one sense it would not be a misrepresentation for public librarians to claim that 'we are all community librarians now'. But the desire for a return to basic, core services is very strong. The more extravagant - as some see them - versions of community librarianship - where librarians 'began to operate more as social or community workers' (Coleman, 1991, p. 20) - always proved difficult for the bulk of the public library profession to swallow. Historically, librarians have shied away from very radical stances. In referring to radical community approaches a former leading public librarian related to us his belief that librarianship mirrored the general political disposition of the nation: 'This country doesn't like extremes. We don't like "outside-Rights" or "outside-Lefts". We like "inside-Right" Labour and "inside-Left" Tory'. Another of our respondents, a community library assistant, regarded the type of work done in certain radical community librarianship authorities, particularly in the 1980s, not as 'proper library work', but as anarchy and chaos. In an early discussion of community librarianship David Liddle (1980, p. 197) saw it as ranging from, at its most innocuous, extension activities, to the other extreme of community librarians being 'perceived as a group of anarchists trying to change society and subverting the public library service to achieve their ends'. By and large, public librarians have unfortunately tended to view community librarianship as tending towards the anarchistic end of the spectrum - a perception shared by the library user who wrote, in respect of certain changes made by one London library authority in the 1980s, 'that their book selection reflects a Camden attitude, too many feminist and pseudo psychology books. A new innovation is the playing of musak all the time, and the place is plastered with leaflets on people's rights etc. and campaigning type posters. On the counter there is always some petition they want you to sign' [16]. Such a flight from neutrality, seen by Thornton (1974, p. 70) as sacred in the classical welfare state era, has proved too much for many public librarians brought up on the idea of servicing the entire political spectrum and generally sympathetic to the ethic, as stated by

Murison, that: 'Personal involvement with particular causes may raise difficulties which may have dire consequences for the whole of their library's service' (Murison, 1988, p. viii). The reactionary cry has been, therefore, to 'get back to basics' [17]. Moreover, running alongside, and perhaps feeding off, the urge to depoliticize and sanitize the public library service - this being the literary equivalent of John Major's 'back to basics' moral crusade of the early 1990s - has been the growing demand for a return to core activities, for librarians have always, for the most part, been happier with traditional roles. As Stanley Jast wrote in 1939 in respect of extension work: 'We must not confuse the branch with the trunk. The first care of the librarian must be the basic services ... Not to do things is sometimes the better part of enthusiasm' (Jast, 1939, p. 156).

More than a mere distaste for radicalism and a liking for professional convention, the move towards a core orientation has essentially been a reaction to the strengthening populism and relativism in public library provision. Although elements of the community librarianship philosophy, populism and relativism - in tandem meaning the satisfaction of demand for popular materials without professional judgement as to their cultural worth or, in simple language, 'giving 'em what they want' (Baltimore County Public Libraries, 1992) - do not constitute its essence. If anything they are the product of the revival in market economics and the consequent need to justify public spending on the grounds of increased throughput. As one of our respondents explained:

> There was a time when you wouldn't have found a Mills and Boon in this library. The lending librarian banned them, effectively. But now we put vast amounts of money into those sections ... because that is where the demand lies ... There is no way you can buy everything. You've got to choose. And if it's a choice between something that has been well reviewed in the *TLS*, and will go out maybe twice a year for the next ten years, and buying the latest book about Princess Di that will go out twelve times a year for the next couple of years and then be pulped, then you buy the second one. And I suspect that will be an increasing trend. You'll be judged on how well you achieve issues. [18]

None the less, for those seeking to beat the heritage drum, populism and relativism, despite their market origins, are useful weapons with which to deter the foe of radical community librarianship. Trumpeting the 'core' inevitably drowns out the new and the popular, including community librarianship; and it is certainly music to the ears of reactionary politicians and conservative cultural commentators who, in an Arnoldian tradition, view many aspects of modern culture as barren and demoralising, if not socially threatening. Ultimately, the price paid for promoting the public library as a heritage institution could be an irreversible lessening of interest in the institution as a forward-looking, radical satisfier of rights, especially for the most disadvantaged members of society - a role which lies at the heart of the community librarianship project. Thus a fundamental choice facing the public library today rests between, on the one hand, mere survival at the expense of expansion [19], which all too easily invites a backward-looking orientation and, on the other, seeking a fresh articulation of purpose which looks not merely to the past, which can be helpful, but also, as advised by Raymond Williams, to a sense of 'making' and 'experimenting' (Williams, 1978, p. 77).

Notes

1 Lowenthal (1985) quoted in Urry (1996, p. 52).
2 So successful was the agenda setting of the Department of National Heritage that the library establishment quickly absorbed the idea that it was highly appropriate to identify core services and, by implication of course, that which was not core also: e.g. see Library Association (1994) and Watson (1995, p. 439).
3 'Retreat of the books', *The Times,* 2 March 1993.
4 Ibid.
5 West's discourse is discussed by Forster (1992) and is supported by Hoggart (1995) who criticises librarians for abandoning literature as their primary focus.
6 Community librarian, Northern, interviewed September 1993.
7 Community librarian, Inner, interviewed September 1993.
8 The privatization of reading, *City Limits,* 13-19 July 1984.
9 Community information librarian, London borough, interviewed September 1992.
10 Community librarian, London borough, interviewed June 1993.
11 Directive on 'Regular Pastimes', Autumn 1988, Mass Observation Archive, University of Sussex, volunteer P1980.
12 Ibid., volunteer D1833.
13 Community librarian, London borough. Volunteers P416 and C1624 for Directive on 'Regular Pastimes', op. cit. expressed similar observations.
14 *Camiscellany; staff magazine of the Cambridgeshire Libraries,* issue 7, March 1981, p. 4.
15 London borough, interviewed September 1992.
16 Directive on 'Regular Pastimes', op. cit., volunteer S1540.

17 Some employ this slogan in a radical not a reactionary way, as a call to return to a public service ethos and to jettison 'accountancy' approaches to service provision; see Pateman (1996).
18 Community librarian, Inner, interviewed September 1993.
19 Seen by Martin (1989, p. vii) as the main crisis in public libraries.

7 Community librarianship in the information society?

A rediscovery of community?

What does the future hold for community librarianship? This question will preoccupy our penultimate chapter, and the answer to it will be by no means straightforward. As we have argued in the foregoing pages, the late eighties and early nineties were characterised by the erosion of the 'community' approach to public librarianship. However, no clear ideology of public library purpose has emerged to replace it. Heritage, consumerism, managerialism, cultural populism - all, we would argue, have played a part in eroding community librarianship as it was commonly understood in 1980, but none of them has attained intellectual or material dominance as the cornerstone of public library policy. Instead, public library futures are often expressed in typically postmodern vein as a series of visions, scenarios, paradigms or functions: an approach which strangely but perhaps inevitably characterised the Department of National Heritage *Public Library Review* (ASLIB, 1995), as well as the Comedia study *Borrowed Time* (Comedia, 1993). Interestingly, much of this futurology incorporates, as we shall see, the discourse and rhetoric of community. The public library of the future is increasingly conceived, and justified, as 'an asset that helps local people identify with their community' (ASLIB, 1995, p.11), as an 'agent for community computing' or even a 'community university' (Batt, 1996).

Superficially, of course, such a rediscovery of the community perspective is extremely promising for community librarianship. The rediscovery arises, in part, as a result of a general reaction to the individualism of the eighties and the preoccupation of that decade with the concept of the market. In the United States, this reaction coincided with the election of the Clinton administration in 1992, and it took the form of a renewal of interest in 'communitarian' social philosophy, popularised by writers such as Amatai Etzioni (Etzioni, 1993). For

Etzioni, the communitarian tradition rejects the liberal model of society which sees it as an aggregation of individuals bound together by various kinds of legal, economic or social 'contract'. Instead, communitarians argue that individuals are in fact 'constituted' by society itself. Hence, the nature of the 'community' in which they exist is fundamental to both individual and societal well being. The alienation, isolation and flux associated with modern individualism is viewed by communitarians as symptomatic of social breakdown and at the root of many social pathologies. They thus argue for a restoration of social conditions conducive to the creation of communities sustained by solidarity and participation (Butcher, 1993, pp. 16-17).

These ideas have been adopted by a surprisingly wide range of opinion leaders, including, predictably, politicians such as Bill Clinton and Tony Blair. Less obviously, paternalist Tories such as Douglas Hurd have also been concerned to distance themselves from the liberal 'new right' of the eighties by focusing attention on the stability of community as a precondition for social harmony and order [1]. At the other extreme, post-industrial utopians such as Brenda Dervin have found in communitarianism the potential for 'the emergence of all kinds of spontaneous and recursive democracies that cut across old conceptions of boundaries and forms'. At their heart, these 'communities' have 'the remarkably inventive use of new communications technologies to support them' (Dervin, 1994, p. 383). Communitarian perspectives can thus underpin not only the imagined communities of the past, but those of the future too: in particular the global/local community of the internet linked not by geography but by cable, satellite and, perhaps, shared values and interests [2].

More immediately in Britain, however, the increasing legitimacy and political acceptability of the communitarian perspective have given renewed impetus to community policy and community work. Butcher (1993) argues that communitarian values provide a basis around which to unify the fragmented ideas and initiatives which characterised British community work and community based services in the eighties. He advocates an holistic approach to community policy based on communitarian values and targeted at communities of either territory or interest. Such policy should seek 'authentic engagement with groups and organisations active at the community level' and give priority to the 'disadvantaged, oppressed and marginalised segments of society'. Importantly, Butcher argues that the latter element can be justified in communitarian terms alone, without recourse to overarching political ideologies such as socialism. 'A bias to the disadvantaged and oppressed' is, for him, an inevitable consequence of the communitarian commitment to community participation, solidarity and empowerment (Butcher, 1993, p. 21).

These ideas are echoed in a series of contemporary policy initiatives at local level which focus on community development. The Association of

Metropolitan Authorities (1993) now advocates a central position for community development as a strategy in local government service provision. Additionally, other agencies such as health authorities, charities, local training and education councils (TECs) and other central government quangos have all shown an increasing interest in community development as a mode of operation at local level. Promoted by organisations such as the Home Office-sponsored Community Development Foundation, the concept has indeed gained a new respectability in the nineties as a method of fostering social improvement at the local level. It is claimed by its protagonists to have shed both the paternalism of its origins in social planning and the stigma of its popular association with extremist political campaigns [3]. For the AMA, it is a 'way in which a local authority deliberately stimulates and encourages groups of people to express their needs, supports them in their collective action and helps with their projects and schemes as part of the authority's overall objectives' (Association of Metropolitan Authorities, 1993, p. 10). According to writers like Blackman (1995, p. 145) this process can incorporate all of community work, community action and the development of both statutory and voluntary community oriented services.

The elements of this 'new' community development of the nineties are often, of course, expressed in the discourse of the 'post-Fordist' or 'disorganised' welfare state. For Alcock and Christiansen (1994, p. 119) 'community based activity requires top down support as well as bottom up initiative'. *Strategic management* is thus seen as a key feature of local authority input, in order to establish continuity and consistency of vision and to guard against 'short termism'. *Partnership, interagency co-operation* and *networking* are further essential prerequisites of successful community development strategies in a mixed economy of welfare. They point to the building of coalitions between various kinds of providers of services; the harnessing of relevant expertise and the active involvement and empowerment of community or user groups.

Empowerment, 'the degree to which or the process by which disadvantaged communities define their own needs or determine the response that is made to them', is at the heart of the new community development (Barr, 1995, pp. 122-3). Indeed, the credibility of community development as a process which works from the 'bottom up' depends on its success. But the process is a difficult and complex mix of negotiation, education and ultimately devolution of power and control from service provider to the community itself. For both parties empowerment involves a learning process and especially the development of a new kind of 'professionalism' among local government and agency workers. According to Barr (1994, p. 130) successful empowerment will require a 'deschooling' of most local government officers whose 'professional aspirations have led them to assert the exclusiveness of their expertise and hence hold themselves at a distance from their consumers ... serious attempts at empowerment strategies must therefore invest heavily in training for staff'.

Notwithstanding the significance of this observation for public librarians, many of these developments seem to bode well for the revival of a community librarianship with community development at its core. Public libraries are, after all, locally based organisations which deal in information: a vital ingredient of the community development mix. They have a recognised, non-partisan and widely respected community presence. The authors of the *Comedia* report claimed that they were 'convinced that the community library has a strategic and enabling part to play in the repertoire of an holistic community development approach' (Greenhalgh, Worpole and Landry, 1995, p. 99), and others have claimed that 'there is increasing recognition, particularly among new local authorities, of the advantages of combining community development principles with local library services' [4]. But how would such a combination work? What sort of prospect for the future of the public library would it hold in store? How realistic, in sum, might it be to talk of a 'new' community librarianship for the late nineties and beyond?

Virtual visions: the public library, information technology and community development

In the debate about futures there is, of course, one overriding perspective which our account has so far underplayed: that of the 'information revolution'. In the nineties, conjecture about the significance of information technology - in particular the internet or 'information superhighway' - has increasingly animated commentators on community development, just as it has public librarians. Many have attempted to articulate a positive future role for information technology (IT) in the rebuilding of community, based on familiar principles of empowerment, partnership and community responsibility on the part of the private sector. Lyon (1990) identifies a number of possible foci of development: IT jobs and training; teleworking; communication and education services (including community information); health and disability; and community development itself. In 1992, an IT and Communities Working Party convened by the Community Development Foundation developed guidelines which attempted to ensure good practice and local participation in community based IT. Its report argued powerfully that IT investment was crucial in the community and voluntary sector, especially in the context of a post-Fordist urban environment characterised by 'decentralised public responsibility for economic development and human services at the local level' (Community Development Foundation, 1992, p.1). More recently, a number of commentators have argued that recent changes in the culture of IT itself open up new possibilities for community access. Harris (1995, p.18) sees the 'mouse as a metaphor' for flexible, user friendly and adaptable systems which might eventually support the demystification and democratisation of information technology.

Partly in response to these kind of ideas, a number of local authorities in the UK have begun to initiate community development strategies linked to the opportunities offered by IT. Manchester, 'the information city', has perhaps been at the forefront of some of these initiatives, pioneering a 'host' computer communications and information network which can be used as a basis for the technical support of a wide range of community based projects. Manchester's strategy involves 'supporting community based economic initiatives and improving community access to information and new technology ... particularly for those sections of the community who face disadvantage and discrimination' (Manchester Telematics Partnership, c.1995, p. 5). Community based schemes include electronic village halls, which provide facilities for IT training and teleworking, and neighbourhood computing networks based on the host system. In addition, a more extensive community information network, under the leadership of the voluntary sector but with links to and outlets in libraries, is currently under development (Coleman, 1996b). As these examples suggest, partnerships between public, private, formalised voluntary and informal community interests are at the heart of the Manchester approach. Such partnerships may be technical, financial and strategic - usually in the guise of a 'coalition' of providers - or they may involve shared management and decision making in the case of schemes which attempt to empower users and community groups.

Perhaps most positively, initiatives like these have begun to help articulate a new rationale for community information provision, broadly conceived, in the information society. For Harris (1991, p. 79), they point to 'the potential of telematics to promote horizontal and informal communication, particularly at local level in the use of electronic mail and bulletin board systems'. Such communication can be seen as the life blood of community development, for it allows communities to develop deinstitutionalised knowledge in their own language and physical or virtual space. However, its effectiveness depends crucially upon what Harris labels the *information capability* of individuals and groups. This 'refers to the capacity of an individual, group, or organisation to acquire and use information for social and economic development' (1991, p. 81). It comprises three main elements: information awareness; access to resources; ability to exploit resources. It follows, therefore, that good practice in community information work involves flexible and relevant provision of resources, based on partnerships which involve local people and deinstitutionalised delivery made possible by the new telematics. It also demands a proactive and predominantly educational stance on the part of the information worker, including a commitment to concentrate on helping the information poor.

How relevant are these ideas to the public library and the practice of community librarianship? In many ways, of course, they represent an updating of a number of the original ideas and principles associated with the community librarianship of the early eighties, especially in its 'radical' form [5]. Observers like McKee (1987) have seen community development and community education as promising an alternative model or paradigm of public library service, and Muddiman (1990, p.93) characterised the consequent role of the public librarian in the information society as 'weaver: someone working at creatively developing cultural networks in a variety of media and settings'. More recently, the *Public Library Review* has sought to stimulate interest in the possible role of the public library as the focus of IT based community networks, and noted a number of American initiatives such as the Cleveland Free Net, the Berkeley 'Community Memory' and the Santa Monica 'Electronic Cafe'. The goals of such networks, according to the review, are to 'enhance community cohesion', create 'a citizenry briefed with high quality, timely and reliable information', promote 'easy access to independent means of education and training', and act as 'an effective processor, so that other needs can be met' (ASLIB, 1995, pp. 68-71). Chris Batt argues that the public library is strategically well placed to act as an agent for such 'free net' computing. He points to plans in his own authority, Croydon, to transfer its document based community information system to its web site (Croydon Online) and link it to connections in schools, libraries, local businesses and voluntary and community agencies. Batt envisages an enabling role for the public library in managing such a system and acting as 'honest broker ... maintaining the canvas and the paints'. Interestingly, however, he notes that the library will never 'be able to retain over a CCN the sort of control we like to retain over the rest of our services' (Batt, 1996, pp. 108-109).

One particular facet of these visions that has gained widespread support is the notion of the future public library as a 'community university'. The influential Comedia Report *Borrowed Time* argued that perhaps one of the most significant consequences of the information revolution to which the public library should respond was the accelerating need for lifelong learning, knowledge renewal and the 'renewal of human capital' (Comedia, 1993, p. 75). Others, like Astbury (1994), have claimed that the public library tradition of the 'people's university' and its long connection with the UK adult education movement place it strategically to become the 'key information and learning centre of the twenty first century'. Developments such as open learning and the claimed forthcoming explosion of educational opportunities on the internet prefigure 'the possibility of being able to introduce our local communities to a world of learning opportunities of which they have never dreamt' (Batt, 1996,

p. 109). Such possibilities obviously connect with those ideas which propose a focus on the information capability of communities and suggest, perhaps, that community education will become a central activity for the community librarian of the future. They suggest also, in the virtual world of the new millennium, a new role, perhaps, for library buildings as 'nerve centres' providing a wide range of informational, educational and cultural services.

Virtual reality? The public interest on the margins

How feasible are such exercises in futurology, and to what extent do they provide a realistic scenario for the future of community oriented public librarianship? In spite of the basis of a number of these ideas in pilot schemes and research initiatives [6], there must be the suspicion that many are tinged with utopianism and wishful thinking. There are two key reasons for such suspicion. First, in general terms, it seems extremely naive to see the 'information' society, as some communitarians do, as providing the social and economic conditions necessary for a rediscovery of a lost 'community', suppressed by modern industrialism. On the contrary, many social scientists such as Castells (1989), Giddens (1990) and Robins and Webster (1992) have argued that the information revolution embodies an expansion of technocratic capitalist *individualism* into ever multiplying areas of economic and social life. These claims are supported by researchers such as Deacon and Golding (1990) and Devins and Hughes (1995) who have concluded that the information society has brought 'division and uncertainty' to the voluntary and community sector, and is likely to bypass communities themselves. Its technological and commercial imperatives inevitably favour, they argue, the development of managed, institutionalised and formalised approaches to information processing at the expense of the democracy and informality of the grass roots. Smith (1996, p. 26) has further speculated that the notion of 'virtual' community might be little more than fool's gold. He notes that many existing attempts to create it are in fact an offshoot of the burgeoning heritage industry: museums, theme parks, virtual villages and other 'environments that evoke nostalgia and vicarious and temporary Gemeinschaft'. 'Whatever benefits may be found in the information society', he concludes, 'the revival of community is not one of them.'

A second problem concerns the public library itself. Even if one accepts the potential of a link between the information revolution and the revival of community development, one must seriously cast doubt upon the ability of the public library to position itself as a catalyst of community revival. As we have seen in the previous two chapters, in the late 1980s the concerns of many public librarians shifted away from 'community' towards the 'customer' on the one hand and towards heritage on the other. Moreover, as one review of recent local authority initiatives in Manchester notes, libraries are now only 'one of a range of agencies involved in providing community information ... the role of the library seems to have become less clear and distinctive ... it is very easy for libraries to be missed out' (Coleman, 1996b, p. 11).

What are the barriers to the development of a new community librarianship based on burgeoning information and communication technologies and networks? Some of them clearly have their origins in the determination of government to oversee a market driven information revolution and to promote the interests of commerce and industry in the design, construction and control of new channels and systems. In spite of the notional support of the Labour Party and, more latterly, a House of Lords Select Committee, it is by no means certain that public libraries will become unproblematically connected to the 'information superhighway' [7]. Indeed, according to Dempsey (1995, p. 8) 'it seems to be generally accepted that the majority of investment will come from the private sector'. In contrast, the public interest in the information superhighway remains in confusion. In public libraries, despite initiatives such as Project Earl, there is 'no explicit vision' of the future (Dempsey, 1995, p.9). Such concern is echoed by the professional establishment. A Library Association policy statement entitled *Information Superhighways* views 'with some alarm public libraries' incipient information poverty relative to academic libraries and information rich individuals'. It recommends 'steps to place public libraries firmly on the broadband information highway' (Library Association, 1995, pp. 11-12).

It is tempting, of course, to explain the silence with which such recommendations are greeted primarily in terms of party politics and the ideological distaste of the right for large scale public institutions and networks. However, whilst this is undoubtedly a factor, we would argue that there are more fundamental and permanent policy pressures at work. As post-Fordist theorists such as Jessop (1994) have noted, in 'information' societies the power of the national state has become increasingly 'hollowed out': eroded on the one hand by global and transnational capital and institutions, and supplanted on the other by local and regional interests who are forced to take the lead in attracting international investment. Like Manchester, 'the information city', the local region as a result becomes the key focus for IT investment, economic regeneration and the provision of community services. Stewart sees a future for the local authority in such a 'post-Fordist' urban environment as one of 'community government', 'confronting the problems and issues faced by local communities'. Such government will need to be, he argues, a 'government of difference', responding flexibly to need through the (now familiar) strategies of coalition, partnership, empowerment and community participation (1995, pp. 253-258).

All of this suggests a future for community librarianship contingent upon the involvement of the public library in local and regional, rather than national, information strategies. The local not the national state will, it seems, be the locus of 'community' in the information society and new definitions of the public interest will, perhaps, be local ones. Initially, this seems promising. As we have shown, many of the nineteenth century traditions of the public library movement lie in local support and participation [8] and, spurred on by the community librarianship of the seventies and early eighties, librarians have continued to participate in local initiatives based on interagency work. Our own fieldwork in 1993-4 looked at schemes such as the development of a healthcare information service in conjunction with an NHS Trust, a community arts strategy, and the successful functioning of a long-standing community information forum and exchange [9]. However, it was also the case that senior library managers we spoke to predominantly conceptualised 'partnership' in terms of a series of deals with official agencies such as TECs, other government agencies and the professionalised voluntary sector. In this landscape, it seemed to us that partnerships were in danger of becoming a series of projects reflecting a kind of local corporatism where 'interests' in the local authority, the private sector and voluntary agencies struggle to simply preserve services in a climate of cuts. Community participation can often be low on the agenda where partnership is driven by such expediency or policy dogma. As Harris warns, 'social exclusion in the information society may well begin as soon as partnerships are formed which do not represent local communities' (1995, p. 17). It seemed to us that this might be beginning to happen.

Nevertheless, we should perhaps not be over pessimistic with regard to the potential of partnership. Library managers are, we suspect, no worse than many other local government officials hard pressed for time and resources. Moreover, as McDowell (1992) indicates, a good number of library authorities have admirable traditions of, and experience in, interagency work. McDowell notes three main kinds of approach:

- networking - the development of links between two or more agencies in order to improve community services

- project based working - the development of a new service or initiative by two or more parties based on an identification of a gap in provision

- strategic planning of information initiatives, incorporating public, academic, business, voluntary sector and community information providers and users.

As we have seen in previous chapters, community librarianship brought with it many manifestations of each type of interagency initiative. The current Library Association/Holt Jackson *Community Initiative Award* provides continuing evidence of a commitment to networking and project based working on the part of many library authorities [10]. Larger scale projects, like Library and Information Plans (LIPS), can also adopt a perspective based on community participation and needs, although this has not always been a priority. A broader kind of local authority strategic management of community information provision is also claimed to benefit local people. John Davies notes that in St Helens the strategic management of community information initiatives improved coherence, co-ordination and direction. Strategic interagency approaches, co-ordinated by the local authority, can provide, he claims, a more 'holistic' and 'catalytic' framework for the development of community information services (1992, p. 278).

However, in spite of a good degree of consensus about these issues, there must be reservations about the ability of the public library to play a full part in the emerging 'local' information society. Many doubts relate to finance and resources. McDowell notes that in public libraries everywhere financial constraints make it ever more difficult to devote staff, time or capital to partnership projects. He concludes that others, however, might forge ahead and 'there is a danger in every part of the country that public libraries may be left behind' (1992, p. 249). As we have noted in Chapter 5, constraints such as these signal a long term policy problem for public libraries. From 1988 onwards, central government has only sanctioned public library funding levels which would support a 'core', 'basic' or traditional service of book lending and print based 'reference'. National government, in effect, refuses to make a commitment to fund 'the essential developments to allow public library authorities to incorporate electronic information handling as part of the basic core service' (McNaught, 1995, p. 156). Without such a commitment, the library service enters into local partnership on the basis of financial instability, short term funding horizons, and service perspectives which address the past rather than the future. Such perspectives and horizons impair planning, undermine the credibility of the public library as partner and in the end nullify initiative and enterprise. As Tester (1993, p. 70) concludes, 'if information provision (in the community) really is to have an enhanced role ... it cannot rely on short term funding and projects, but must be allocated mainstream funding'.

The refusal to allow that innovation (in general) and community initiative (in particular) should be part of the mainstream programme of public library work has, in our view, a further ossifying effect. Its consequence is to confer legitimacy on what we have called in Chapter 6 'the lure of heritage' - the view that the real purposes of the public library are somehow bound up with the heritage of 'the book' rather than the complexities of education and information in the postmodern world. This is not merely a problem of funding. On balance, the public library policymakers have failed to heed the warning of the Comedia report that 'unless libraries responded much more rapidly and dynamically to the changing times we live in they were ... living on borrowed time' (Comedia, 1993, p. 81). Subsequent debate, and in particular the Department of National Heritage review of public libraries in 1994-95, has revealed a public library community that is hesitant, divided and unable to articulate a consistent set of progressive principles. The *Review* itself predominantly defined policy and purpose in terms of existing library functions, and for McNaught (1995, p. 155), 'does a great disservice to the future of the public library by suggesting that the development of new services is not absolutely essential to (its) survival'. In effect, the chance to seriously construct a new consensus about the kind of public information and educational support services needed in the twenty first century was lost in the review. Libraries remain, as a consequence, uncertain partners at local, regional and indeed national level, without a clear sense of their mission, identity and purpose. As Comedia (1993, p. 79) suggests, many remain 'invisible and undernetworked' and 'insular and inward looking'. Unlike the public libraries of Victorian or even post-1945 Britain, they invite caricature as 'relics of a bygone age' (Pirie, 1995) and thus provide convenient alibis for continuing underfunding and neglect.

Like all caricatures, this one is surely a distortion. But it is effective, in our view, in drawing attention to the resilient conservatism in public libraries which we noted in Chapter 4 [11]. As we have seen, such conservatism resides not only in caution about policy but also in elements of the professional and institutional culture of the public library service. These elements, delineated by Jones (1984), persist, albeit in modified form, today. They combine technical conservatism, rule bound institutionalism and a relatively narrow perspective on the role of the professional librarian balanced by the persistence of a very positive culture of 'service' to individual library users, and by an assimilation of some elements of the 'new' managerialism and consumerism. Their overall effect is 'conservative' in the sense that they favour the continuance of a heavily institutionalised and professionally 'managed' library service which increasingly resembles commercial and retail models. We have already argued that the bureaucratic conservatism of the welfare state set limits on the impact of community librarianship during the decade 1975-85; we would want to argue again that a modified form of this organisational culture persists in the nineties and plays a major part in determining the kind of changes which are actually possible on the ground in the contemporary library service. It is this institutional culture, rather than extraneous visions, strategies or policy statements, which in the end will determine the nature of community involvement of the public library.

How does this institutional culture manifest itself in today's public library? In all of our field studies we found evidence of a perception of community librarianship which was very different from that of its apologists, theorists and futurologists. Essentially this was a conservative perception which combined a strong sense of the institutional identity of the library with its need to 'justify' its existence in a local 'market' of community provision. In many local authorities it was evident that there was pressure to sharpen the corporate image of the service and highlight its responsibility to the 'community'. Buildings were back in fashion: even in 'Inner', a London borough struggling to maintain a commitment to outreach, a focus on the improvement of library buildings for all kinds of community use was being restored. Local (or 'community') information systems were also a preoccupation for many managers, and one told us that the delivery of accurate, up to date, 'quality' local information was important for the corporate identity and the credibility of the library service and the council as an information provider. Like Harris (1995), however, we found little evidence of community involvement in the development of any of the computerised local information services we looked at, and in all of them content and delivery remained under the control of the library service or local authority as a whole.

As well as image, 'quality' of service seemed to be a key ingredient of what many staff understood by a 'community' approach. Most library staff we spoke to, especially at clerical and junior professional levels, were extremely supportive of initiatives such as customer care which stressed the maximisation of satisfaction of customers or users. Whatever intellectuals think, library staff in general seem to have little difficulty in assimilating ideas of 'community' and consumerism. In one of our case study authorities, library operations managers were being actively recruited from the retail sector and one of our informants linked customer care with community librarianship by asking 'isn't that what community librarianship is all about?' [12]. More seriously, other librarians argued that ideas about 'quality' should apply equally to 'community' services. The majority had organised impressively maintained and indexed community information and rights collections, in contrast to the relative chaos that predominated in many such collections fifteen or twenty years ago. Some community librarians were keen to improve the general 'quality', or responsiveness, of services through liaison with community group leaders, user surveys and the like, although for most reality fell short of ambition. Most concurred, however, with the sentiments of one group librarian, who told us, 'I want my library to be the focal point of the local community, that's all. If that's CL, fine' [13].

Such a community librarianship undoubtedly has its empirical merits. It relates, more obviously than theories and visions do, to the 'real world'. It speaks of modest achievements and achievable goals in a declining and

141

underfunded public service: the improvement of community information collections, a gradual acceptance of the legitimacy of multicultural approaches to service, the modernisation of local information systems, sporadic improvements in community profiling and market research. Perhaps more public library staff than ever are aware of the need for 'community' involvement and contact, certainly all are aware of the rhetoric of customer care. There is a new consciousness, perhaps, of the significance of the public library as a place and of the need to justify its claim to be a 'community asset'. But there were limits, in this librarianship, to community involvement. In general, it took place on the basis of existing (and traditional) library functions rather than innovation. Allhouse (1995), in a study of public library initiatives and experiments involving the internet, found little interest the new networks among public library staff. Significantly, in our many interviews conducted for this book, no-one offered us a vision of *community librarianship*, as opposed to the public library, in the 'information' society. Moreover, many dismissed the attempts of librarians to become advice workers, adult educators and the like as a failure and a dilution of the professional role. Will the same fate befall networked information advisors? It seemed for many that community involvement no longer incorporated an active and interpersonal engagement with communities and their problems as part of the librarian's role. Rather, with some exceptions, librarians were seen as managers of resources purveyed efficiently and consistently to meet 'community' demands [14].

Such a new, rather bland, conception of community librarianship seems to us ill equipped to meet the challenges of the information society. It offers little in response to the technological revolution, hampered as the public library is by political indifference and professional caution and dissent. It speaks the rhetoric of community, but is puzzled by its fragmentation and flux, and it is hesitant about asserting a commitment to social justice and social change. In an age when those concerned with communities and their development preach decentralisation, partnership and empowerment, public librarians seem in danger of reverting to a conservative, insular and defensive stance. Like the public library as an institution, they have become in the main passive and reactive: they respond to constraints and contingencies, but fail to articulate a clear and purposive narrative of their future role. Visions and utopias they may have, but in the end, these may not be enough to save the public library from a future on the margins of social and community life.

We believe there is, however, an alternative. If there is to be a future for community librarianship in the 'information' society, it will surely be in the context of developing informational and cultural policies and provision in the local state. Libraries have much to offer the developing local public sphere, not least because of the experience gained in the 1970s and 1980s when many seriously attempted a 'community' approach to provision. The basic philosophical traditions of the public library - equal opportunity and universal access to knowledge - remain inviolable and need to be accepted, applied and adopted throughout the public sphere as the cornerstone of a just information society. However, as a result of both social and technical change and diversification, public libraries desperately need to innovate if such a goal is to be pursued. Such innovation, it seems certain, will have to be on the basis of a mix of local and regional funding and partnership arrangements which will inevitably undermine and weaken their institutional core. They will need to adapt to interagency modes of provision involving, not only governmental and professionalised voluntary agencies, but increasingly 'communities', themselves. 'Librarians', if they are still called that, will need to take on new interpersonal and technical skills and roles. These challenges, as some librarians and library authorities are belatedly recognising, must be seen as opportunities rather than threats. They provide, in the end, the most positive route towards a restructuring and reinvention of the public library (or whatever our children might call it) in the twenty first century. Perhaps if librarians can rekindle some of the radical traditions of their past, they might yet embark upon such a project.

Notes

1   See, for example, Hurd's pamphlet *Conservatism in the 1990s* (Hurd, 1991).

2   See the collection of papers edited by Wilcox (1996) for an overview and assessment of the potential of such 'virtual' communities.

3   See Cockburn (1977) and our own discussion in Chapter 3 on the politics of community development in the 1970s. Alison West, Chief Executive of the Community Development Foundation, commented in 1993 on a 'new realism about community development' in which it can be seen as 'a cost effective and realistic way of reaching certain limited social goals, particularly at the time of resource constraints' (Community Development Foundation, 1993, p. 14).

4   The quotation is taken from the publicity leaflet for a conference entitled 'Public Libraries and Communities' held in London on 16th November 1995. The conference was co-sponsored by the Community Development Foundation and the Library Association Community Services Group.

5   See Chapter 3 for a detailed discussion of the 'radical' model of community librarianship.

6   A special edition of *Vine* (vol.98, March 1995) is devoted to reports and discussion of initiatives involving the public library and the internet.

7   See a report in *Library Association Record*, September 1996, which usefully, although perhaps over optimistically, reviews the most recent developments including the report of the House of Lords Select Committee (Watson, 1996, pp. 440-1).

8   See Chapter 2 and also Black (1996a) for a more detailed exploration of the 'civic' involvement of the early public library.

9   In Loamshire, Northern and Inner respectively.

10 The award was instituted in 1992 and provides for a prize of £5000 each year to be given to a library based initiative which has a 'measurable beneficial impact' on the local community. See Featherstone (1992) for an overview and introduction. Subsequent reports in *Community Librarian* and *Public Library Journal* have carried details of prize winners, finalists and so on.

11 See the section of Chapter 4 - 'The public library as professional bureaucracy: the limits of community librarianship'.

12 Interview with Library Operations Manager, Loamshire, December 1993.

13 Interview with Group Librarian, Outer, February 1994.

14 This idea of a more passive role was particularly resisted by a group of children's librarians in Inner, at a group interview in October 1993. Children's librarians are, of course, along with 'special' services librarians, perhaps the only group for whom a proactive community stance has been generally accepted by the whole of the library profession. Other librarians, too, lamented the move to a more 'managerial' role. Two Assistant Librarians in Loamshire told us that their job satisfaction had declined significantly as a result of extra responsibilities for stock management and information provision within the library and a reduced commitment to outreach (group interview, December 1993).

8 Conclusion: The public library in postmodern Britain

Many accounts of the contemporary public library and its problems begin with the notion of the 'information revolution'. Typically, such a revolution is seen to be 'as profound in its effects as the industrial revolution' (ASLIB, 1995, p. 3) and as disorientating and destabilising for the traditional institutions of modernity. Electronic media, networked communications and computerised information processing together constitute a revolutionary 'knowledge environment' that threatens to overwhelm the world of paper and print. Unless public libraries 'expand their roles, and seize the opportunities that are emerging' (ASLIB, 1995, p.3), like impotent dinosaurs, they will die. Unless they 'address the critical issues of tomorrow', the tides of historical change threaten to sweep over them and consign them to oblivion (Greenhalgh, Worpole and Landry, 1995, p. 167).

Such technological determinism undoubtedly has its elements of truth, but in the end, we would argue, offers only a relatively superficial diagnosis of the problems of the contemporary public library. As we have seen, these problems can be traced back at least as far as the 1970s, to the clamour of professional dissatisfaction at that time with the McColvin model of public library provision - what we have called the 'modern' or 'welfare state' library service. Such dissatisfaction was concerned, not with the failure of libraries to adopt information technology (IT), but with their failure to adopt a sufficiently *pluralistic* model of service that incorporated the interests of all their potential users. The public sphere as represented by the public library, in spite of its evident 'modernity' and its attempts to shake off its closed Victorian image, was variously seen as elitist, eurocentric, homocentric and mirroring the prejudices of a predominantly conservative national culture and profession. Out of such disquiet, community librarianship, of course, emerged. It adopted a variety of guises: the welfarist, concerned with redressing the balance of resources to the 'disadvantaged'; the responsive, concerned with popularising and expanding public library services; the radical, concerned with deinstitutionalisation and community control. Each of these shared a commitment to pluralism and innovation in service provision and the break up of the 'modern', or monolithic, institutionalised service model.

In hindsight it is, of course, possible to relate these changes to a more general crisis of public institutions in the late twentieth century. For many commentators, such a crisis stems fundamentally from the fragmentation of the idea of 'community' as social solidarity and the consequent erosion of the idea of a 'public sphere' of discourse which was seen as binding social groups in common communication. The causes and consequences of this crisis are complex, but its elements encompass the growth of cultural relativism and pluralism, a loss of faith in centralised planning and the institutions of the state, social fragmentation, and the rise of individualism and the politics of difference. David Harvey (1989) claims that such social conditions are those of 'postmodernity' in which the modern, or 'enlightenment', project, based on humanism, benevolent science and technology and professional expertise, is in danger of collapse. Others, focusing on the economic and political dimensions of the crisis use the label 'post-Fordism' [1]. Continually, in this book we have used these terms to explore the problems of the contemporary public library. This is quite deliberate. Cuts, and the continuing run down of public service; the pressures towards commercialism and cultural populism; the flirtation with privatisation; the lure of heritage: all, we believe, can convincingly be traced at root to the breakdown of a consensus about 'modern' public life.

What is perhaps rather less obvious is the view that the community librarianship of the 1970s and early 1980s was a remarkably positive response to this 'postmodern' turn. Radical librarians realised, it seems, quite independently of social and cultural theorists, the limitations of a monolithic public institution and made laudable efforts to change it. Some of these efforts involved simply a diversification and refocusing of services around the conception of 'need', and in some areas of provision, such as services directed at ethnic minorities or people with disabilities, the resultant specialised provision has survived and been expanded. However, other more radical initiatives largely failed. In particular, attempts to 'deinstitutionalise' the public library in order that it might respond to the new realities of cultural difference only ever in reality took root in a small minority of public library authorities. Even in these, outreach, the major practical expression of deinstitutionalisation and part of the more radical tradition of public library service, has fallen into decline. Nevertheless, radical community librarianship remains as an important early attempt to reconcile the universalist principles of public provision with diversifying and fragmenting conceptions of community. Perhaps, however, it was ahead of its time.

The marginality and subsequent retreat of community librarianship as a total approach to library provision can, of course, partly be attributed to its own contradictions. Community librarians shunned elitist and bureaucratic conceptions of professionalism, but in the end they could do little to escape from the straightjacket of being professional employees of the state. They espoused deinstitutionalisation, but their own interests and survival depended on the health of the public library as an institution. They flirted with, but in the end were reluctant to adopt, adventurous roles which broke professional boundaries such as animateur, community worker, advice worker or educator. In the final analysis, as public choice theorists would argue, their institutional conservatism perhaps does explain the enduring stability of the 'core', 'basic', book borrowing function of the public library. Community librarianship, as a result, arguably always remained on the margins rather than at the centre of public library work, at the mercy of short term commitment and short term money. From an organisational perspective, its roots are relatively shallow.

To claim, however, that community librarianship 'failed' as a whole, or indeed to claim that it was a contradiction in terms, would be, we believe, a harsh and arguably premature judgement. As a movement, it revived the possibility that libraries could initiate and support change and improvement in a shifting and diversifying society. In spite of its intellectual diversity, community librarianship was essentially an idealistic movement drawing to a degree on nineteenth century and welfare state notions of self-realisation through collective action. It was consequently underpinned by a number of principles which we associate with cultural democracy in its most complex and positive sense. These incorporate:

- a recognition that the diffusion of knowledge throughout all sectors of society represents the primary and *civilising* purpose of the public library movement

- a recognition of the complexity of the many formulations of knowledge and an acceptance of *cultural pluralism* (but not relativism): the notion that the service exists to nurture not one 'culture' but many

- the formulation of service on the basis of *equal rights of citizenship*: the recognition that some sectors of society are less powerful than others and therefore may require affirmative action in service provision

- a commitment to the development of service on the basis of *communal involvement* on the part of librarians in order to underpin the library's position as a facilitator of the shared culture of its users.

These principles, we believe, can still offer a positive basis for the future of the public library service in 'new', or 'postmodern', times. They are based, unlike the McColvinite model, on an emphatic attempt to respond to social diversification and plurality of interests and cultures. Yet they reinforce, at the same time, the underlying commitment of the public interest to social justice and equity, especially through the concept of equal opportunity. For political theorists like Mouffe (1992) and Lipietz (1994), such a dual commitment, idealistic and utopian though it may be, must form the starting point for any radical democratic politics today. For us, it is perhaps the most durable legacy of early community librarianship, which was born of the recognition that, despite its rhetoric of universalism, too many citizens were, and still are, excluded from the public library ideal.

Nevertheless, a different kind of postmodernity - what Jameson (1984) labels 'the cultural logic of late capitalism' - has now muted such radical commitment. Our account of the public library of the 1980s has charted the impact of such a postmodernity of the market. It is present, we would argue, in the pressures towards consumerism and individualism which impel the public library to be managed 'like a business' responding primarily to 'customer' demand. It is present, too, in the pressures towards cultural relativism which accompany such marketing approaches and threaten to detach the public library from its educative and civilising purpose. Paradoxically too, we would argue, it is present in those ideas which seek to restore the 'golden age' of the public library and focus its activities on books and heritage rather than contemporary need. As we have warned, these pressures threaten a hollow community librarianship which is in danger of becoming little more than an exercise in rhetoric and nostalgia, uninterested in social justice and social change. They threaten to marginalise a public library which has always justified its existence in terms of social, educational and even economic *progress*. Above all, conservative postmodernity brings with it the possibility of the collapse and fragmentation of the public sphere altogether. It promises the rise of an information and communications industry which sees itself, and the market, as the guarantor of 'freedom' of access to information and of global educational advance. It threatens institutions such as the public library with, at best, irrelevance and, at worst, extinction.

Defenders of the public library service have, as we have seen, put forward sometimes imaginative alternatives to this scenario of private sector dominance and public decline. Many of them, like the arguments and visions relating to the notion of the 'community university' sketched out in Chapter 7, utilise communitarian ideas and are well grounded in traditional justifications of public library service in terms of universal access to information and education. Other arguments, like those reviewed by Dempsey (1995), seek to justify the *modernisation* of the public sphere as a whole and the creation of a public

148

library for the twenty first century, complete with internet access, interactive open learning facilities and community computing. However, it seems to us that such a wholesale modernisation of the public library as an institution is an unlikely event, however much the profession might argue for it. Politically, as we saw in Chapter 5, central government has signalled its intention not to fund the expansion of electronic communication services in public libraries, insisting that such funding be generated from the private sector or other kinds of partnerships. Dempsey (1995, p. 7) notes sanguinely that 'it seems to be generally accepted that the majority of investment will come from the private sector'. However, public librarians generally are at a loss as to how such finance might be raised [2], and in any event worry about the price that the private sector might exact. While most concur with Usherwood (1996, p. 205) that the 'idea of a just information society' is at the heart of the public library movement, no-one seems to have any idea of how the public library can bring this about.

The postmodern perception of the public institution lies, we would argue, at the real root of this dilemma. In postmodern Britain, as elsewhere, the old narrative of the 'public interest' is one that it is increasingly difficult to sustain as what is 'public' diversifies and fragments. In particular, the notion that a single institution - the public library - can act pre-eminently as a guarantor of public access to knowledge is one that is rooted in the classical era of the welfare state, state planning and universal provision. It now carries doubtful credibility, increasingly as the kinds of 'knowledge' that libraries have come to purvey sometimes bear scant relation to the needs of the communities they are supposed to serve. More than ever, in an electronic age of multiple channels, fragmented communities and diversified needs, it looks as though the 'public interest', however defined, will need to turn to new institutional forms of delivery if it is to survive. As we have noted in Chapter 7, such forms will probably consist of flexible and shifting networks and partnerships, utilising, perhaps on the Manchester model, different kinds of information 'system' and a rich and varied technological and skills mix. Their focal point will probably be the local or regional, rather than the national, network, under the guidance, if the public interest is to be preserved, of democratically elected local or 'community' government (Stewart, 1995). Most important of all, if such coalitions are to maintain a clear sense of local or 'community' interests, they will need to incorporate and not exclude local people, including those who speak for the disadvantaged and the dispossessed.

The public library, if it is to survive in postmodern Britain, will need to increasingly reinvent itself as a part of such public partnerships and networks. As history teaches, reinvention is possible: after 1918, and more rapidly after 1945, the public library speedily adapted to its role as a national, rather than civic, institution. In the twenty-first century, it will need to be prepared for innovation, deinstitutionalisation and even more rapid change. It will need to shed many of its traditions of statist modernity and professional bureaucracy, and commit itself to plural, flexible and democratic models of service provision. If it does so, it will have its radical and innovative traditions to draw on, including those of community librarianship itself. Indeed, from our perspective, the commitment of community librarianship to equal rights of citizenship, education and access on the one hand, balanced by pluralism and communitarianism in provision on the other, provides the basic rationale for a 'public interest' in postmodern culture. The alternative is the dominance of the market, a bland future for the public librarian as technocrat or resource manager, and a community librarianship that is little more than rhetoric or nostalgia. But, as someone said along the way, its ideas are 'not dead yet'. Community librarianship might in the end thrive and flourish, maybe as it was always intended to do, outside the bounds of the public library itself.

Notes

1   For an overview of these developments see Amin (1995).
2   In general the consensus suggests that new finance will have to be raised from 'external' or 'non-mainstream' sources. The *Public Library Review* recommended charging for 'new services' and non-book materials; national lottery and heritage funds; 'partnership' funding, including a 'Future Generations' Trust; sponsorship; EU funding; vouchers; 'smart cards'; and a fines recovery service (ASLIB, 1995, pp. 27-29).

Appendix: A note on research methods

It is not our intention to offer here a lengthy justification and defence of the theoretical and conceptual aspects of our research methodology. As we have noted in the preface, the main thrust of our overall approach is critical and interpretative: we consider that an understanding of contemporary community librarianship can only be achieved as a result of the consideration of the wider societal forces which have shaped public library development in the late twentieth century. To this end we have brought to bear on the topic a wide range of ideas drawn from the literatures of community; socio-cultural theory; political economy; local government and politics; and contemporary history. These ideas are grounded firmly in social science, and indeed many of them are central to the current debate concerning a claimed 'information society'. We believe that as a result they are crucially applicable and relevant to the public library and can help build a theory of its contemporary crisis. But, in the end, we can only leave the reader to judge.

Beyond theory, however, other readers may be interested in the details of some of the more practical and empirical aspects of our study: questions of sources and data, activity in the field, data analysis and so on. In fact, this book began in 1992 as a relatively small scale empirical project funded on a very limited budget. Entitled *Community Librarianship, Rhetoric or Reality*, it was designed to investigate a supposed decline or 'death' of community librarianship which a number of practitioners of our acquaintance claimed to be in progress. Such a claim, and the reasons for it, seemed to us to raise all kinds of interesting questions which led to a need for a re-assessment of community librarianship as a whole. We thus devised a fourfold research strategy aimed at tracking the historical trajectory of community librarianship from its formative period in the late-1960s and 1970s to the present day. The elements of the strategy were as follows:

- Depth interviews with approximately twenty practitioners who had been and/or are still centrally involved with the development of community based approaches to public library provision. Most of these interviews were tape recorded and lasted for a period of around one hour, although some were much longer in duration. Informants were selected on the basis of their experience of community librarianship, but we made a special effort to interview librarians practising at a variety of 'levels': from 'strategic' managers and planners at one end of the scale to community librarians working in the field at the other. Interviews took the form of loosely structured depth interviews which covered a number of common themes but which allowed informants freedom to develop ideas, lines of narrative and description. However, typically they began with a 'career history' perspective and ended with a discussion regarding the prospects for community/public librarianship.

- Documentary research focusing on the origins of community librarianship was based on archival evidence drawn from the The British Library Information Science Service and the local studies departments in the public libraries of Westminster, Cambridge, Stevenage, Croydon, Manchester, Darlington, Chelsea and Southwark. Considerable though selective use was also made of the general public's views on the public library contained in the archives of Mass Observation, housed by the University of Sussex, in particular the Autumn 1988 Directive on 'Regular Pastimes' where hundreds of volunteer observers offered unprompted, and therefore uncontaminated, evidence of public library use.

- A content analysis of public library authority policy and service strategy documents. In late 1993 we circulated 120 English and Welsh library authorities [1] with a request for recent policy and service statements relevant to 'community library services'. The request was deliberately framed in this broadly based way because we anticipated problems with the label 'community librarianship' - a problem confirmed in correspondence from a number of public librarians. 74 public library authorities responded to our request, many providing us with voluminous packages of material including customer service documents; mission statements; statements of strategy and objectives; committee documents; as well as detailed documents relating to outreach, services to particular user groups and materials selection. All of this material was analysed qualitatively with the objective of identifying patterns of policy change experienced by community library services since the mid-1980s. The resultant models and typologies of change are described in Chapter 5.

152

- Four, more detailed, case studies were undertaken. Their key purpose was to test the hypothesis of decline and to look for new and emergent models of the community approach. Public library authorities who were known to have been active protagonists of community librarianship in the early and mid-1980s were specifically chosen for these studies, but they also offered geographical and organisational contrasts. Two (referred to as 'Inner' and 'Outer' in our notes) were London Boroughs of contrasting socio-economic and political complexion, 'Northern' was a predominantly working class metropolitan district and 'Loamshire' an English county with a varied socio-economic structure and base. Within each case a variety of fieldwork tactics were employed, ranging from observation and occasionally participation in meetings through to group interviews and individual depth interviews. However, care was taken to speak to a range of staff from directorate level on the one hand through to community librarians, library assistants and van drivers on the other. Conversation was tape recorded where possible and where permission was given, otherwise field diaries were compiled to provide an immediate record of data.

There were, of course, a good number of less structured and sometimes opportunistic visits to other projects, people and locations where these seemed interesting or appropriate. In addition, we have occasionally made use of data obtained by both our undergraduate and postgraduate students, many of whom we encourage to undertake small scale research in this field. More specifically, however, in Chapters 6 and 7, we owe a debt to the PhD research of Pen Jenkinson and Paul Johnson focusing on libraries and heritage and on emerging technologies and community development respectively.

It almost goes without saying that our dominant mode of data analysis has been qualitative. In general we have followed the sort of techniques recommended by writers such as Burgess (1984) and Finch (1990) in handling the data we have amassed. We have attempted to identify thematic patterns, build conceptual models and (not least) link the specifics of the world of the public library to the wider landscape of contemporary history and theory. We have almost totally resisted the temptation to quantify, except once, in Table 5.1. On that occasion, it seemed rather churlish to refuse to share with readers the results of an exploratory classification of public library authorities according to our impressions of their response to local government restructuring. However, it is the categories and models, not the figures, that are of importance here. The figures are suggestive only, and we claim no statistical significance or validity for them.

Methodologically literate readers will, no doubt, be able to identify many other detailed shortcomings in our work. One facet of community librarianship which we would ourselves like to have explored more fully, but lacked both time and resources to do so, was the 'user', 'public' or 'client' perspective. This was attempted in only a limited way in respect of the Mass Observation material noted above. Very few studies exist (still) which focus qualitatively and in depth on the informational and cultural needs of citizens, community organisations and especially the marginalised and the dispossessed. As the gap between 'information' rich and poor widens and deepens, the potential of the radical tradition of library and information work remains as a result understated and underexplored. We hope at least that this study, limited though it is, might help to place such a radical perspective once again on local and national information policy agendas.

Note

1   Scottish Library authorities were omitted for reasons of cost and time, and because our study never intended to explore the local government environment in Scotland. We recognise, however, that many important initiatives relevant to community librarianship emanate from Scotland and these are reported where we review the literature.

Bibliography

Abell, A. (1996), 'Ready to move centre stage', *Library Association Record*, vol.98, no.5, May.

Adam Smith Institute (1986), *Ex Libris*, Adam Smith Institute, London.

Addison, P. (1975), *The Road to 1945*, Cape, London.

Alcock, P. and Christiansen, L. (1995), 'In and against the state: community based organisations in Britain and Denmark in the 1990s', *Community Development Journal*, vol.30, no.2.

Alexander, Z. (1982), *Library Services and Afro-Caribbean Communities*, Association of Assistant Librarians, Newcastle under Lyme.

Allen, J. (1992), 'Post-industrialism and Post-Fordism' in Hall, S., Held, D. and McGrew, T. (eds.), *Modernity and its Futures*, Polity and Open University Press, Cambridge.

Allhouse, M. (1995), *An Examination of the Provision of Public Access to the Internet in Public Libraries in England and Wales*, unpublished MSc. dissertation, Leeds Metropolitan University.

Allred, J. (1990), 'The public library as an educational resource', *Public Library Journal*, vol.5. no.1, January-February.

Altick, R.D. (1957), *The English Common Reader: a Social History of the Mass Reading Public 1800-1900*, University of Chicago Press, Chicago.

Amin, A. (ed.) (1995), *Post-Fordism: a Reader*, Blackwell, Oxford.

Andrew, G. (1995), 'Pointing to the future: how one community's experience can benefit the country', *Vine*, no.98.

Armour, J. (1975), 'The why and how of outreach: reach out or be forced out' in Martin, W. (ed.), *Library Services to the Disadvantaged*, Bingley, London.

ASLIB (1995), *Review of the Public Library Service in England and Wales for the Department of National Heritage*, ASLIB, London.

Association of Assistant Librarians (1981), 'Libraries and racialism', *Assistant Librarian,* vol.74, no.9.

Association of Metropolitan Authorities (1993), *Local Authorities and Community Development: A Strategic Opportunity for the 1990s,* Association of Metropolitan Authorities, London.

Astbury, R. (ed.) (1983), *Libraries and the Unemployed: Needs and Responses,* Special Community Services Sub-Committee of the Library Association, London.

Astbury, R. (ed.) (1989), *Putting People First: Some New Perspectives on Community Librarianship,* AAL, Newcastle under Lyme. .

Astbury, R. (1994), 'The public library of the twenty first century: the key information and learning centre in the community', *Libri,* vol.44, no.2.

Atton, C. (1993), 'The tragedy of Comedia: libraries and the free market', *Assistant Librarian,* September.

Avineri, S. and de-Shalit. A. (eds.) (1992), *Communitarianism and Individualism,* Oxford University Press, Oxford.

Bailey, P. (1978), *Leisure and Class in Victorian England: Rational Recreation and the Contest for Control 1830-1885,* Routledge and Kegan Paul, London.

Baker, E. (1922), *The Public Library,* Daniel O'Connor, London.

Baltimore County Public Libraries (1992), *Give 'Em What They Want,* American Library Association, Chicago.

Banks, J.A. (1973), 'The contagion of numbers' in Dyos, H.J. and Wolff, M., *The Victorian City: Images and Reality,* vol. 1, Routledge and Kegan Paul, London.

Barlow, R. (1989), *Team Librarianship: the Advent of Public Library Team Structures,* Bingley, London.

Barnett, C.C. (1977), 'Library surveys and user surveys' in Whatley, H.A. (ed.), *British Librarianship and Information Science 1971-75,* Library Association, London.

Barr, A. (1995), 'Empowering communities - beyond fashionable rhetoric? Some reflections on the Scottish experience', *Community Development Journal,* vol.30, no.2.

Barugh J. and Woodhouse, R. (1987), *Public Libraries and Organisations Serving the Unemployed,* British Library, London.

Barugh, J. (1984), 'Community information and the public library', *Journal of Librarianship,* vol.16, no.2.

Barugh, J. (1989), 'The relationship between community librarianship and community information' in Astbury, R. (ed.), *Putting People First: Some New Perspectives on Community Librarianship,* Association of Assistant Librarians, Newcastle under Lyme.

Batt, C. (1988), *Information Technology in Public Libraries*, Library Association, London.

Batt, C. (1994), *Information Technology in Public Libraries*, 5th ed., Library Association, London.

Batt, C. (1996), 'The cutting edge 29: the four paradigms', *Public Library Journal*, vol.11, no.4.

Beal, C. (1985), *Community Profiling for Librarians*, Centre for Research into User Studies Occasional Paper no. 12, University of Sheffield.

Beauchamp, P. (1992), 'All change and no change', *Assistant Librarian*, July.

Bell, E.M. (1942), *Octavia Hill: a Biography*, Constable and Co., London.

Bendix, D. (1969), 'Urban ferment - libraries, what drummer?', *Pennsylvania Library Association Bulletin*, no.24, November.

Berriman, S.G. and Harrison, K.C. (1966), *British Public Library Buildings*, Deutsch, London.

Berry, L. (1988), 'The rhetoric of consumerism and the exclusion of community', *Community Development Journal*, vol.23, no.4.

Black, A. (1996a), 'Local politics and national provision' in Kinnell, M. and Sturges, P. (eds.), *Continuity and Innovation in the Public Library. The Development of a Social Institution*, Library Association Publishing, London.

Black, A. (1996b), *A New History of the English Public Library: Social and Intellectual Contexts 1850-1914*, Leicester University Press, Leicester.

Blackman, T. (1995), *Urban Policy and Practice*, Routledge, London.

Blunkett, D. and Jackson, H. (1987), *Democracy in Crisis: the Town Halls Respond*, Hogarth Press, London.

Boaden, N. et. al. (1982), *Public Participation in Local Services*, Longman, London.

Board of Education, Public Libraries Committee (1927), *Report on Public Libraries in England and Wales* [Kenyon Report].

Bowen, J. and Dee, M. (1986), *Library Services for Older People*, British Library, London.

Broady, J. and Usherwood, B. (1985), 'Public expenditure policies and the public library: changing the rules of the revenue game', *Journal of Librarianship*, vol.17, no.1.

Bunch, A. (1982) *Community Information Services: their Origin, Scope and Development*, Bingley, London.

Bundy, M.L. (1972), 'Urban information and public libraries', *Library Journal*, vol.97, no.2.

Burgess, R. (1984), *In the Field: An Introduction to Field Research*, Routledge, London.

Burns, D., Hambleton, R. and Hoggett, P. (1994), *The Politics of Decentralization: Revitalizing Local Democracy*, Macmillan, Basingstoke.

Burrows, R. and Loader, B. (1994), *Towards a Post-Fordist Welfare State*, Routledge, London.

Butcher, H. (1993), 'Introduction: some examples and definitions' in Butcher, H., Glen, A., Henderson, P. and Smith, J. (eds.), *Community and Public Policy*, Pluto, London.

Butcher, H., Glen, A., Henderson, P. and Smith, J. (eds.) (1994), *Community and Public Policy*, Pluto, London.

Cambridgeshire Libraries (1984), *Policy Document No. 8*, March.

Castells, M. (1989), *The Informational City: Information Technology, Economic Restructuring and the Urban/Regional Process*, Blackwell, Oxford.

Central Office of Information (1994), *Britain 1995: an Official Handbook*, HMSO, London.

Cheshire County Council, Central Policy and Research Unit (1985), *The Cheshire Library Survey 2. Out of a Job, into a Library?*, British Library, London.

Clarke, A. (1991), 'A focus for change: the role of community newspapers' in *Making the News: Libraries and Community Media*, Community Services Group (Scotland).

Clough, E. and Quarmby, J. (1978), *A Public Library Service for Ethnic Minorities in Great Britain*, Library Association, London.

Cochrane, A. (1989), 'Restructuring the state: the case of local government', in Cochrane, A. and Anderson, J. (eds.), *Politics in Transition*, Sage/Open University, London.

Cockburn, C. (1977), *The Local State: Management of Cities and People*, Pluto, London.

Coe, N. and Parsons, S. (1989), 'The post-green paper public library service', *Library Association Record*, vol.91, no.9.

Cohen, A.P. (1989), *The Symbolic Construction of Community*, Routledge, London.

Coleman, P. (1981), *Whose Problem? The Public Library and the Disadvantaged*, Association of Assistant Librarians, Newcastle under Lyme.

Coleman, P. (1986), 'Community information policy and provision', *Aslib Proceedings*, vol.38, no.9.

Coleman, P. (1991), 'Much more than books: the clarion call or the death knell for public libraries?' in Ashcroft, M. and Wilson, A. (eds.), *Public Library Policy and Strategic Planning for the '90s*, Capital Planning Information Ltd., Stamford, Lincolnshire.

Coleman, P. (1992), 'Past to Future - the Public Library's Changing Role' in Kinnell, M., *Informing Communities: the Role of Library and Information Services*, Community Services Group of the Library Association, London.

Coleman, P. (1996a) 'Widening the vision - improving access to information: part 1', *Assistant Librarian*, January.

Coleman, P. (1996b), 'Widening the vision - improving access to information: part 2', *Assistant Librarian*, February.

Collins, J. (1995), *Architecture of Excess: Cultural Life in the Information Age*, Routledge, London.

Collison, R.L. (1950), *Library Assistance to Readers*, Library Association, London.

Comedia (1993), *Borrowed Time: the Future of Public Libraries in the UK*, Comedia, Stroud Green.

Communities in Crisis: a Resource Programme for Local Organizations and Leaders (1985), Ruskin College, Oxford and the William Temple Organization.

Community Development Foundation (1992), *Press Enter. Information Technology in the Voluntary and Community Sector. Report of the IT and Communities Working Party*, CDF, London.

Community Development Foundation (1993), *Annual Review 1992-3*, CDF, London.

Community Information Project (1988), *Ten Year Report*, CIP, London.

Community Relations Commission (1976), *Public Library Services for a Multi-cultural Society*, CRC, London.

Cooke, M. (1980), 'Providing for ethnic minorities: need for co-operation and information', *Library Association Record*, vol.82, no.8.

Cooke, M. (1987), 'The recruitment and training of library and information workers of ethnic minority background', *Training and Education*, vol.4, no.3.

Cope, C. (1990), 'Performance indicator work in public libraries in the UK', *Public Library Journal*, vol.5, no.4.

Corner, J. and Harvey, S. (eds.), *Enterprise and Heritage: Crosscurrents of National Culture*, Routledge, London.

Cronin, B. (1984), 'The marketing of public library services in the United Kingdom: the rationale for a marketing approach', *European Journal of Marketing*, vol.18, no.2.

Crossick, G. (1978), *An Artisan Elite in Victorian Society: Kentish London 1840-80*, Croom Helm, London.

Crow, G. and Allan, G. (1994), *Community Life: an Introduction to Local Social Relations*, Harvester Wheatsheaf, London.

Dale, S.M. (1980), 'Another way forward for adult learners: the public library and independent study', *Studies in Adult Education*, vol.12, no.1, April.

Darcy, B. and Ohri, A. (1978), *Libraries are Ours: the Public Library as a Source of Information for Community Groups*, Community Projects Foundation, London.

Davies, J. (1992), 'Strategic management' in M. Kinnell (ed.), *Informing Communities*, Library Association Community Services Group, Newcastle under Lyme.

Dawes, L. (1973), 'Libraries, culture and blacks', *Assistant Librarian*, July.

Deacon, D. and Golding, P. (1991), 'The voluntary sector in the information society: a study in division and uncertainty', *Voluntas*, vol.2, no.2.

Dean, S.C. (1981), 'Tackling unemployment: the Consett experience', *Assistant Librarian*, December.

Dempsey, L. (1995), 'The public library and the information superhighway', *Vine*, no.98.

Dennes, R. and Daniels, S. (1981), 'Community and the social geography of Victorian cities', *The Urban History Yearbook*.

Department of Education and Science (1962), *Standards of Public Library Service in England and Wales* [Bourdillon Report].

Department of Education and Science (1978), *The Libraries Choice*, HMSO, London.

Dervin, B. (1994), 'Information < > democracy: an examination of underlying assumptions', *Journal of the American Society for Information Science*, vol.45, no.6.

Devereux, M. (1972), 'Libraries in working class areas', *Assistant Librarian*, November

Devins, D. and Hughes, G. (1995), 'Down the superhighway to urban information inequality', Paper presented at the B.S.A. Contested Cities Conference, 10th-14th April 1995, University of Leicester, Leeds Metropolitan University Policy Research Unit, Leeds.

Digby, A. (1989), *British Welfare Policy: workhouse to workfare*, Faber and Faber, London.

Dolan, J. (1989), 'Community librarianship in a northern inner city' in Astbury, R. (ed.), *Putting People First: Some New Perspectives on Community Librarianship*, Association of Assistant Librarians, Newcastle under Lyme.

Dolan, J. (1992), 'Birmingham - as a whole' in Alexander, Z. and Knight, T. (eds.), *The Whole Library Movement: Changing Practice in Multicultural Librarianship*, Association of Assistant Librarians, Newcastle under Lyme.

Donadgrodski, A.P. (1977), *Social Control in Nineteenth Century Britain*, Croom Helm, London.

Dye, T.R. (1986), 'Community Power and Public Policy' in Waste, R.J. (ed.), *Community Power: Directions for Future Research*, Sage, London.

Ealing Public Libraries (1964), *Respice-Prospice: a Report on the Ealing Public Library Service from its Beginnings in 1883 to 1964*.

Edwards, E. (1869), *Free Town Libraries*, Trubner, London.

Elliott, P. (1984), *Public Libraries and Self Help Ethnic Minority Organisations*, Polytechnic of North London School of Librarianship and Information Studies, London.

Etzioni, A. (1993), *The Spirit of Community. Rights, Responsibilities and the Communitarian Agenda*, Crown Publishing Group, New York.

Evans, E.J. (1978), *Social Policy 1830-1914*, Routledge and Kegan Paul, London.

Featherstone, T. (1979), 'Team librarianship in Tameside' in Major R. and Judd, P. (eds.), *Team librarianship. Papers given at the Library Association Northern Branch/Association of Assistant Librarians Northern Division Joint Annual Weekend School*, Association of Assistant Librarians Northern Division, Newcastle upon Tyne.

Featherstone, T. (1992), 'Community librarianship challenged. The Library Association/Holt Jackson community initiative award', *Public Library Journal*, vol.7, no.6.

Finch, H. (1990), 'Analysing qualitative material' in Slater, M. (ed.), *Research Methods in Library and Information Studies*, Library Association Publishing, London.

Forster, I. (1992), 'Life on the shelf', *New Statesman and Society*, 13 March.

Fraser, D. (1984), *The Evolution of the British Welfare State*, Macmillan, Basingstoke.

Fryer, D. and Payne, R. (1983), 'Book borrowing and unemployment', *Library Review*, Autumn.

Fryer, P. (1984), *Staying Power: the History of Black People in Britain*, Pluto, London.

Gerard, D. (1962), *Book Provision for Special Needs*, London and Home Counties Branch of the Library Association.

Gerard, D. (ed.) (1978), *Libraries in Society: a Reader*, Clive Bingley, London.

Gibson, T. (1979), *People Power: Community and Work Groups in Action*, Penguin, Harmondsworth.

Giddens, A. (1985), *The Nation State and Violence*, Polity, Cambridge.

Giddens, A. (1990), *The Consequences of Modernity*, Polity Press, Cambridge.

Glen, A. (1993), 'Methods and themes in community practice' in Butcher, H., Glen, A., Henderson, P. and Smith, J. (eds.), *Community and Public Policy*, Pluto, London.

Godwin, T.M. (1981), 'Developments in Manchester's public libraries as a result of the inner city programme', *Journal of Librarianship*, vol.13, no.3.

Golighty, C.L. (1970), 'Examining Our Attitudes Towards the Unserved' in Sherrill, L.L. (ed.), *Library Service to the Unserved*, Bowker, New York.

Gorz, A. (1982), *Farewell to the Working Class: an Essay on Post-industrial Socialism*, Pluto, London.

Green, D. (1987), *The New Right: the Counterrevolution in Social, Economic and Political Thought*, Wheatsheaf, Hove.

Greenhalgh, L. (1995), 'A new lease of shelf-life', *Library Association Record*, vol.97, no.8, August.

Greenhalgh, L., Worpole, K. and Landry, C. (1995), *Libraries in a World of Cultural Change*, UCL Press, London.

Grenz, S.J. (1996), *A Primer on Postmodernism*, William B. Eerdmans Publishing Co., Cambridge.

Groombridge, B. (1964), *The Londoner and his Library*, The Research Institute for Consumer Affairs.

Grundt, L. (1972), 'Metropolitan Area Library Problems: an Annotated Bibliography' in Conant, R.W. and Molz, K. (eds.), *The Metropolitan Library*, Massachusetts Institute of Technology.

Gundara, J. and Warwick, R. (1981), 'Myth or reality', *Assistant Librarian*, vol.74, no.5.

Gutman, A. (1992), 'Communitarian Critics of Liberalism' in Avineri, S. and de-Shalit, A. (eds.), *Communitarianism and Individualism*, Oxford University Press, Oxford.

Habermas, J. (1985), 'Modernity: an Incomplete Project', in Foster, H. (ed.), *Postmodern Culture*, Pluto, London.

Hall, S. and Jacques, M. (eds.) (1983), *The Politics of Thatcherism*, Lawrence and Wishart, London.

Hampden-Turner, C. and Trompenaars, F. (1995), *The Seven Cultures of Capitalism*, Piatkus, London.

Handy, C (1976), *Understanding Organisations*, Penguin, Harmondsworth.

Hardy, J. (1981), *Values in Social Policy: Nine Contradictions*, Routledge and Kegan Paul.

Harris, J. (1993), *Private Lives, Public Spirit: a Social History of Britain 1870-1914*, Penguin, Harmondsworth.

Harris, J. (1995), 'Between Civic Virtue and Social Darwinism' in Englander, D. and O'Day, R. (eds.), *Retrieved Riches: Social Investigation in Britain 1840-1914*, Scolar Press, Aldershot.

Harris, K. (1991), 'Information and social change in the 1990s', *International Journal of Information and Library Research*, vol.3, no.1.

Harris, K. (1996), 'Social inclusion in the information society' in Wilcox, D. (ed.), *Inventing the Future: Communities in the Information Society*, Partnership Books, Brighton.

Harrison, K.C. (1963a), *The Library and the Community*, Andre Deutsch, London.

Harrison, K.C. (1963b), *Public Libraries Today*, Crosby Lockwood, London.

Harrison, K.C. (1973), *Public Relations for Librarians*, Andre Deutsch, London.

Harvey, D. (1989), *The Condition of Postmodernity*, Blackwell, Oxford.

Hebbert, M. (1980), *The Inner City Problem in Historical Context*, Social Science Research Council.

Hendry, J. (1973), 'A positive prejudice: serving the culturally disadvantaged', *Assistant Librarian*, December.

Hendry, J. (1979), 'Team librarianship, scoring goals' in Major R. and Judd, P. (eds.), *Team librarianship. Papers given at the Library Association Northern Branch/Association of Assistant Librarians Northern Division Joint Annual Weekend School*, Association of Assistant Librarians Northern Division, Newcastle upon Tyne.

Hendry, J. (1981), 'How little we really do: library services for the unemployed in the Renfrew district', *Assistant Librarian*, December.

Hendry, J. (1986), 'Jill's pure brill. Johnstone Information and Leisure Library: the development of a project', *Library Association Record*, vol.88, no.2.

Hendry, J. (1988), 'The right twigs for an eagle's nest: caring libraries in a caring society', *Library Association Record*, vol.90, no.7.

Hennessey, J. A. (1979), 'Choices for library services: the socio-economic dimension', *Journal of Librarianship*, vol.11, no.2.

Hewison, R. (1987), *The Heritage Industry*, Methuen, London.

Hill, J. (1973), *Children are People: the Librarian in the Community*, Hamish Hamilton, London.

Hill, J. (1992), 'The new management ethic: developing services for children and schools', in Alexander, Z. and Knight, T. (eds.), *The Whole Library Movement: Changing Practice in Multicultural Librarianship*, AAL, Newcastle under Lyme.

Hoggart, R. (1991a), 'The abuses of literacy', *The Guardian*, 27 June.

Hoggart, R. (1991b), 'A public library is not a burger bar', *Independent on Sunday*, 20th June.

Hoggart, R. (1995), *The Way We Live Now*, Chatto, London.

Hoggett, P. (1990), *Modernisation, Political Strategy, and the Welfare State*, School of Advanced Urban Studies, University of Bristol, Bristol.

Hoggett, P. and Hambleton, R. (eds.) (1987), *Decentralization and Democracy: Localizing Public Services*, University of Bristol, School of Advanced Urban Studies Occasional Paper No. 28.

Howard, E.N. (1978), *Local Power and the Community Library*, American Library Association, Chicago.

Hurd, D. (1991), *Conservatism in the 1990s*, Conservative Political Centre, London.

Illich, I. et al (1977), *Disabling Professions*, Marion Boyars, London.

Inglis, F. (1993), 'So farewell then, citizen servant', *The Times Higher*, 6 August.

Jackaman, P. (1972), 'The library and the illiterate', *Assistant Librarian*, July.

Jameson, F. (1984), 'Postmodernism or the cultural logic of late capitalism', *New Left Review*, no.146.

Jast, S. (1935), 'Public Libraries' in Laski, H.J., Jennings, W.I. and Robson, W.A., *A Century of Municipal Progress 1835-1935*, Allen and Unwin, London.

Jast, S. (1939), *The Library and the Community*, Thomas Nelson, London.

Jenkinson, P. (1995), 'Heritage: implications of the concept for public library services', *Public Library Journal*, vol.10, no.3, May.

Jenks, C. (ed.) (1992), *The Post-modern Reader*, Academy Editions, London.

Jessop, B. (1994), 'The transition to post-Fordism and the Schumpterian workfare state' in Burrows, R. and Loader, B. (eds.), *Towards a Post-Fordist Welfare State?*, Routledge, London.

Johnman, M.A. and Kendall, H. (c. 1885), *A Commission Appointed to Inquire into the Condition and Workings of Free Libraries of Various Towns in England.* Darlington Public Library Local Studies Department.

Joint Working Party of the Library Advisory Council and the Community Relations Commission (1976), *Public Library Service for a Multicultural Society*, Community Relations Commission, London.

Jones, K. (1984), *Conflict and Change in Library Organisations: People, Power and Service*, Bingley, London.

Jones, K. (1994), *The Making of Social Policy in Britain 1830-1990*, Athlone Press, London.

Jordan, P. (1972), 'Social class, race relations and the public library', *Assistant Librarian*, March.

Kamenka, E. (1982), *Community as a Social Ideal*, Edward Arnold, London.

Kelly, T. (1966), 'Public libraries and public opinion', *Library Association Record*, vol.68.

Kelly, T. (1977), *A History of Public Libraries in Great Britain 1845-1975*, Library Association, London.

Kelly, T. and Kelly, E. (1977), *Books for the People: an Illustrated History of the British Public Library*, Andre Deutsch, London.

Kendall, M. (1992), 'Section 11 changes in funding criteria: the implications for public library services for black and minority ethnic groups', *Public Library Journal*, vol.7, no. 2.

Kinnell Evans, M. (1991), *All Change? Public Library Management Strategies for the 1990s*, Taylor Graham, London.

Kinnell, M. and MacDougal, M. (1992), 'Libraries and leisure services: marketing and reality', *Public Library Journal*, vol.7, no.4.

Klein, G. (1985), *Reading into Racism: Bias in Children's Literature and Learning Materials*, Routledge, London.

KPMG and Capital Planning Information (1995), *DNH Study: Contracting Out in Public Libraries*, KPMG, London.

Lahav, R. (1989), 'The use of public libraries: is class still an issue?', *Public Library Journal*, vol.4, no.2, March-April.

Lambert, C. (1969), 'Library provision for the Indian and Pakistani communities in Britain', *Journal of Librarianship*, vol.1, no.1.

Lambert, C. (1985), *Expenditure Cuts in Public Libraries and their Effect on Services. A Report for the Library Campaign*, Library Campaign, London.

Lathrope, D. (1989), 'Restructuring for community librarianship in a county library service' in Astbury, R. (ed.), *Putting People First: Some New Perspectives on Community Librarianship*, Association of Assistant Librarians, Newcastle under Lyme.

Lewis, M.J. (1987), 'History, development, change ' in Ryder, J. (ed.), *Library Services to Housebound People*, Library Association, London.

Lewis, O. (1949), *Life in a Mexican Village*, University of Illinois Press, Urbana.

Library Association (1938), A *Survey of Libraries*, Library Association, London.

Library Association (1950), *A Century of Public Libraries 1850-1950*, Library Association, London.

Library Association (1977), *Public Libraries in Multicultural Britain*, Library Association, London.

Library Association (1980), *Community Information: What Libraries Can Do. A Consultative Document*, Library Association, London.

Library Association (1983), 'Public libraries duty to the unemployed', *Library Association Record*, vol.85, no.6.

Library Association (1985), *Library and Information Services for Our Multicultural Society*, Library Association, London.

Library Association (1988), *The Government's Green Paper on Public Library Finance: a Digest of the Library Association's Response*, Library Association, London.

Library Association (1993), *A Charter for Public Libraries*, Library Association, London.

Library Association (1994), *The Future of Your Public Library Service: Time to Make Your Own Views Known*, Library Association, London. Circular leaflet.

Library Association (1995), 'Information superhighways: library and information services and the internet - a statement by the Library Association', *ITs News*, no.32.

Library Association Community Services Group (1986), 'Group Rules (Constitution)', *Community Librarian*, vol.3, no.4.

Liddle, D. (1980), 'Community librarianship', *New Library World*, vol. 81, no.964.

Line, M.B. (1967), *Library Surveys*, Clive Bingley, London.

Lipietz, A. (1994), 'Post-Fordism and democracy' in Amin, A (ed.), *Post-Fordism: a Reader*, Blackwell, Oxford.

Lowe, R. (1994), 'The welfare state in Britain since 1945', *ReFRESH* [Recent Findings of Research in Economic and Social History], no. 18, Spring.

Lowenthal, D. (1985), *The Past is a Foreign Country*, Cambridge University Press, Cambridge.

Luce, R. (1993), 'Libraries: a ticket to civilization', *The Independent*, 27 October.

Luckham, B. (1971), *The Library in Society*, Library Association, London.

Luckham, B. (1978), 'The Public Library: for Whom and How?' in Gerard, D. (ed.), *Libraries in Society: a Reader*, Clive Bingley, London.

Lyon, D. (1990), *Information Technology and Community Development*, Community Development Foundation, London.

Macdonald, K.M. (1995), *The Sociology of the Professions*, Sage, London.

Macnicol, J. (1987), 'In pursuit of the underclass', *Journal of Social Policy*, vol. 16, no. 3, July.

Manchester Telematics Partnership (c.1995), *Manchester the Information City. Promoting Economic Regeneration through the Use of Telematics*, Manchester Telematics Partnership, Manchester.

Mann, K. (1992), *The Making of an English Underclass*, Open University Press, Milton Keynes.

Marriott, J. (1996), 'Sensation of the Abyss: the Urban Poor and Modernity' in Nava, N. and O'Shea, A. (eds.), *Modern Times: Reflections on a Century of English Modernity*, Routledge, London.

Marsden, G. (ed.) (1990), *Victorian Values: Personalities and Perspectives in Nineteenth Century Society*, Longman, London.

Marshall, T.H. (1975), *Social Policy*, Hutchinson and Co., London.

Martin, B. (1981), *A Sociology of Contemporary Cultural Change*, Blackwell, Oxford.

Martin, W. (1974), 'The Highfield community library, Belfast', *New Library World*, vol.75, no.893.

Martin, W. (ed.) (1975), *Library Services to the Disadvantaged*, Bingley, London.

Martin, W. (1989), *Community Librarianship: Changing the Face of Public Libraries*, Bingley, London.

Marwick, A. (1982), *British Society Since 1945*, Penguin, Harmondsworth.

Mayo, M. (1995), 'Rediscovering community development: some prerequesites for working "in and against the state"', *Community Development Journal*, vol.30, no.2.

McCann, A. (1994), 'Libraries - are they dangerous places?', *Assistant Librarian*, May.

McColvin, L. (1942), *The Public Library System of Great Britain*, Library Association, London.

McColvin, L. (1950), *Public Library Extension*, United Nations Educational, Scientific and Cultural Organization, Paris.

McDowell, O. (1992), 'Inter-agency co-operation' in Kinnell, M. (ed.), *Informing Communities*, Library Association Community Services Group, Newcastle under Lyme.

McIntosh, A. (1979), 'Urban Deprivation and the Library Response' in Loosley, J. (ed.), *Serving All The Community: Library Services to the Disadvantaged*, Library Association South Western Branch.

McKee, B. (1987), *Public Libraries into the 1990s*, AAL, Newcastle under Lyme.

McKee, B. (1989), *Planning Library Service*, Bingley, London.

McLennan, G. (1992), 'The Enlightenment Project Revisited' in Hall, S., Held, D. and McGrew, T. (eds.), *Modernity and its Futures*, Polity Press and Open University Press, Cambridge.

McNaught, B. (1995), 'Partnership, strategy and leadership: what we have, what we need, and what we lack, respectively', *Public Library Journal*, vol.10, no.6.

Meller, H. (1996), 'The Leisure Revolution' in Kinnell, M. and Sturges, P. (eds.), *Continuity and Innovation in the Public Library: the Development of a Social Institution*, Library Association, London.

Midwinter, A. (1990), 'Setting public library objectives: a critical perspective', *Public Library Journal*, vol.5 no.6.

Midwinter, E. (1994), *A Century of Social Welfare in Britain*, Open University Press, Milton Keynes.

Ministry of Education (1959), *The Structure of the Public Library Service in England and Wales* [Roberts Report].

Ministry of Education (1962), *Inter-library Co-operation in England and Wales* [Baker Report].

Minto, J. (1932), *A History of the Public Library Movement in Great Britain and Ireland*, George Allen and Unwin and the Library Association, London.

Moore, N. and Steele, J. (1991), *Information Intensive Britain: a Review of the Policy Issues*, Policy Studies Institute, London.

Morris, L. (1994), *Dangerous Classes: the Underclass and Social Citizenship*, Routledge, London.

Mouffe, C. (ed.) (1992), *Dimensions of Radical Democracy*, Verso, London.

Muddiman, D. (1990), 'Towards a definition of public library purpose', *Public Library Journal*, vol.5, no.4.

Muddiman, D. and Black, A. (1993), *Public Library Policy and Purpose*, Comedia, Stroud Green.

Mulgan, G. (1993), *The Public Service Ethos and Public Libraries*, Comedia, Stroud Green.

Mulgan, G. and Worpole, K. (1986), *Saturday Night or Sunday Morning. From Arts to Industry - New Forms of Cultural Policy*, Comedia, London.

Munford, W. (1951), *Penny Rate: Aspects of British Public Library History 1850-1950*, Library Association, London.

Murison, W.J. (1988), *The Public Library: its Origins, Purpose and Significance*, Clive Bingley, London.

Murray, C. (1990), *The Emerging British Underclass*, Institute of Economic Affairs (Health and Welfare Unit), London.

Myers, J. (1994), 'Stable quiet retreats or bustling with innovation', *Library Association Record*, vol.96, no.8, August.

Nairn, T. (1977), *The Break Up of Britain: Crisis and Neo-Nationalism*, New Left Books, London.

National Consumer Council (1977), *The Fourth Right of Citizenship: a Review of Local Advice Services*, NCC, London.

Newby, H. (1985), 'Recession and reorganisation in industrial society' in Newby, H. et al (eds.), *Restructuring Capital: Recession and Restructuring in Industrial Society*, Macmillan, Basingstoke.

Nisbet, R.A. (1969), *The Quest for Community*, Oxford University Press, Oxford.

Nisbet, R.A. (1970), *The Sociological Tradition*, Heinemann, London.

Norman, P.L. (1972), 'Library services for immigrants', *Library Association Record*, vol.74, no.10.

Nottinghamshire County Labour Party (1985), *Services, Jobs and Democracy. The Policy of the Labour Party for the County Council Elections, 2nd May, 1985*, Nottinghamshire County Labour Party, Brinsley, Nottinghamshire.

Noyce, J. (1974), *Libraries and the Working Classes in the Nineteenth Century*, Smoothie Publications, Brighton.

Office of Arts and Libraries (1988), *Financing Our Public Library Service: Four Subjects for Debate*, HMSO, London.

Office of Arts and Libraries (1990), *Keys to Success: Performance Indicators for Public Libraries*, HMSO, London.

Office of Arts and Libraries (1991), *Setting Objectives for Public Library Services*, HMSO, London.

Orton, G. (1980), *An Illustrated History of Mobile Library Services in the UK*, Branch and Mobile Libraries Group of the Library Association.

Oulton, T. (1991), *Strategies in Action: Public Library Management and Public Expenditure Constraints*, Library Association Publishing, London.

Parekh, B. (1991), 'British citizenship and cultural difference' in Andrews, G. (ed.), *Citizenship*, Lawrence and Wishart, London.

Pateman, J. (1996), 'Public libraries: let's get back to basics', *The Library Campaigner*, no. 54, Summer.

Peters, T. and Waterman, R. (1982), *In Search of Excellence: Lessons from America's Best-Run Companies*, Harper and Row, New York.

Pirie, M. (1995), 'Subsidised entertainment for the middle classes', *Independent*, 24th February.

Pluse, J. (1991), 'Customer focus: the salvation of service organisations', *Public Library Journal*, vol.6, no.1.

Pollitt, C. (1993), *Managerialism and the Public Services: Cuts or Cultural Change in the 1990s*, 2nd ed., Blackwell, Oxford.

Price, N. (1989), 'What price Section 11: the demise of the ethnic librarian?', *Library Association Record*, vol.91, no.11.

Raddon, R. (1987), 'Black and ethnic minority staff: issues of recruitment and training', *Public Library Journal*, vol. 2, no. 4.

Redfern, M. (1989), 'Community librarianship: an historical perspective', in Astbury, R. (ed.), *Putting People First: Some New Perspectives on Community Librarianship*, Association of Assistant Librarians, Newcastle under Lyme.

Redfield, R. (1947), 'The folk society', *American Journal of Sociology*, vol.1, no.3.

Redhead, B. (1993), *Country Living*, October.

Relton, F. (1887), *Report of Visits to Provincial Free Libraries on Behalf of the Chelsea Public Library Commissioners*, Chelsea Public Library Local Studies Department.

Ritchie, S. (ed.) (1982), *Modern Library Practice*, ELM Publications, Buckden, Cambridgeshire.

Robins, K. and Webster, F. (1992), *The Technical Fix: Computers, Education and Industry*, Macmillan, London.

Room, G. (1990), *New Poverty in the European Community*, Macmillan, Basingstoke.

Rosenau, P.M. (1992), *Post-modernism and the Social Sciences: Insights, Inroads and Intrusions*, Princeton University Press, Princeton, New Jersey.

Rubinstein, W.D. (1993), *Capitalism, culture and decline in Britain 1750-1990*, Routledge, London.

Rusbridger, A. (1988), 'Charge of the write brigade', *The Guardian*, January 7th.

Russell, D. (1995), *A Social History of Public Libraries in London 1939-1945*, unpublished MA (Information Studies) dissertation, University of North London.

Ryder, J. (ed.) (1987), *Library Services to Housebound People*, Library Association, London.

Sahai, S. (1973), *The Library and the Community*, Today and Tomorrow Publishers, New Delhi.

Samuel, R. (1992a), 'In defence of potboilers', *The Times*, 7 March.

Samuel, R. (1992b), 'No mythic golden age', *New Statesman and Society*, 6 March.

Samuel, R. (1994), *Theatres of Memory. Vol. 1: Past and Present in Contemporary Culture*, Verso, London.

Saunders, J. (1981) 'The empire strikes back', *Information and Library Manager,* vol.1, no.2.

Saunders, J. (1986), 'Mission imperceptible', *Library Association Record,* vol.88, no.3

Sayers, W.B.C. (1935-6), 'What people read', *The Library World*, vol. 38.

Select Committee on Public Libraries (1849), *Report.*

Shimmon, R. (1995), 'Views of the review', *Library Association Record,* vol.97, no.7, July.

Slater, M. (1980), *Career Patterns and the Occupational Image*, ASLIB, London.

Smith, B. (1983), *Marketing Strategies for Libraries,* MCB University Press, Bradford.

Smith, B. (1985), *Decentralization: the Territorial Dimension of the State,* Allen and Unwin, London.

Smith, G. (1996), 'Virtual community in real reality .....' in Wilcox, D. (ed.), *Inventing the Future: Communities in the Information Society,* Partnership Books, Brighton.

Smith, V. (1987), 'Reviving the People's University', *Library Association Record,* vol.89, no.11, November.

Snaith, S. (1942), 'A tube shelter lending library', *Library Review,* Spring.

Snape, R. (1995), *Leisure and the Rise of the Public Library,* The Library Association, London.

Stewart, J. (1995), 'A future for local authorities as community government' in Stewart, J. and Stoker, G. (eds.), *Local Government in the 1990s,* Macmillan, London.

Stewart, J. and Clarke, M. (1987), 'The public service orientation: issues and dilemmas', *Public Administration,* vol.65, no.2.

Stewart, J. and Stoker, G. (eds.) (1995), *Local Government in the 1990s,* Macmillan, London.

Stoker, G. and Mossberger, K. (1995), 'The post-fordist local state: the dynamics of its development' in Stewart, J. and Stoker, G. (eds.), *Local Government in the 1990s,* Macmillan, London.

Stoker, G. and Young, S. (1993), *Cities in the 1990s: Local Choice for a Balanced Strategy,* Longman, Harlow.

Stokes, P. (1978), 'The public library in the corporate state', *Assistant Librarian*, December.

Sturges, P. (1996), 'The Public Library and its Readers, *Library History*, vol.12.

Talbot, C. (1990), 'What is a multicultural library service?' *Library Association Record*, vol.92, no.7.

Talbot, C. (1991), *Libraries in a Multicultural Society: the Role of Libraries in Promoting 'Good Relations Between Persons of Different Racial Groups'*, Manchester Polytechnic Department of Library and Information Studies, Manchester.

Tester, S. (1992), *Common Knowledge: A Co-ordinated Approach to Information-Giving*, Centre for Policy on Ageing, London.

Thompson, E.P. (1968), *The Making of the English Working Class*, Penguin, Harmondsworth.

Thompson, F.M.L. (1981), 'Social Control in Victorian Britain', *Economic History Review*, vol.34, May.

Thompson, J. (1977), *A History of the Principles of Librarianship*, Clive Bingley, London.

Thompson, V. (1989), 'A community library service for ethnic minority groups' in Astbury, R. (ed.), *Putting People First: Some New Perspectives on Community Librarianship*, Association of Assistant Librarians, Newcastle under Lyme.

Thornton, J. (1974), *Library Power*, Clive Bingley, London.

Tonks, D. (1975), *The Library Services in the New Towns of North East England*, unpublished Fellowship of the Library Association thesis.

Totterdell, B. (1981), 'Public Libraries in a Changing World' in Harrison, K.C. (ed.), *Public Library Policy*, K.G. Saur, London.

Totterdell, B. and Bird, J. (1976), *The Effective Library: Report of the Hillingdon Project on Public Library Effectiveness*, Library Association, London.

Tyerman, K. and Russell, N. (1992), 'Moulding a new generation', *Assistant Librarian*, November.

Urry, J. (1996), 'How Societies Remember the Past' in Macdonald, S. and Fyfe, G. (eds.), *Theorizing Museums*, Blackwell/The Sociological Review, Oxford.

Usherwood, B. (1981), *The Visible Library: Practical Public Relations for Public Librarians*, Library Association, London.

Usherwood, B. (1991), 'The visible library in the 1990s', *Assistant Librarian*, December.

Usherwood, B. (1992a), 'Community information' in M. Kinnell (ed.), *Informing Communities*, Library Association Community Services Group, Newcastle under Lyme.

Usherwood, B. (1992b), 'Managing public libraries as a public service', *Public Library Journal*, vol.7, no.6.

Usherwood, B. (1993), *Success Stories: Libraries are Full of Them*. A celebration of libraries published for National Library Week by the Yorkshire and Humberside Branch of the Library Association.

Usherwood, B. (1996), 'Public libraries and political purpose' in Kinnell, M. and Sturges, P. (eds.), *Continuity and Innovation in the Public Library. The Development of a Social Institution*, Library Association Publishing, London.

Van Riel, R. (ed.) (1992), *Reading the Future: a Place for Literature in Public Libraries*, Arts Council of Great Britain and the Library Association, London.

Venner, D. and Cotton, S. (1986), *Information for a Rural Community: the South Moulton Community Information Project*, British Library, London.

Vincent, J. (1986), *An Introduction to Community Librarianship*, Association of Assistant Librarians, Newcastle under Lyme.

Waters, H. and Wilkinson, J. (1974), 'A poverty of thinking', *Library Association Record*, vol.76, no.1.

Watson, D. (1995), 'Public library debate flourishes', *Library Association Record*, vol.97, no.8, August.

Watson, D. (1996), 'Techno future and the mixed economy', *Library Association Record*, vol.98, no.9.

Watson, J., Bowen, J. and Walley, E. (1980), *The Management of Community Information Services in the Public Library*, Leeds Polytechnic, Leeds.

Webster, F. (1995), *Theories of the Information Society*, Routledge, London.

White, J. (1993), *Frogs or Chameleons: the Public Library Service and the Public Librarian. A Research Report Investigating the Status of Public Libraries and the Careers of Public Librarians in England*. Report to the Library Association, CURS, University of Birmingham.

White, L. (1983), *The Public Library in the 1980s: the Problems of Choice*, Lexington Books, Lexington, Mass..

White, M. (1992), *Against Unemployment*, Policy Studies Institute, London.

Wiener, M. (1981), *English Culture and the Decline of the Industrial Spirit*, Penguin, Harmondsworth.

Wilcox, D. (ed.) (1996), *Inventing the Future: Communities in the Information Society*, Partnership Books, Brighton.

Wilde, N. (1996), 'Is there a postmodern public librarianship?', *Public Library Journal*, vol.11, no.3, May-June.

Williams, F. (1994), 'Social relations, welfare and the post-Fordism debate' in Burrows, R. and Loader, B. (eds.), *Towards a Post-Fordist Welfare State*, Routledge, London.

Williams, G. (1993), 'Unemployment in Clwyd: the responses of the local authority and the library service' in Astbury, R. (ed.), *Libraries and the Unemployed: Needs and Responses*, Special Community Services Sub Committee of the Library Association, London.

Williams, R. (1973), *The Country and the City*, Chatto and Windus, London.

Williams, R. (1978), 'The Library's Relation to the Community' in Gerard, D. (ed.), *Libraries in Society: a Reader*, Clive Bingley, London.

Willmott, P. and Thomas, D. (1984), *Continuity in Social Policy*, Policy Studies Institute, London.

Wilson, P. (1977), *A Community Elite and the Public Library: the Uses of Information in Leadership*, Greenwood, London.

Wirth, L. (1938), 'Urbanism as a way of life', *American Journal of Sociology*, vol.44, no.1.

Woodhouse, R. (1983), 'Local authority and library initiatives in the North region' in Astbury, R. (ed.), *Libraries and the Unemployed: Needs and Responses*, Special Community Services Sub Committee of the Library Association, London.

Wright, P. (1985), *On Living in an Old Country*, Verso, London.

Yeo, E. and Yeo, S. (1988), 'On the Uses of Community: from Owenism to the Present' in Yeo, S. (ed.), *New Views of Cooperation*, Routledge, London.

Yorke, D. (1977), *Marketing the Library Service*, Library Association, London.

Yorke, D. and Colley, D. (1973), 'Meet the public: public libraries and marketing research', *Library Association Record*, vol.75, no.10.

Young, M. and Willmott, P. (1962), *Family and Kinship in East London*, Pelican, Harmondsworth.

.